MW00824286

Vegetarian Instant Pot Cookbook for Beginners #2020

700 Mouthwatering, Quick and Easy Plant Based Recipes for Your Pressure Cooker

By Louis Mitchell

Copyrights©2020 By Louis Mitchell

All Rights Reserved

This document is geared towards providing exact and reliable information in regards to the topic and issue covered. The publication is sold with the idea that the publisher is not required to render accounting, officially permitted, or otherwise, qualified services. If advice is necessary, legal or professional, a practiced individual in the profession should be ordered.

Legal Notice: The book is copyright protected. This is only for personal use. You cannot amend, distribute, sell, use, quote or paraphrase any part or the content within this book without the consent of the author.

Under no circumstance will any legal responsibility or blame be held against the publisher for any reparation, damages, or monetary loss due to the information herein, either directly or indirectly.

Disclaimer Notice: Please note the information contained within this document is for educational and entertainment purpose only. Every attempt has been made to provide accurate, up to date and reliable complete information. No warranties of any kind are expressed or implied. Reader acknowledge that the author is not engaging in the rendering of legal, financial, medical or professional advice. The content of this book has been derived from various sources. Please consult a licensed professional before attempting any techniques outlined in this book.

Table of Content

Introduction

Hello! Thank you for taking the time to browse and buy this eBook on vegetarian recipes using the Instant Pot. You may be having doubts if the Instant Pot is useful for cooking vegetables and vegetarian recipes. The answer is a resounding Yes! You can definitely cook veggies using your Instant Pot.

With the onslaught of problems concerning weight, convenience, and the skill of cooking—the Instant Pot has been a great ally in resolving these issues. It has a lot of user-friendly buttons that help busy people, like you and me, make deliciously homecooked meals. Pairing your Instant Pot with vegetarian approved recipes is a great step in helping you lead a healthy lifestyle. And you do not have to be Ramsay Gordon in order to whip up these mouth-watering dishes in your own home. All you need is your nifty Instant Pot and this amazing vegetarian recipe eBook that contains 400 different pieces of recipes. The recipes range from ovo-vegetarian, lacto-vegetarian, lacto-ovo-vegetarian, and even vegan recipes! If you want to understand more about what I am talking about, read on…

I hope this eBook will help you conquer your kitchen. It takes a bit of effort in the beginning, like any endeavor does, and once you get the hang of it. Cooking vegetarian meals in your Instant Pot becomes easy, healthy, and even more affordable for you and your family.

Good Luck and most of all enjoy the process!

Chapter 1 Understanding the Vegetarian Diet

There are many ways that people can do in order to stay healthy. Aside from getting enough exercise, eating the right kinds of food can also boost one's health. While there are so many types of diet regimens that people can adapt, perhaps the healthiest and easiest diet of all is the vegetarian diet. As the name implies, the vegetarian diet is all about eating mostly plant-based foods. But unlike other popular diets such as strict plant-based and vegan diets, vegetarian diet offers more freedom to people. Thus, this section is dedicated to providing you with the right information on what this diet is all about.

Types of Vegetarian Diet

Being a vegetarian involves abstaining from meat, poultry, and fish. Many people adopt this diet regimen for various reasons including religion, environmental, and ethical considerations aside from health considerations. While it is true that being a vegetarian means abstaining from meat and other related products, there are several forms of vegetarianism that people can adopt. Below are the different types of vegetarianism that are popular across the globe.

- Lacto-ovo-vegetarian diet: This type of vegetarian diet restricts one from eating meat, poultry, and fish but not dairy products and eggs.
- Lacto-vegetarian diet: This type of vegetarian diet restricts one from eating meat, poultry, fish, and eggs but allows the consumption of dairy products.
- Ovo-vegetarian diet: This type of vegetarian diet restricts the consumption of meat, poultry, fish, and dairy but not eggs.
- Pescatarian diet: This diet restricts the consumption of meat and poultry but allows one to consume fish and sometimes dairy products and eggs.
- Vegan diet: The vegan diet is a type of vegetarian diet, but it restricts the consumption of all animal products and by-products including honey.
- Flexitarian diet: This is a mostly vegetarian diet that also incorporates the consumption of fish, meat, and poultry on occasional moments.

Health Benefits of Vegetarian Diet

The vegetarian diet is touted for its many health benefits. In fact, many studies have been published that have concluded that this particular diet is better than other types of diets. Below are the different health benefits that you can obtain following the vegetarian diet.

- Better nutritional intake: Studies show that those who eat more plant-based foods have a higher intake of important nutrients such as Vitamin C, E, and Magnesium. These nutrients are often found deficient among meat-eaters.
- Better digestion: Studies have noted that an average American has poor fiber intake as they consume more meat and other animal products. Low fiber intake often leads to constipation and other digestive issues. Shifting to a vegetarian diet can avoid digestion problems.
- Encourage weight loss: Shifting to this diet can encourage weight loss. The thing is that most plant-based foods are calorie deficient although they are jam-packed with nutritional content. You would have to eat more food in bulk to get the same number of calories than you would eat a plate of steak. This is the reason why many people who want to lose weight healthily are encouraged to adopt a vegetarian diet.
- Reduce the risk for cancer: Many observational studies have associated the vegetarian diet with reduced risk for developing many types of cancer. Most plants – fruits and vegetables – contain high

amounts of antioxidants that can help stave off inflammation and improve the immune system responses of the body.

- **Stabilize blood sugar levels:** Because eating more fruits and vegetables improves one's fiber intake, this can help stabilize the blood sugar levels as fiber and complex carbohydrates are not immediately metabolized by the body after meals.
- **Better heart health:** The vegetarian diet can help reduce the risk of developing heart diseases by reducing the low-density lipoproteins (LDL) or bad cholesterol. Studies have shown that the vegetarian diet is better at reducing bad cholesterol than the Mediterranean diet.

Foods to Eat

A vegetarian diet should comprise of a diverse type of foods to get the most nutritional value. So, if you are wondering what types of foods you can eat when following the vegetarian diet, below are some examples of the food that you can eat while following this diet.

- Fruits: Fruits are good sources of fiber and natural sugars. They also contain high amounts of antioxidants, vitamins, and minerals. Vegetarians are encouraged to consume different kinds of fruits such as berries, citruses, bananas, melons, and many others.
- Vegetables: Vegetables, particularly green leafy vegetables, contain high amounts of antioxidants and other compounds beneficial for the body. They also contain high amounts of fiber. Consume leafy greens, tomatoes, and many colorful vegetables for the best results.
- Grains: Grains are calorie-dense foods that provide energy to sustain your activities throughout the day. Examples of grains include barley, quinoa, buckwheat, oats, and rice.
- Legumes: Legumes such as beans, lentils, chickpeas, and peas are great alternative sources of protein. They are also calorie-dense that can provide energy to the body to sustain daily activities.
- Nuts: Nuts such as almonds, cashews, walnuts, chestnuts are calorie-dense so they can be great snack items.
- Seeds: Vegetarians can also snack on seeds such as hemp seeds, chia seeds, and flaxseeds. Not only do they contain high amounts of fiber and nutritional content, but they are also rich in good oil particularly Omega-3 fatty acid.
- Healthy fats: Vegetarians can also consume fats as long as they are sourced from healthy ingredients including coconut oil, avocado, and olive oil.
- Others: Other products that you can consume if you follow this diet include tofu, tempeh, natto, nutritional yeast, and seitan. Eggs and dairy are also allowed depending on the type of vegetarian diet you adopt.

Foods to Avoid

Similar to other types of diets, becoming a vegetarian also restricts you from eating certain types of foods. Thus, it is important to know the types of foods that should be avoided.

- Meat: Meat such as beef, pork, veal, and all meat products should be avoided at all costs.
- Poultry: Poultry such as turkey and chicken are not allowed. This is also true for poultry products available in the market.
- Fish and shellfish: Unless you are a pescatarian, you should avoid eating fish and shellfish if you follow other variations of vegetarianism.
- Meat derivatives: Meat derivatives such as lard, gelatin, oleic acid, and suet are not allowed in the vegetarian diet.
- Eggs: Restricting eggs applies to lacto-vegetarians and vegans.
- Dairy products: Dairy products such as milk, cream, yogurt, ghee, and cheese are restricted to ovo-vegetarians and vegans.

- Others: Other animal products such as honey, pollen, beeswax are restricted particularly among vegans.

How to Be Successful in Adapting the Vegetarian Diet

Being a well-rounded vegetarian can be healthy and good for you. But some caveats will make anyone fail in this diet especially that food restriction may increase your risk of nutritional deficiencies particularly iron, vitamin B12, zinc, and selenium. Below are the different things that you can do to be successful in following the vegetarian diet.
fff

Using the Instant Pot in Tandem with The Vegetarian Diet

Becoming a vegetarian can be challenging for many people. One of the reasons is that some find it difficult to cook delicious vegetarian foods because they believe that they would have to buy different kitchen appliances to be able to enjoy a variety of foods. Conventional vegetarian recipes call for different cooking methods including steaming, broiling, roasting, and slow cooking to name a few. Plus, you get to cook faster than you would use a stovetop burner and you don't need to slave in the kitchen whenever you prepare your meals. But with the Instant Pot, you will only need this kitchen device to make sumptuous vegetarian meals anyone will enjoy.

While the Instant Pot is a perfect kitchen appliance for those who are starting with their vegetarian diet, it is not entirely fail-proof. There are some possible obstacles that you may encounter when you are using the Instant Pot. Nevertheless, the advantages of the Instant Pot still outweigh the obstacles, but it is still important to take note of the possible challenges when using the Instant Pot and how to deal with them.

- Not smell-proof: Although the Instant Pot comes with a rubber seal to keep the flavor and most of the smell of food in, it cannot be helped that some of the smell may escape from the pressurized inner pot. This is especially true if you are cooking foods with a lot of spices. Although the smell can linger on the Instant Pot for a few days, it does not give off off-taste on your food. To handle the strong smell, you can soak the inner pot and other washable items in water mixed with baking soda for at least 30 minutes.
- Sputtering liquid: Sputtering liquid is an indication that the inner pot is full of ingredients. Not only will sputtering make a huge mess in your kitchen but it may damage the electric components of your Instant Pot. Aside from cleaning up the accidental sputter, it is also crucial to use enough liquid when cooking food. Make sure that you do not fill the inner pot beyond the max line.
- Get a larger Instant Pot: The Instant Pot comes in different sizes so make sure that you get a larger Instant Pot if you are cooking for your family. If you are cooking only for yourself, you can get the smallest Instant Pot in the market.

A Short Guide to Using Your Instant Pot

Cooking with an Instant Pot is no rocket science. As one of the most intuitive kitchen appliances in the market, all there is to it is for you to put your ingredients inside the inner pot, close the lid, choose the cooking button that you want, and forget about it until your food is cooked. But for the benefit of everyone, below is a guide on how to use your Instant Pot.

- Use the minimum amount of liquid required: You need to use at least a cup of liquid in your Instant Pot when you cook food with it. However, if you are cooking grains and beans, make sure that you soak them first at least for an hour (or overnight) before cooking them in the Instant Pot.
- Fill only until the recommended fill level: The Instant Pot comes with recommended fill levels and you will see ½ or 2/3 line marked in the inner pot. DO not fill the Instant Pot with liquid beyond the 2/3 level. For foods that will expand, do not fill the Instant Pot with ingredients above the ½ line.
- Choose the right cooking button: The Instant Pot comes with many cooking buttons that you can choose from. Below are the different

kinds of cooking buttons that you can use when cooking with your Instant Pot.

o Manual: This button allows you to choose the cooking time to cook your food. When you choose this button, you need to press the +/- button to adjust the cooking time.

o Keep Warm/Cancel: This button allows you to end the cooking program or keep your food warm until ready to be consumed.

o Sauté: This button allows you to sauté or brown foods in the Instant Pot. With this button, you don't need to use the stove to sauté spices. You can also use this button to thicken sauces. When you press this button, the default time is 30 minutes, but you can press the Cancel button to end sautéing your ingredients.

o Adjust: This button allows you to switch between the Less, Normal, and More cooking modes. This is a great button to use when you are using the Sauté button as it allows you to control the amount of heat when cooking.

o Pressure: This button allows you to toggle between High and Low pressure when cooking your food.

o Program: The Instant Pot comes with a myriad of buttons that allows you to cook different kinds of food perfectly (minus the guesswork). Examples of the pre-set program buttons include Soup/Broth, Meat/Stew, Bean/Chili. Cake, Rice, Egg, Multigrain, Yogurt, Steam, Slow Cook, and Porridge.

• Use the trivet: When you want to raise your food, use the metal trivet to avoid the food from coming into contact with the bottom of the pot thereby avoiding burning.

• Close the lid: Close the lid by turning it clockwise. The arrow on the front of the lid of the Instant Pot should line up with the arrow next to the locked symbol on the body unit.

• Seal the Instant Pot: To cook food faster, the pressure inside the Instant Pot needs to build up. This can be achieved by turning the steam release valve to the sealing position. However, if you are going to use the Yogurt and Slow Cook button, you don't need to set the steam release valve into the sealing position.

• Do pressure release: There are two types of pressure release that you can do – natural pressure release (NPR) and quick pressure release (QPR). Natural pressure release allows the Instant Pot to release pressure naturally after the cook cycle ends. This takes about 10 to 20 minutes. On the other hand, QPR allows you to release the pressure quickly so that you can open the lid. When doing QPR, make sure that the steam release vent is facing away from you.

Chapter 2 Vegetable Recipes

Instant Pot Veggie Curry

Prep time: 5 minutes, cook time: 10 minutes; Serves 4

Ingredients:

1 tablespoon coconut oil
1 onion, diced
1 teaspoon mustard seeds
4 cloves of garlic, minced
2 tablespoons Indian curry powder
1 teaspoon grated ginger
1 cup vegetable broth
1 cup light coconut milk
1 butternut squash, seeded and diced
1 red bell pepper, diced
1 14-ounce canned chickpeas, drained and rinsed
2 tablespoons brown sugar
½ teaspoon salt
Chopped cilantro for garnish

Instructions

1. Set the Instant Pot to the Sauté mode and add oil. Stir in the onion, mustard seeds, garlic, curry powder, and ginger. Keep stirring for 1 minute until fragrant.
2. Add in the broth, coconut milk, squash, bell pepper, and chickpeas. Season with brown sugar and salt.
3. Close the lid and set the vent to the Sealing position.
4. Press the Pressure Cook or Manual button and cook on high. Adjust the cooking time to 10 minutes.
5. Do quick pressure release.
6. Garnish with cilantro before serving.

Nutrition Facts Per Serving

Calories 353, Total Fat 21g, Saturated Fat 16g, Total Carbs 37g, Net Carbs 27g, Protein 10g, Sugar: 11g, Fiber: 10g, Sodium: 397mg, Potassium: 515mg, Phosphorus: 173mg

Potato Curry

Prep time: 10 minutes, cook time: 30 minutes; Serves 5

Ingredients:

1 teaspoon oil
1 yellow onion, chopped
4 cloves of garlic, minced
5 cups baby potatoes, scrubbed clean
2 tablespoons curry powder
2 cups water
1 can coconut milk, full fat
Salt and pepper to taste
1 teaspoon chili pepper flakes
2 cups green beans, chopped into inch-thick pieces
3 tablespoons arrowroot powder + 4 tablespoons water

Instructions

1. Set the Sauté button on the Instant Pot and Heat oil. Sauté the onion and garlic for 30 seconds until fragrant.
2. Stir in the potatoes and curry powder. Keep stirring for 3 minutes.
3. Add water and coconut milk. Season with salt, pepper, and chili flakes.
4. Close the lid and set the vent to the Sealing position.
5. Press the Pressure Cook or Manual button and cook on high. Adjust the cooking time to 20 minutes.
6. Do quick pressure release.
7. Once the lid is open, press the Sauté button and add in the green beans. Cook for 5 minutes.
8. Stir in the arrowroot slurry and allow to thicken for 5 more minutes.

Nutrition Facts Per Serving

Calories 187, Total Fat 4g, Saturated Fat 0.6g, Total Carbs 36g, Net Carbs 29g, Protein 5g, Sugar: 6g, Fiber: 7g, Sodium: 61mg, Potassium: 917mg, Phosphorus: 133mg

Vegan Tofu and Little Potato Stew

Prep time: 10 minutes, cook time: 28 minutes; Serves 5

Ingredients:

2 tablespoons olive oil
1 block (350g) extra-firm tofu, cubed
½ cup chopped yellow onion
2 cloves of garlic
1 ½ cups carrots
1 ½ cup chopped celery
1 ½ pounds baby potatoes, scrubbed
1 cup frozen peas
2 tablespoons soy sauce
6 cups vegetable broth
3 tablespoons tomato paste
1 cup water
salt and pepper to taste
2 tablespoons cornstarch + 3 tablespoons water

Instructions

1. Press the Sauté button on the Instant Pot and heat the oil.
2. Sear the tofu on all sides until lightly golden.
3. Stir in the onion and garlic until fragrant.
4. Add the carrots, celery, potatoes, and peas. Stir-fry the vegetables for 2 minutes.
5. Pour in the water and season with soy sauce, salt and pepper. Add the tomato paste.
6. Close the lid and set the vent to the Sealing position.
7. Press the Meat/Stew button and adjust the cooking time to 20 minutes.
8. Do quick pressure release.
9. Once the lid is open, press the Sauté button and stir in the cornstarch slurry and cook for 5 minutes until the sauce thickens.

Nutrition Facts Per Serving

Calories 152, Total Fat 7g, Saturated Fat 2g, Total Carbs 17g, Net Carbs 14g, Protein 6g, Sugar: 3g, Fiber: 3g, Sodium: 880mg, Potassium: 975mg, Phosphorus: 436mg

Instant Pot Cabbage

Prep time: 10 minutes, cook time: 9vminutes; Serves 6

Ingredients:

1 onion, diced
2 cups vegetable broth
1 teaspoon oregano
½ teaspoon thyme
1 head of green cabbage, chopped
salt and pepper to taste

Instructions

1. Press the Sauté button on the Instant Pot and cook the onion with a tablespoon of vegetable broth for 3 minutes. Stir in the oregano and thyme and cook for another minute.
2. Stir in the remaining broth and cabbages. Season with salt and pepper to taste.
3. Close the lid and set the vent to the Sealing position.
4. Press the Pressure Cook or Manual button and cook on high. Adjust the cooking time to 5 minutes.
5. Do natural pressure release.

Nutrition Facts Per Serving

Calories 69, Total Fat 3g, Saturated Fat 0.5g, Total Carbs 11g, Net Carbs 8g, Protein 2g, Sugar: 5g, Fiber: 3g, Sodium: 416mg, Potassium: 340mg, Phosphorus: 57mg

Instant Pot Vegetable Soup

Prep time: 10 minutes, cook time: 19 minutes; Serves 8

Ingredients:

1 teaspoon canola oil
1 onion, diced
2 teaspoons minced garlic
2 teaspoons Italian seasoning mix
1-pound potatoes, chopped
3 large carrots, peeled and chopped
2 celery ribs, sliced

1 ½ cups fire-roasted diced tomatoes
1 cup green beans
salt and pepper to taste
6 cups vegetable broth
1 cup spinach

Instructions

1. Press the Sauté button on the Instant Pot and heat the oil.
2. Sauté the onion and garlic for 30 seconds until fragrant.
3. Add in the Italian seasoning mix and stir for another 30 seconds.
4. Add the potatoes, carrots, celery, tomatoes, and beans. Season with salt and pepper to taste.
5. Pour in the broth.
6. Close the lid and set the vent to the Sealing position.
7. Press the Pressure Cooker or Manual button and cook on high. Adjust the cooking time to 15 minutes.
8. Do quick pressure release. Once the lid is open, press the Sauté button and stir in the spinach. Continue cooking for 3 minutes.

Nutrition Facts Per Serving
Calories 101, Total Fat 1g, Saturated Fat 0g, Total Carbs 17g, Net Carbs 14g, Protein 6g, Sugar: 3g, Fiber: 3g, Sodium: 743mg, Potassium: 566mg, Phosphorus: 213mg

Instant Pot Homestyle Veggies

Prep time: 5 minutes, cook time: 20 minutes; Serves 4
Ingredients:
1 cup vegetable broth
½ pound whole carrots, peeled and roughly chopped
1-pound fresh green beans, trimmed
1 ½ pounds red potatoes, cut in half
salt and pepper to taste
Instructions
1. Pour broth in the Instant Pot.
2. Place the vegetables on a steamer basket or trivet and season with salt and pepper to taste.
3. Close the lid and set the vent to the Sealing position.
4. Press the Steam button and cook using the pre-set cooking time.
5. Do natural pressure release.

Nutrition Facts Per Serving
Calories 122, Total Fat 0g, Saturated Fat 0g, Total Carbs 26g, Net Carbs g, Protein 4g, Sugar: 4g, Fiber: 4g, Sodium: 39mg, Potassium: 673mg, Phosphorus: 235mg

Instant Pot Steamed Vegetables

Prep time: 10 minutes, cook time: 5 minutes; Serves 6
Ingredients:
1 cup water
2 cups raw baby carrots
2 cups raw cauliflower florets
2 cups raw broccoli florets
Instructions
1. Pour water in the Instant Pot and place a steamer basket or trivet inside.
2. Place the vegetables in the steamer basket.
3. Close the lid and set the vent to the Sealing position.
4. Press the Steam button and cook using the pre-set cooking time.
5. Do natural pressure release.

Nutrition Facts Per Serving
Calories 27, Total Fat 0.3g, Saturated Fat 0g, Total Carbs 6g, Net Carbs 4g, Protein 2g, Sugar: 2g, Fiber:2 g, Sodium: 40mg, Potassium: 250mg, Phosphorus: 38mg

Summer Vegetable Dinner

Prep time: 5 minutes, cook time: 15 minutes; Serves 8
Ingredients:
4 large ears of corn, shucked and cleaned
1 cup water
3 cups potatoes, cut into chunks
4 cups summer squash, sliced thickly
4 cups kale
Instructions
1. Arrange the corn in the Instant Pot and pour water.
2. Arrange the potato pieces on top of the corn. Toss in the squash and add in the kale last.

3. Close the lid and set the vent to a sealing position.
4. Press the Pressure Cook or Manual button and cook on high. Adjust the cooking time to 15 minutes.
5. Do natural pressure release.

Nutrition Facts Per Serving
Calories 123, Total Fat 1g, Saturated Fat 0g, Total Carbs 27g, Net Carbs 22g, Protein 4g, Sugar: 4g, Fiber: 5g, Sodium: 23mg, Potassium: 573mg, Phosphorus: 126mg

Creamy Cauliflower and Broccoli Medley

Prep time: 5 minutes, cook time: 5 minutes; Serves 8
Ingredients:
2 pounds bag of cauliflower and broccoli florets mix
1 can coconut milk
Zest of 1 lemon
Juice from ½ lemon
¼ teaspoon garlic powder
¼ teaspoon oregano
¼ teaspoon dried parsley
¼ teaspoon dried basil
1/8 teaspoon onion powder
salt and pepper to taste
Instructions
1. Place all ingredients in the Instant Pot.

2. Stir to combine everything.
3. Close the lid and set the vent to the Sealing Position.
4. Press the Pressure Cooker or Manual button and cook on high. Adjust the cooking time to 5 minutes.
5. Do natural pressure release.

Nutrition Facts Per Serving
Calories 32, Total Fat 0.6g, Saturated Fat 0g, Total Carbs 5g, Net Carbs 2g, Protein 4g, Sugar: 1g, Fiber:3 g, Sodium: 65mg, Potassium: 299mg, Phosphorus: 89mg

Parsnips and Carrots

Prep time: 5 minutes, cook time: 10 minutes; Serves 4
Ingredients:
1 tablespoon olive oil
2 cloves of garlic, minced
2 pounds carrots, peeled and sliced
2 pounds parsnips, peeled and sliced
½ cup water
¼ cup maple syrup
Salt and pepper to taste
Fresh parsley, chopped
Instructions
1. Press the Sauté button on the Instant Pot and heat the oil.
2. Sauté the garlic for 30 seconds until fragrant. Stir in the carrots and parsnips for 3 minutes.

3. Pour in water and maple syrup. Season with salt and pepper to taste.
4. Close the lid and set the vent to the Sealing position.
5. Press the Pressure Cooker or Manual button and adjust the cooking time to 6 minutes.
6. Do natural pressure release.
7. Once the lid is open, garnish with parsley.

Nutrition Facts Per Serving
Calories 356, Total Fat 5g, Saturated Fat 0.7g, Total Carbs 78g, Net Carbs 60g, Protein 6g, Sugar: 34g, Fiber: 18g, Sodium: 192mg, Potassium: 1745mg, Phosphorus: 257mg

Potato and Carrot Medley

Prep time: 10 minutes, cook time: 19 minutes; Serves 6
Ingredients:
2 tablespoons extra virgin olive oil
1 onion, chopped
3 cloves of garlic, minced
4 pounds Yukon potatoes, cut into chunks
2 pounds carrots, sliced

1 teaspoon Italian seasoning mix
salt and pepper to taste
1 ½ cup vegetable broth
Fresh parsley for garnish
Instructions

1. Press the Sauté button on the Instant Pot and heat the oil.
2. Sauté the onion and garlic. Stir for 30 seconds until fragrant.
3. Stir in the potatoes and carrots. Season with salt, pepper, and Italian seasoning mix. Stir for 3 minutes.
4. Add in the broth.
5. Close the lid and set the vent to the Sealing position.
6. Press the Pressure Cooker or Manual button and cook on high. Adjust the cooking time to 15 minutes.
7. Do natural pressure release.
8. Once the lid is open, garnish with parsley before serving.

Nutrition Facts Per Serving
Calories 341, Total Fat 4g, Saturated Fat 0.8g, Total Carbs 71g, Net Carbs 60g, Protein 9g, Sugar: 11g, Fiber: 11g, Sodium: 354mg, Potassium: 1810mg, Phosphorus: 242mg

Vegetable Lo Mein

Prep time: 10 minutes, cook time: 15 minutes; Serves 4
Ingredients:
8 ounces spaghetti noodles
2 cups vegetable broth
1 teaspoon sesame oil
1 teaspoon ginger paste
1 teaspoon minced garlic
1 tablespoon soy sauce
1 tablespoon vinegar
1 teaspoon red chili paste
1 teaspoon brown sugar
1 teaspoon coconut oil
½ cup carrots, thinly sliced
½ cup cabbages, thinly sliced
½ cup broccoli florets
salt and pepper to taste
½ cup green scallions
Toasted sesame seeds for garnish

Instructions
1. Place the spaghetti noodles and vegetable broth in the Instant Pot.
2. Close the lid and set the vent to the Sealing position. Press the Pressure Cook or Manual button and adjust the cooking time to 8 minutes. Do quick pressure release and drain the noodles. Set the noodles aside to cool.
3. Meanwhile, mix together the sesame oil, ginger paste, garlic, soy sauce, vinegar, chili pasta, and brown sugar. Set aside.
4. Clean the inner pot and place in the Instant Pot.
5. Press the Sauté button and heat the oil. Sauté the carrots, cabbages and broccoli florets. Season with salt and pepper to taste. Stir for 3 minutes.
6. Add in the noodles and the sauce prepared earlier.
7. Toss to coat the noodles and vegetables.
8. Press the Cancel button to turn off the cooking.
9. Garnish with scallions and sesame seeds before serving.

Nutrition Facts Per Serving
Calories 120, Total Fat 3g, Saturated Fat 1g, Total Carbs 20g, Net Carbs 16g, Protein 4g, Sugar: 3g, Fiber: 4g, Sodium: 75mg, Potassium: 155mg, Phosphorus: 74mg

Instant Pot Vegetable Spaghetti

Prep time: 5 minutes, cook time: 6 minutes; Serves 6
Ingredients:
1 tablespoon olive oil
2 cloves of garlic, minced
4 ounces mushrooms, diced
1 large carrot, chopped
2 zucchinis, chopped
1 green bell pepper, diced
½ cup chopped basil
2 cups water
8 ounces spaghetti noodles
24 ounces pasta sauce
salt and pepper to taste

Instructions
1. Press the Sauté button on the Instant Pot.
2. Heat the oil and stir in the garlic once the oil is hot. Add in the mushrooms and sauté for 4 minutes.

3. Add the carrots, zucchini, and bell pepper. Stir for another 3 minutes. Add the basil.
4. Deglaze the pot with water to remove the browned bits.
5. Break the spaghetti pasta into the Instant Pot. Pour over the remaining water and pasta sauce. Season with salt and pepper to taste.
6. Close the lid and set the vent to the Sealing position.
7. Press the Pressure Cooker or Manual button and cook on high for 6 minutes.
8. Do quick pressure release.
9. Once the lid is open, give the pasta a good mix to combine everything.

Nutrition Facts Per Serving
Calories 114, Total Fat 3g, Saturated Fat 0.4g, Total Carbs 21g, Net Carbs 16g, Protein 5g, Sugar: 6g, Fiber: 5g, Sodium: 812mg, Potassium: 491mg, Phosphorus: 102mg

Veggie Fried Rice

Prep time: 10 minutes, cook time: 25 minutes; Serves 4

Ingredients:
2 cups brown rice
2 cups vegetable broth
2 carrots, diced
1 tablespoon olive oil
1 white onion, chopped
2 cloves garlic, minced
½ cup frozen peas
salt and pepper to taste
Diced green scallions for garnish

Instructions
1. To the Instant Pot, add the brown rice, broth, and diced carrots. Stir to combine.
2. Close the lid and set the vent to the Sealing position.
3. Press the Rice button and cook on low pressure using the pre-set cooking time.
4. Once the timer goes off, do natural pressure release and open the lid. Fluff the rice and transfer into a bowl.
5. Clean the inner pot and place in the Instant Pot.
6. Press the Sauté button and heat the olive oil.
7. Sauté the onion and garlic until fragrant.
8. Add in the peas and stir for 3 minutes.
9. Stir in the cooked rice and season with salt and pepper to taste. Garnish with green scallions before serving.

Nutrition Facts Per Serving
Calories 405, Total Fat 6g, Saturated Fat 1g, Total Carbs 79g, Net Carbs g74, Protein 9g, Sugar: 3g, Fiber: 5g, Sodium: 30mg, Potassium: 385mg, Phosphorus: 338mg

Herb and Vegetable Brown Rice

Prep time: 10 minutes, cook time: 25 minutes; Serves 6

Ingredients:
1 ½ tablespoon olive oil
1 cup onion, chopped
4 cloves of garlic, minced
½ cup red bell pepper, chopped
½ cup celery, chopped
¼ teaspoon dried oregano
1 ½ cup long grain brown rice
1 ¾ cup water
salt and pepper to taste
½ cup fresh parsley, minced

Instructions
1. Press the Sauté button on the Instant Pot and heat the olive oil. Sauté the onion and garlic until fragrant. Stir in the bell pepper, celery, and oregano for 2 minutes until the celery has wilted.
2. Stir in the brown rice, water, salt and pepper. Stir everything to combine.
3. Press the Rice button and cook using the pre-set cooking time. Do natural pressure release.
4. Once the lid is open, fluff the rice and garnish with chopped parsley.

Nutrition Facts Per Serving
Calories 233, Total Fat 6g, Saturated Fat 1g, Total Carbs 40g, Net Carbs 37g, Protein 6g, Sugar: 2g, Fiber: 3g, Sodium: 35mg, Potassium: 242mg, Phosphorus: 181mg

Kung Pao Brussels Sprouts

Prep time: 5 minutes, cook time: 4 hours and 5 minutes; Serves 4

Ingredients:

2 pounds Brussels sprouts, halved
½ cup water
2 tablespoons extra-virgin olive oil
salt and pepper to taste
1 tablespoon sesame oil
2 cloves of garlic, minced
½ cup soy sauce
2 teaspoons apple cider vinegar
1 tablespoon hoisin sauce
1 tablespoon brown sugar
2 teaspoons garlic chili sauce
1 tablespoon cornstarch + 2 tablespoons water
Sesame seeds for garnish
Green onions for garnish
2 tablespoons chopped roasted peanuts

Instructions

1. Place the Brussels sprouts and water in the Instant Pot and drizzle over the olive oil. Season with salt and pepper to taste. Close the lid but do not seal the vent.
2. Press the Slow Cook button and adjust the cooking time to 4 hours.
3. Take the broccoli out and set aside.
4. To the inner pot, stir in the sesame oil and press the Sauté button. Stir in the garlic for 30 seconds.
5. Add in the water and bring to a boil.
6. Stir in the soy sauce, apple cider vinegar, hoisin sauce, brown sugar, and garlic sauce. Bring to a boil and add in the cornstarch slurry until the sauce thickens.
7. Add in the slow cooked broccoli into the sauce.
8. Garnish with sesame seeds, green onions, and roasted peanuts before serving.

Nutrition Facts Per Serving

Calories 343, Total Fat 16g, Saturated Fat 3g, Total Carbs 43g, Net Carbs 32g, Protein 13g, Sugar: 20g, Fiber: 11g, Sodium: 757mg, Potassium: 1151mg, Phosphorus: 257mg

Vegetarian Pad Thai

Prep time: 10 minutes, cook time: 9 minutes; Serves 4

Ingredients:

½ cup soy sauce
1 tablespoon fresh lime juice
2 tablespoons rice wine vinegar
3 tablespoons coconut aminos
1/3 cup granulated sugar
1 tablespoon vegetable oil
12 ounces extra-firm tofu, sliced
1 onion, chopped
1 clove garlic, minced
10 ounces Pad Thai rice noodles
2 cups vegetable stock
2 tablespoons shredded radish
1 cup bean sprouts
1 medium carrot, peeled and shredded
¼ cup unsalted peanuts, roasted
3 scallions, chopped
1 medium lime, cut into wedges

Instructions

1. In a mixing bowl, combine the soy sauce, lime juice, wine vinegar, coconut aminos, and sugar. Set aside.
2. Press the Sauté button on the Instant Pot and heat the olive. Brown the tofu for 3 minutes on each side. Set aside.
3. Sauté the onion and garlic for 30 seconds until fragrant.
4. Add the rice noodles, tofu, and vegetable stock. Close the lid and set the vent to the Sealing position.
5. Press the Pressure Cooker or Manual button and adjust the cooking time to 6 minutes.
6. Do quick pressure release. Once the lid is open, drain the noodles and set aside.
7. Place the noodles in bowls and top with radish, bean sprouts, carrots, peanuts, scallions, and lime wedges.
8. Drizzle with the prepared sauce.

Nutrition Facts Per Serving

Calories 559, Total Fat 12g, Saturated Fat 4g, Total Carbs 93g, Net Carbs g, Protein 17g, Sugar: 23g, Fiber: 4g, Sodium: 432mg, Potassium: 521mg, Phosphorus: 125mg

Red Curry Vegetables

Prep time: 5 minutes, cook time: 15 minutes; Serves 4

Ingredients:

1 onion, chopped
3 cloves garlic, minced
2 ½ cups chopped cauliflower florets
2 ½ cups cubed sweet potato
1 can coconut milk
1 can diced tomatoes
3 tablespoon red curry paste
2 teaspoons soy sauce
1 teaspoon turmeric
1 cup water
A bunch of kale leaves
Fresh lime juice
Fresh cilantro leaves

Instructions

1. Place the onions and garlic in the Instant Pot. Add a teaspoon of water. Press the Sauté button and do water sauté for 1 minute.
2. Stir in the cauliflower, sweet potato, milk, tomatoes, red curry paste, soy sauce, and turmeric. Add water.
3. Close the lid and set the vent to the Sealing position.
4. Press the Pressure Cooker or Manual button and adjust the cooking time to 10 minutes.
5. Do quick pressure release.
6. Once the lid is open, press the Sauté button and add the kale leaves. Cook for 3 more minutes until the kale leaves are wilted.
7. Serve with lime juice and cilantro leaves.

Nutrition Facts Per Serving

Calories 70, Total Fat 1g, Saturated Fat 0g, Total Carbs 14g, Net Carbs 9g, Protein 3g, Sugar: 6g, Fiber:5 g, Sodium: 172mg, Potassium: 615mg, Phosphorus: 84mg

Instant Pot Carrots

Prep time: 5 minutes, cook time: 8 minutes; Serves 4

Ingredients:

2 pounds fresh carrots, cut into thick strips
1 cup water
1 tablespoon olive oil
1 teaspoon fresh thyme

Instructions

1. Place the carrots and water in the Instant Pot.
2. Lock the lid and set the vent to the Sealing position.
3. Press the Pressure Cooker or Manual button and adjust the cooking time to 5 minutes.
4. Once the timer sets off, do quick pressure release and drain the carrots.
5. Clean the inner pot.
6. Press the Sauté button and heat the oil. Stir in the thyme to toast and add in the carrots. Stir fry for 3 minutes.

Nutrition Facts Per Serving

Calories 109, Total Fat 4g, Saturated Fat 0.5g, Total Carbs 19g, Net Carbs 12g, Protein 2g, Sugar: 8g, Fiber: 7g, Sodium: 132mg, Potassium: 534mg, Phosphorus: 68mg

Vegetable Chow Mein

Prep time: 5 minutes, cook time: 10 minutes; Serves 5

Ingredients:

4 cups vegetable broth
2 tablespoon dark soy sauce
1 teaspoon sesame oil
1 tablespoon vinegar
1 tablespoons sriracha sauce
1 tablespoon brown sugar
16 ounces hakka noodles
1 teaspoon grated ginger
1 teaspoon grated garlic
1 cup cabbage, thinly sliced
½ cup celery, chopped
2 carrots, peeled and julienned
1 cup snow peas, trimmed
1 cup broccoli florets
½ cup green onion, chopped

Instructions

1. In a bowl, mix the vegetable broth, soy sauce, sesame oil, sriracha sauce, and brown sugar. Whisk and set aside.

2. Press the Sauté button on the Instant Pot and pour the prepared sauce. Spread the noodles over the sauce. Top with grated ginger, garlic, cabbage, celery, and carrots.
3. Close the lid and set the vent to the Sealing position.
4. Press the Pressure Cooker or Manual button. Adjust the cooking time to 5 minutes.
5. Do quick pressure release.
6. Once the lid is open, press the Sauté button and stir in the snow peas and broccoli. Cook for 5 minutes.
7. Garnish with green onion.

Nutrition Facts Per Serving
Calories 172, Total Fat 2g, Saturated Fat 0.4g, Total Carbs 33g, Net Carbs 31g, Protein 5g, Sugar: 5g, Fiber: 2g, Sodium: 295mg, Potassium: 201mg, Phosphorus: 56mg

Instant Pot Vegetable Soup

Prep time: 10 minutes, cook time: 20 minutes; Serves 4
Ingredients:
1 tablespoon olive oil
1 onion, chopped
4 cloves garlic, minced
1 carrot, peeled and diced
1 teaspoon dried oregano
½ teaspoon paprika
½ teaspoon cumin
½ teaspoon chopped mint
½ cup coarse bulgur
salt and pepper to taste
4 cups vegetable stock
2 cups baby spinach
1 lemon juice, freshly squeezed
Instructions
1. Press the Sauté button on the Instant Pot and heat the oil.
2. Sauté the onion and garlic for 30 seconds or until fragrant.
3. Stir in the carrot, oregano, paprika, cumin, mint, bulgur, and vegetable stock. Season with salt and pepper to taste.
4. Close the lid and set the vent to the Sealing position.
5. Press the Pressure Cook or Manual button and adjust the cooking time to 15 minutes.
6. Do quick pressure release.
7. Once the lid is open, press the Sauté button and stir in the spinach. Cook for 3 minutes or until the spinach has wilted.
8. Drizzle with lemon juice before serving.

Nutrition Facts Per Serving
Calories 118, Total Fat 6g, Saturated Fat g, Total Carbs 11g, Net Carbs g, Protein 7g, Sugar: 2g, Fiber: 2.5g, Sodium: 33mg, Potassium: 273mg, Phosphorus:79 mg

Summer Vegetable Soup

Prep time: 10 minutes, cook time: 20 minutes; Serves 4
Ingredients:
4 cups vegetable broth
1 14-ounce can dice tomatoes
2 tablespoon tomato paste
1 small yellow onion, diced
1 red bell pepper, diced
1 small zucchini, chopped
2 ears of corn, shucked
1 tablespoon fresh lemon juice
1 tablespoon fresh parsley, chopped
salt and pepper to taste
Instructions
1. Place all ingredients in the Instant Pot and give a good stir.
2. Press the Broth/Soup button and adjust the cooking time to 20 minutes. Cook on high pressure.
3. Do quick pressure release.

Nutrition Facts Per Serving
Calories 97, Total Fat 1g, Saturated Fat 0.2g, Total Carbs 22g, Net Carbs 17g, Protein 4g, Sugar: 7g, Fiber: 5g, Sodium: 132mg, Potassium: 547mg, Phosphorus: 100mg

Hibachi Mushroom Steak

Prep time: minutes, cook time: minutes; Serves 2

Ingredients:

1/3 cup soy sauce

2 tablespoons white vinegar

1 tablespoon grated ginger

1 tablespoon minced garlic

1-pound large chestnut mushrooms, stems removed

1 zucchini, sliced in rounds

1 yellow onion.

1 tablespoon granulated sugar

Salt and pepper to taste

Instructions

1. Place all ingredients in a bowl and allow ingredients to marinate in the fridge for at least 30 minutes.

2. Pour in the Instant Pot all ingredients.

3. Close the lid and set the vent to the Sealing position.

4. Press the Pressure Cook or Manual button and cook on high. Adjust the cooking time to 5 minutes.

5. Do natural pressure release.

Nutrition Facts Per Serving

Calories 208, Total Fat 8g, Saturated Fat 2g, Total Carbs 26g, Net Carbs 22g, Protein 11g, Sugar: 18g, Fiber: 4g, Sodium: 650mg, Potassium: 950mg, Phosphorus: 265mg

Lemony Rice and Vegetable Soup

Prep time: 10 minutes, cook time: 20 minutes; Serves 4

Ingredients:

1 tablespoon extra-virgin olive oil

1 yellow onion, chopped

2 cloves of garlic, minced

2 large carrots, diced

2 stalks celery, diced

½ large fennel bulb, diced

½ teaspoon ground cumin

1 cup brown basmati rice

2 handful spinach

6 cups vegetable broth

salt and pepper to taste

4 tablespoons fresh lemon juice

Instructions

1. Press the Sauté button on the Instant Pot and heat the oil.

2. Sauté the onion and garlic for 30 seconds until fragrant.

3. Stir in the carrots, celery, fennel, and cumin. Stir for 2 minutes until the vegetables are wilted.

4. Add in the rice, spinach, and broth. Season with salt and pepper to taste.

5. Stir the ingredients until well-combined.

6. Close the lid and set the vent to the Sealing position.

7. Press the Rice button and cook using the preset cooking time.

8. Do natural pressure release.

9. Once the lid is open, drizzle with lemon juice then fluff the rice.

Nutrition Facts Per Serving

Calories 245, Total Fat 5g, Saturated Fat 0.8g, Total Carbs 45g, Net Carbs 41g, Protein 5g, Sugar: 5g, Fiber: 4g, Sodium: 84mg, Potassium: 418mg, Phosphorus: 196mg

Vegetable Pho Soup

Prep time: 10 minutes, cook time: 40 minutes; Serves 4

Ingredients:

2 tablespoons olive oil

1 onion, quartered

5 whole star anise pods

1 tablespoon fennel seeds

1 tablespoon coriander seeds

1 cinnamon stick

½ tablespoon whole black peppercorns

1 cup dried mushrooms

1 1-inch ginger, peeled

2 kaffir lime leaves

2 bay leaves

2 celery stalks, chopped roughly

1 large carrot, chopped roughly

4 cups water

salt to taste

2 cup broccoli florets

2 tablespoons cilantro, chopped
1 cup straw mushrooms
8 ounces shiitake mushrooms
1 small zucchini, chopped
1 cup mung bean sprouts
1 cup basil leaves
1 lime, cut into wedges
Sriracha sauce

Instructions

1. Press the Sauté button and heat the oil. Toast the onion, anise, fennel seeds, coriander, cinnamon stick, black peppercorns, dried mushrooms, ginger, kaffir lime leaves, and bay leaves. Stir for 2 minutes until fragrant.
2. Add in the celery and carrots and stir for another 3 minutes before pouring in water. Season with salt to taste.
3. Close the lid and set the vent to the Sealing position.
4. Press the Broth/Soup button and cook using the preset cooking time. Do quick pressure release once the timer has set off.
5. Once the lid is open, remove the solids. Add in the broccoli, cilantro, mushrooms, and zucchini.
6. Close the lid again and set the vent to the Sealing position. Press the Pressure Cook or Manual button and adjust the cooking time to 5 minutes.
7. Do natural pressure release.
8. Garnish with bean sprouts, basil leaves, and lime wedges before serving. Drizzle with sriracha sauce if desired.

Nutrition Facts Per Serving
Calories 171, Total Fat 9g, Saturated Fat 1g, Total Carbs 23g, Net Carbs 17g, Protein 6g, Sugar: 6g, Fiber: 6g, Sodium: 215mg, Potassium: 511mg, Phosphorus: 143mg

Veggie Macaroni

Prep time: 10 minutes, cook time: 20 minutes; Serves 4

Ingredients:
2 cups dry macaroni
2 cups water
1 ½ cups marinara sauce
½ cup coconut milk
1 cup frozen veggies of your choice
2 tablespoons nutritional yeast
salt and pepper to taste

Instructions

1. Add all ingredients in the Instant Pot and give a good stir.
2. Close the lid and set the vent to the Sealing position.
3. Press the Multigrain button and cook on high. Adjust the cooking time to 20 minutes.
4. Do natural pressure release.

Nutrition Facts Per Serving
Calories 330, Total Fat 9g, Saturated Fat 7g, Total Carbs 51g, Net Carbs 56g, Protein 11g, Sugar: 8g, Fiber: 5g, Sodium: 306mg, Potassium: 692mg, Phosphorus: 171mg

Instant Pot Broccoli

Prep time: 10 minutes, cook time: 10 minutes; Serves 4

Ingredients:
2 heads broccoli, cut into florets
2 tablespoons coconut oil
salt and pepper to taste
3 tablespoons nutritional yeast

Instructions

1. Pour a cup of water in the Instant Pot and place a steamer basket or trivet.
2. Place the broccoli florets in the steamer basket.
3. Close the lid and set the vent to the Sealing position.
4. Press the Steam button and cook for 10 minutes.
5. Do quick pressure release.
6. Once the lid is open, take the broccoli out and place in a bowl.
7. Drizzle with oil and season with salt, pepper, and nutritional yeast.
8. Toss to combine everything.

Nutrition Facts Per Serving
Calories 88, Total Fat 7g, Saturated Fat 4g, Total Carbs 3g, Net Carbs 2g, Protein 4g, Sugar: 0.3g, Fiber: 1g, Sodium: 406mg, Potassium: 323mg, Phosphorus: 29mg

Vegan Jambalaya

Prep time: 10 minutes, cook time: 25 minutes; Serves 4

Ingredients:
1 tablespoon oil
1 onion, diced
1 green bell pepper, seeded and diced
3 ribs of celery, diced
4 cloves of garlic, minced
1 ½ cup long grain white rice
1 can small diced tomatoes
1 tablespoon Cajun seasoning
2 teaspoons smoked paprika
3 cups vegetable broth
¼ cup chopped parsley
salt and pepper to taste

Instructions
1. Press the Sauté button on the Instant Pot and heat the oil.
2. Sauté the onion, green bell pepper, celery, and garlic. Stir for 2 minutes until fragrant.
3. Add in the rest of the ingredients and give a good stir.
4. Close the lid and set the vent to the Sealing position.
5. Press the Rice button and cook on low pressure.
6. Do natural pressure release.

Nutrition Facts Per Serving
Calories 319, Total Fat 4g, Saturated Fat 0.7g, Total Carbs 63g, Net Carbs 60g, Protein 6g, Sugar: 3g, Fiber: 3g, Sodium: 165mg, Potassium: 293mg, Phosphorus: 109mg

Vegetables in Tomatoes

Prep time: 5 minutes, cook time: 24 minutes; Serves 4

Ingredients:
1 tablespoon olive oil
2 cloves of garlic
1 large onion, chopped
1 cup diced carrots
½ cup peas
32 ounces vegetable broth
1 cup broccoli florets
1 14-ounce can dice tomatoes
2 tablespoons fresh basil
3 cups water
salt and pepper to taste

Instructions
1. Press the Sauté button on the Instant Pot and heat the oil. Sauté the garlic and onion until fragrant for 30 seconds or until fragrant.
2. Stir in the carrots and peas and stir for 2 minutes.
3. Add in the rest of the ingredients. Give a good stir.
4. Close the lid and set the vent to the Sealing position.
5. Press the Broth/Soup button and cook on high. Adjust the cooking time to 20 minutes.
6. Do natural pressure release.

Nutrition Facts Per Serving
Calories 77, Total Fat 4g, Saturated Fat 0.5g, Total Carbs 10g, Net Carbs 6g, Protein 2g, Sugar: 6g, Fiber: 4g, Sodium: 142mg, Potassium: 363mg, Phosphorus: 48mg

Vegetarian Mushroom Soup

Prep time: 5 minutes, cook time: 6 minutes; Serves 4

Ingredients:
8 ounces sliced cremini mushrooms
1 cup frozen peas
1 onion, chopped
1 14-ounce diced tomatoes
½ cup water
½ teaspoon ground cumin
1 ½ cup coconut milk
1 tablespoon grated ginger
salt to taste
1 tablespoon sugar
½ cup cilantro, chopped

Instructions
1. In the Instant Pot, combine the mushrooms, peas, onions, tomatoes, water, cumin, coconut milk, and ginger. Season with salt, and sugar.

2. Close the lid and set the vent to the Sealing position. Press the Pressure Cook or Manual button and adjust the cooking time to 6 minutes.
3. Do natural pressure release.
4. Once the lid is open, stir in the cilantro before serving.

Nutrition Facts Per Serving
Calories 240, Total Fat 7g, Saturated Fat 5g, Total Carbs 35g, Net Carbs 28g, Protein 12g, Sugar: 13g, Fiber: 7g, Sodium: 440mg, Potassium: 930mg, Phosphorus: 310mg

Lemon Veggie Risotto

Prep time: 10 minutes, cook time: 25 minutes; Serves 4

Ingredients:
1 bunch asparagus, sliced thin
1 cup broccoli, florets
1 cup fresh peas
1 tablespoon + 2 tablespoons olive oil
1 onion, diced
1 cup leek, diced
2 garlic, cloves
salt and pepper to taste
1 teaspoon fresh thyme
1 ½ cups arborio rice
4 cups vegetable broth
1 cup spinach
½ bunch chives, chopped
¼ teaspoon red pepper flakes
1 teaspoon lemon zest
2 tablespoons lemon juice

Instructions
1. Preheat the oven to 400⁰F and line a baking sheet with parchment paper. To the baking sheet, add the asparagus, broccoli, and peas. Drizzle with oil and place in the oven for 20 minutes until the vegetables are tender. Set aside.
2. In the Instant Pot, press the Sauté button and heat the remaining oil. Sauté the onion, leeks, and garlic for 30 seconds or until fragrant.
3. Add rice and continue stirring for 2 minutes until lightly toasted.
4. Stir in the broth and season with salt and pepper.
5. Press the Cancel button and close the lid. Make sure that the vent is set to the Sealing position.
6. Press the Pressure Cook or Manual button and cook on high for 7 minutes.
7. Once the timer sets off, do quick pressure release.
8. Once the lid is open, press the Sauté button and add the rest of the ingredients including the toasted vegetables.
9. Serve warm.

Nutrition Facts Per Serving
Calories 204, Total Fat 13g, Saturated Fat 2g, Total Carbs 30g, Net Carbs 19g, Protein 7g, Sugar: 3g, Fiber: 11g, Sodium: 18mg, Potassium: 827mg, Phosphorus: 774mg

Instant Pot Vegetable Korma

Prep time: 10 minutes, cook time: 27minutes; Serves 4

Ingredients:
1 large sweet onion, chopped
15 raw cashews, soaked in water overnight
1 1-inch ginger, sliced
4 cloves garlic, peeled
2 tablespoons coconut oil
6 whole black peppercorns
4 green cardamoms
4 whole cloves
1 bay leaf
½ cup tomato puree
2 tablespoons garam masala or curry powder
½ teaspoon sugar
1 large potato, peeled and diced
2 medium carrots, peeled and diced
¼ cup frozen green peas
1 cup coconut milk
½ cup water
Juice from half of lemon
salt and pepper to taste
2 tablespoons chopped cilantro

Instructions

1. Place the onion, cashews, ginger, and garlic in a blender and pulse until smooth. Set aside.
2. Press the Sauté button on the Instant Pot and heat the oil. Toast the peppercorns, cardamoms, cloves, bay leaf for 2 minutes until fragrant.
3. Stir in the onion-cashew paste and stir for 3 minutes. Add the tomato puree and stir to remove the brown bits at the bottom.
4. Add the garam masala and sugar. Stir in the vegetables. Continue stirring for 2 minutes.
5. Stir in the coconut milk, water, and lemon juice. Season with salt and pepper to taste.
6. Press the Cancel button and close the lid. Set the vent to the Sealing position.
7. Press the Meat/Stew button and cook on the lowest pre-set cooking button.
8. Do natural pressure release.
9. Serve with chopped cilantro.

Nutrition Facts Per Serving
Calories 189, Total Fat 21g, Saturated Fat 11g, Total Carbs 14g, Net Carbs 11g, Protein 4g, Sugar: 4g, Fiber: 3g, Sodium: 341mg, Potassium: 509mg, Phosphorus: 236mg

One Pot Vegetarian Linguine

Prep time: 10 minutes, cook time: 10 minutes; Serves 6

Ingredients:
1 tablespoon olive oil
2 small onions, chopped
1 clove garlic, minced
½ pound fresh cremini mushrooms, sliced
1 large tomato, chopped
2 medium zucchinis, thinly sliced
4 tablespoons nutritional yeast
salt and pepper
6 ounces uncooked linguine
3 cups water
2 tablespoons cornstarch + 3 tablespoons water

Instructions
1. Press the Sauté button on the Instant Pot. Heat the oil and sauté the onions and garlic for 1 minute until fragrant.
2. Stir in the mushrooms and tomato. Stir for a minute.
3. Add in the zucchini and season with nutritional yeast, salt and pepper to taste.
4. Add the linguine and water. Stir to combine.
5. Close the lid and set the vent to the Sealing position.
6. Press the Pressure Cook or Manual button and cook on high. Adjust the cooking time to 6 minutes.
7. Do quick pressure release once the timer sets off.
8. Open the lid and press the Sauté button. Stir in the cornstarch slurry and continue to stir until the sauce thickens.

Nutrition Facts Per Serving
Calories 239, Total Fat 3g, Saturated Fat 0.4g, Total Carbs 52g, Net Carbs 44g, Protein 8g, Sugar: 18g, Fiber:8 g, Sodium: 366mg, Potassium: 1286mg, Phosphorus: 162mg

Lemon Couscous

Prep time: 10 minutes, cook time: 24 minutes; Serves 4

Ingredients:
1 cup pearl couscous
1 ¼ cup water
1 tablespoon olive oil
¾ cup sliced scallions
1 clove garlic, minced
¾ teaspoon salt
¼ teaspoon pepper
1 teaspoon lemon zest

Instructions
1. Place couscous and water in the Instant Pot.
2. Close the lid and set the vent to the Sealing position. Press the Rice button and cook using the preset cooking time.
3. Once the timer sets off, open the lid and fluff the couscous. Remove from the Instant Pot and clean the inner pot.
4. Return the inner pot into the Instant Pot and press the Sauté button. Heat the oil and sauté the scallions and garlic for 30 seconds until fragrant.

5. Stir in the couscous and season with salt, pepper, and lemon zest.
6. Stir for 3 minutes.
7. Serve warm.

Nutrition Facts Per Serving
Calories 81, Total Fat 3g, Saturated Fat g0.5, Total Carbs 11g, Net Carbs 10g, Protein 2g, Sugar: 0.5g, Fiber: 1g, Sodium: 5mg, Potassium: 79mg, Phosphorus: 17mg

Veggie Pasta Shells

Prep time: 10 minutes, cook time: 10 minutes; Serves 6
Ingredients:
2 tablespoons olive oil
1 small onion, chopped
1 clove garlic, minced
½ bunch broccoli, cut into florets
1 cup shredded carrot
¼ cup basil leaves
½ cup marinara sauce
1 box pasta shells
4 tablespoons nutritional yeast
salt and pepper to taste
Instructions
1. Press the Sauté button on the Instant Pot and heat the oil.
2. Sauté the onion and garlic until fragrant. Stir in the rest of the ingredients.
3. Give a stir to combine.
4. Close the lid and set the vent to the Sealing position.
5. Press the Pressure Cook or Manual button and cook on high. Adjust the cooking time to 8 minutes.
6. Once the timer sets off, do quick pressure release.

Nutrition Facts Per Serving
Calories 98, Total Fat 5g, Saturated Fat 0.7g, Total Carbs 8g, Net Carbs5 g, Protein 5g, Sugar: 3g, Fiber: 3g, Sodium: 396mg, Potassium: 523mg, Phosphorus: 60mg

Butternut Squash and Thyme

Prep time: 5 minutes, cook time: 6 minutes; Serves 4
Ingredients:
2 tablespoons olive oil
2 cloves of garlic, minced
1 sprig of thyme
½ medium butternut squash, peeled and sliced
½ cup vegetable broth
salt and pepper to taste
Instructions
1. Press the Sauté button on the Instant Pot and heat the oil.
2. Sauté the garlic for 30 seconds until fragrant.
3. Stir in the rest of the ingredients.
4. Close the lid and set the vent to the Sealing position.
5. Press the Pressure Cook or Manual button and cook on high for 5 minutes.
6. Do natural pressure release.

Nutrition Facts Per Serving
Calories 120, Total Fat 7g, Saturated Fat 1g, Total Carbs 15g, Net Carbs 12g, Protein 1g, Sugar: 3g, Fiber: 3g, Sodium: 74mg, Potassium: 446mg, Phosphorus: 44mg

Veggies with Herbed Mushrooms

Prep time: 5 minutes, cook time: 8 minutes; Serves 6
Ingredients:
1 tablespoon coconut oil
1 onion, chopped
4 cloves garlic, minced
3 ounces shiitake mushrooms, sliced
3 ounces cremini mushrooms, sliced
3 ounces button mushrooms, sliced
1 teaspoon dried thyme
1 teaspoon Italian oregano
salt and pepper to taste
12 ounces frozen vegetables
1 cup vegetable broth
Instructions

1. Press the Sauté button on the Instant Pot and heat the oil. Sauté the onion and garlic for 30 seconds until fragrant.
2. Stir in the mushrooms and season with thyme, oregano, salt, and pepper. Stir for 2 minutes.
3. Add in the rest of the ingredients.
4. Close the lid and set the vent to the Sealing position.
5. Press the Pressure Cook or Manual button and cook on high. Set the cooking time to 5 minutes.
6. Do natural pressure release once the timer sets off.

Nutrition Facts Per Serving
Calories 159, Total Fat 3g, Saturated Fat 2g, Total Carbs 33g, Net Carbs 26g, Protein 5g, Sugar: 4g, Fiber: 7g, Sodium: 25mg, Potassium: 585mg, Phosphorus: 125mg

Lemony Artichokes with Olives Pasta

Prep time: 10 minutes, cook time: 12 minutes; Serves 4
Ingredients:
6 ounces linguine pasta
4 cups water
2 tablespoon olive oil
1 onion, minced
2 cloves garlic, minced
1 14-ounce can artichoke hearts, drained and halved
Salt and pepper to taste
1 tablespoon grated lemon zest
3 tablespoons lemon juice
½ cup green olives, pitted and chopped
1 teaspoon red pepper flakes
2 tablespoon parsley, chopped
Instructions
1. Place the pasta and water in the Instant Pot.
2. Close the lid and set the vent to the Sealing position. Press the Pressure Cook or Manual button and adjust the cooking time to 6 minutes. Do quick pressure release. Once the lid is open, drain the pasta then set aside. Clean the inner pot.
3. Press the Sauté button on the Instant and heat olive oil.
4. Sauté the onion and garlic for a minute or until lightly golden.
5. Stir in the artichokes and season with salt and pepper to taste. Stir for 3 minutes.
6. Add in the rest of the ingredients.
Stir for 3 minutes or until everything is combined.

Nutrition Facts Per Serving
Calories 184, Total Fat 8g, Saturated Fat 1g, Total Carbs 28g, Net Carbs 17g, Protein 5g, Sugar: 3g, Fiber: 11g, Sodium: 68mg, Potassium: 371mg, Phosphorus: 118mg

Simple Steamed Butternut Squash

Prep time: 10 minutes, cook time: 10minutes; Serves 4
Ingredients:
1 cup water
1 medium butternut squash, peeled and sliced thickly
2 tablespoons extra virgin olive oil
1 tablespoon vegetable bouillon, cracked into powder
salt and pepper to taste
Instructions
1. Place a cup of water in the Instant Pot and place a trivet or steamer basket inside.
2. In a bowl, season the butternut squash with olive oil, vegetable bouillon, salt, and pepper.
3. Place in a heat-proof dish that will fit inside the Instant Pot.
4. Place inside the Instant Pot and close the lid. Set the vent to the Sealing position.
5. Press the Steam button and cook on high for 10 minutes.
6. Do natural pressure release.

Nutrition Facts Per Serving
Calories 57, Total Fat 6g, Saturated Fat 3g, Total Carbs 1g, Net Carbs 0.5g, Protein 0.01g, Sugar: 0.005g, Fiber: 0.5g, Sodium: 60mg, Potassium: 9mg, Phosphorus:2 mg

Summer Squash and Mint Pasta

Prep time: 10 minutes, cook time: 10 minutes; Serves 5

Ingredients:

2 tablespoons olive oil
1 shallot, minced
1 cup sliced squash
1/3 cup mint, chopped
1 tablespoon lemon juice
12 ounces rigatoni pasta
4 tablespoons nutritional yeast
salt and pepper to taste
1 ½ cups water

Instructions

1. Press the Sauté button on the Instant Pot. Heat the oil.
2. Sauté the shallots until fragrant. Add in the squash, mint and the rest of the ingredients.
3. Give a good stir.
4. Close the lid and set the vent to the Sealing Position.
5. Press the Pressure Cook or Manual button. Adjust the cooking time to 7 minutes.
6. Do natural pressure release.

Nutrition Facts Per Serving

Calories 183, Total Fat 7g, Saturated Fat 1g, Total Carbs 22g, Net Carbs 18g, Protein 8g, Sugar: 0.3g, Fiber: 4g, Sodium: 432mg, Potassium: 364mg, Phosphorus: 90mg

Miso-Glazed Eggplants

Prep time: 5 minutes, cook time: 5 minutes; Serves 2

Ingredients:

4 medium eggplants, sliced into 1-inch pieces
2 cloves garlic, minced
1 teaspoon miso paste
1 teaspoon brown sugar
1 teaspoon soy sauce
1 teaspoon sesame oil
Salt and pepper to taste
1 teaspoon toasted sesame seed

Instructions

1. Place all ingredients except for the toasted sesame seeds in the Instant Pot and give a good stir.
2. Close the lid and set the vent to the Sealing position.
3. Press the Pressure Cook or Manual button. Adjust the cooking time to 5 minutes.
4. Do natural pressure release.
5. Garnish with sesame seeds before serving.

Nutrition Facts Per Serving

Calories 324, Total Fat 6g, Saturated Fat 1g, Total Carbs 68g, Net Carbs 35g, Protein 12g, Sugar: 41g, Fiber: 33g, Sodium: 117mg, Potassium: 2540mg, Phosphorus: 286mg

One-Pot Curried Butternut Squash

Prep time: 5 minutes, cook time: 5 minutes; Serves 4

Ingredients:

1 14-ounce coconut milk
1 1-inch ginger, sliced
1 onion, minced
2 cloves garlic, minced
½ butternut squash, peeled and sliced
1 tablespoon turmeric powder
1 tablespoon garam masala powder
2 tablespoons lemon juice
salt and pepper to taste

Instructions

1. Place all ingredients in the Instant Pot. Give a good stir.
2. Close the lid and set the vent to the Sealing Position.
3. Press the Pressure Cook or Manual button.
4. Adjust the cooking time to 5 minutes.
5. Once the timer sets off, do natural pressure release.

Nutrition Facts Per Serving

Calories 42, Total Fat 0.3g, Saturated Fat 0g, Total Carbs 9g, Net Carbs 7g, Protein 1g, Sugar: 4g, Fiber: 2g, Sodium: 106mg, Potassium: 354mg, Phosphorus: 38mg

Instant Pot Maple Glazed Carrots

Prep time: 5 minutes, cook time: 8 minutes; Serves 4

Ingredients:

1 cup water

2 large carrots, peeled and julienned

1 tablespoon oil

1 clove garlic, minced

1 shallot, minced

¼ cup maple syrup

Salt and pepper to taste

Instructions

Pour water into the Instant Pot and place trivet or steamer basket inside.

1. Place carrots in the steamer basket.
2. Close the lid and set the vent to the Sealing position.
3. Press the Steam button and cook for 5 minutes.
4. Do quick pressure release. Remove the carrots from the steamer basket then set aside. Clean the inner pot.
5. Press the Sauté button on the Instant Pot and heat the oil.
6. Sauté the garlic and shallots.
7. Stir in the steamed carrots and maple syrup.
8. Stir for 2 minutes. Season with pepper and salt.
9. Serve and enjoy.

Nutrition Facts Per Serving

Calories 97, Total Fat 4g, Saturated Fat 0.5g, Total Carbs 17g, Net Carbs 16g, Protein 0.4g, Sugar: 14g, Fiber: 1g, Sodium: 27mg, Potassium: 160mg, Phosphorus: 14mg

Cider Glazed Brussels Sprouts

Prep time: 5 minutes, cook time: 10 minutes; Serves 8

Ingredients:

1 cup apple cider

½ cup dried cranberries

2 pounds Brussels sprouts

salt to taste

2 tablespoons extra virgin oil

Instructions

1. Place the apple cider in the Instant Pot. Press the Sauté button and bring to a boil.
2. Add the cranberries and Brussels sprouts. Season with salt.
3. Press the Cancel button and close the lid. Set the vent to the Sealing position.
4. Press the Pressure Cook or Manual button. Adjust the cooking time to 5 minutes.
5. Do quick pressure release.
6. Once the lid is open, drizzle with extra virgin olive oil.

Nutrition Facts Per Serving

Calories 94, Total Fat 4g, Saturated Fat 0.6g, Total Carbs 14g, Net Carbs 9g, Protein 4g, Sugar: 6g, Fiber: 5g, Sodium: 29mg, Potassium: 458mg, Phosphorus: 80mg

Instant Pot Ratatouille

Prep time: 10 minutes, cook time: 10 minutes; Serves 4

Ingredients:

1 ½ tablespoon extra-virgin olive oil

1 tablespoon minced garlic

1 cup chopped red onion

1 cup chopped red bell pepper

2 14-ounce cans diced tomatoes

1 large zucchini, sliced into 1inch pieces

1 large yellow squash, sliced into 1-inch pieces

1 small eggplant, peeled and slice into 1-inch pieces

1 tablespoon red wine vinegar

½ teaspoon smoked paprika

salt to taste

2 tablespoons fresh basil leaves

Instructions

1. Press the Sauté button on the Instant Pot and heat the oil. Sauté the garlic, onion, and bell pepper until fragrant.
2. Stir in the tomatoes and cook for another 3 minutes.
3. Add in the zucchini, yellow squash, and eggplant.
4. Season with red wine vinegar, paprika, and salt. Top with basil.

5. Close the lid and set the vent to the Sealing position.
6. Press the Pressure Cook or Manual button and adjust the cooking time to 5 minutes.
7. Do natural pressure release.

Nutrition Facts Per Serving
Calories 354, Total Fat 7g, Saturated Fat 0.8g, Total Carbs 58g, Net Carbs 45g, Protein 15g, Sugar: 13g, Fiber: 13g, Sodium: 558mg, Potassium: 891mg, Phosphorus: 321mg

Steamed Asian Brussels Sprouts

Prep time: 10 minutes, cook time: 10 minutes; Serves 4
Ingredients:
1 cup water
2 tablespoons sesame oil
4 teaspoons soy sauce
2 teaspoon rice vinegar
1 ½ cups Brussels sprouts, thinly sliced
salt to taste
2 tablespoons chopped peanuts, toasted
Instructions
1. Pour water in the Instant Pot and place a steamer basket or trivet inside.
2. In a heat-proof dish, mix all ingredients except for the peanuts. Toss to coat the Brussels sprouts with the ingredients.
3. Place the dish with the Brussels sprouts on the trivet.
4. Close the lid and set the vent to the Sealing position.
5. Press the Steam button and cook for 10 minutes.
6. Do natural pressure release to open the lid.
7. Garnish with toasted peanuts before serving.

Nutrition Facts Per Serving
Calories 137, Total Fat 11g, Saturated Fat 2g, Total Carbs 8g, Net Carbs 6g, Protein 4g, Sugar: 3g, Fiber: 2g, Sodium: 137mg, Potassium: 205mg, Phosphorus: 63mg

Steamed Eggplant Salad

Prep time: minutes, cook time: minutes; Serves 2
Ingredients:
1 cup water
4 medium-sized Chinese eggplants
½ cup chopped tomatoes
1 red onions, chopped
1 tablespoon grated ginger
Juice from ½ lemon, freshly squeezed
1 tablespoon chopped green onions
salt and pepper to taste
Instructions
1. Pour water in the Instant Pot and place a steamer basket or trivet inside.
2. Place the Chinese eggplants on the basket.
3. Close the lid and set the vent to the Sealing position.
4. Press the Steam button. Cook for 10 minutes.
5. Do natural pressure release.
6. Once the lid is open, take the eggplants out and allow to cool.
7. Once cool, shred with two forks. Place in a bowl and add the rest of the ingredients.

Nutrition Facts Per Serving
Calories 309, Total Fat 2g, Saturated Fat 0.5g, Total Carbs 73g, Net Carbs 39g, Protein 12g, Sugar: 42g, Fiber: 34g, Sodium: 27mg, Potassium: 2708mg, Phosphorus: 291mg

Spaghetti Squash

Prep time: 5 minutes, cook time: 10 minutes; Serves 2
Ingredients:
1 cup water
1 spaghetti squash, cut lengthwise and seeds removed
Salt and pepper to taste
Instructions
1. Pour water in the Instant Pot and place a steamer basket or trivet inside.
2. Season the spaghetti squash with salt and pepper.
3. Place on the steamer basket.

4. Close the lid and set the vent to the Sealing position.
5. Press the Steam button cook for 10 minutes.
6. Do natural pressure release.
7. Once the lid is open, remove the squash and fluff using fork.

Nutrition Facts Per Serving
Calories 9, Total Fat 0.05g, Saturated Fat 0g, Total Carbs 2g, Net Carbs 1.7g, Protein 0.5g, Sugar: 1g, Fiber: 0.3g, Sodium: 4mg, Potassium: 77mg, Phosphorus: 10mg

Korean Braised Potatoes

Prep time: 5 minutes, cook time: 30 minutes; Serves 4
Ingredients:
1-pound baby potatoes, scrubbed clean
3 tablespoons soy sauce
2 tablespoons sugar
3 cloves garlic, minced
1 cup water
Sesame seeds for garnish
Instructions
1. Place all ingredients except for the sesame seeds in the Instant Pot.
2. Close the lid and set the vent to the Sealing position.
3. Press the Meat/Stew button and adjust the time to 20 minutes.
4. Once the timer sets off, do quick pressure release to open the lid.
5. Once the lid is open, press the Sauté button and allow the sauce to simmer until it has reduced to a glaze. Stir constantly.
6. Garnish with sesame seeds before serving.

Nutrition Facts Per Serving
Calories 141, Total Fat 2g, Saturated Fat 0.4g, Total Carbs 28g, Net Carbs 25g, Protein 3g, Sugar: 7g, Fiber: 3g, Sodium: 188mg, Potassium: 518mg, Phosphorus: 83mg

Broccoli and Rice

Prep time: 5 minutes, cook time: 8 minutes; Serves 6
Ingredients:
1 teaspoon coconut oil
2 cloves garlic, minced
3 cups broccoli florets
8 ounces shiitake mushrooms
10 ounces pre-cooked or leftover rice
1 cup roasted cashews
3 tablespoons soy sauce
pepper to taste
3 tablespoons toasted sesame oil
Instructions
1. Press the Sauté button on the Instant Pot and heat the coconut oil.
2. Stir in the garlic and sauté for 30 seconds until fragrant.
3. Add in the broccoli and shiitake mushrooms. Cook for 3 minutes until the broccoli has wilted.
4. Add in the leftover rice and cashew and season with soy sauce and pepper to taste.
5. Stir for 3 minutes.
6. Drizzle with sesame oil before serving.

Nutrition Facts Per Serving
Calories 428, Total Fat 32g, Saturated Fat 6g, Total Carbs 33g, Net Carbs 30g, Protein 8g, Sugar: 7g, Fiber: 3g, Sodium: 264mg, Potassium: 301mg, Phosphorus: 212mg

Vegetable Paella

Prep time: 10 minutes, cook time: 35 minutes; Serves 6
Ingredients:
3 tablespoons olive oil
1 onion, chopped finely
6 cloves garlic, minced
2 teaspoons smoked paprika
1 15-ounces diced tomatoes
2 cups short-grain rice
1 can chickpeas
3 cups vegetable broth

½ cup dry white wine
½ teaspoon saffron threads
salt and pepper to taste
1 14-ounce artichokes, drained
½ cup Kalamata olives, pitted and halved
½ cup frozen peas
2 red bell peppers, seeded and cut into strips
2 tablespoons lemon juice
¼ cup fresh parsley, chopped

Instructions

1. Press the Sauté button on the Instant Pot and heat the oil. Sauté the onion and garlic until fragrant. Stir in the paprika, tomatoes, rice and chickpeas. Stir for 2 minutes. Add in the broth, white wine, and saffron. Stir to combine or until the liquid is simmering. Season with salt and pepper to taste.
2. Arrange the artichokes, olives, peas, and bell pepper on top. Drizzle with lemon juice.
3. Close the lid and set the vent to the Sealing position.
4. Press the Rice button and cook on low until the timer sets off.
5. Do natural pressure release.
6. Garnish with parsley before serving.

Nutrition Facts Per Serving
Calories 546, Total Fat 13g, Saturated Fat 3g, Total Carbs 93g, Net Carbs 81g, Protein 18g, Sugar: 8g, Fiber: 12g, Sodium: 339mg, Potassium: 908mg, Phosphorus: 306mg

Cauliflower in Cashew Chipotle Sauce

Prep time: 5 minutes, cook time: 6 minutes; Serves 4

Ingredients:
1 cup cashew nut, soaked overnight and drained
3 tablespoons nutritional yeast
2 tablespoons lime juice
3 tablespoons adobo or chipotle hot sauce
2 tablespoons olive oil
salt and pepper to taste
1 large head cauliflower, cut into florets
1 cup water

Instructions

In a blender, place the cashew nuts, water, nutritional yeast, lime juice, adobo or chipotle sauce, and olive oil. Season with salt and pepper to taste. Pulse until smooth. Set aside.

1. Place the cauliflower and water in the Instant Pot and pour over the cashew chipotle sauce.
2. Close the lid and set the vent to the Sealing position.
3. Press the Pressure Cook or Manual button and adjust the cooking time to 6 minutes.
4. Once the timer sets off, do quick pressure release.

Nutrition Facts Per Serving
Calories 294, Total Fat 22g, Saturated Fat 4g, Total Carbs 17g, Net Carbs 13g, Protein 10g, Sugar: 4g, Fiber: 4g, Sodium: 615mg, Potassium: 733mg, Phosphorus: 220mg

Slow Cooked Veggie Enchilada Casserole

Prep time: 5 minutes, cook time: 5 hours; Serves 5

Ingredients:
½ medium head of cauliflower, cut into florets
1 large sweet potato, peeled and cubed
2 red bell peppers, cut into squares
3 tablespoons extra virgin olive oil
1 teaspoon ground cumin
8 ounces red salsa
salt and pepper to taste
2 handful baby spinach leaves
½ cup fresh cilantro
9 corn tortillas, halved

Instructions

1. Place the cauliflower, sweet potato, bell peppers, olive oil, cumin, and salsa in the Instant Pot. Season with salt and pepper to taste. Add in the baby spinach on top.
2. Close the lid but do not seal the vent.
3. Press the Slow Cook function and adjust the cooking time to 5 hours.
4. Once cooked, serve with cilantro and tortillas.

Nutrition Facts Per Serving
Calories 94, Total Fat 4g, Saturated Fat 0.5g, Total Carbs 14g, Net Carbs 11g, Protein 2g, Sugar: 6g, Fiber: 3g, Sodium: 416mg, Potassium: 456mg, Phosphorus: 58mg

Bok Choy With Mushrooms

Prep time: 5 minutes, cook time: 10 minutes; Serves 4

Ingredients:

3 tablespoons olive oil
1 small yellow onion, chopped
2 cloves garlic, minced
5 ounces fresh shiitake mushrooms
1 red bell pepper, seeded and sliced into strips
1-pound bok choy, torn
1 cup vegetable broth
2 tablespoons soy sauce
salt and pepper to taste
1 tablespoon sesame seed oil
1 tablespoon cornstarch + 2 tablespoons water

Instructions

1. Press the Sauté button on the Instant Pot. Heat the oil and sauté the onion and garlic for 30 seconds or until fragrant.
2. Stir in the mushrooms and red bell pepper. Sauté for 3 minutes.
3. Add in the bok choy and vegetable broth. Season with soy sauce, salt and pepper to taste.
4. Close the lid and set the vent to the Sealing position.
5. Press the Pressure Cook or Manual button and adjust the cooking time to 3 minutes.
6. Do quick pressure release.
7. Once the lid is open, press the Sauté button and stir in the sesame oil and cornstarch slurry. Stir for 3 minutes until the sauce thickens.

Nutrition Facts Per Serving

Calories 138, Total Fat 11g, Saturated Fat 2g, Total Carbs 10g, Net Carbs 8g, Protein 3g, Sugar: 4g, Fiber: 2g, Sodium: 131mg, Potassium: 447mg, Phosphorus: 63mg

Stuffed Acorn Squash

Prep time: 10 minutes, cook time: 20 minutes; Serves 4

Ingredients:

1 cup water
2 medium acorn squash
2 tablespoons olive oil
½ cup quinoa, rinsed
¼ cup dried cranberries, chopped
¼ cup raw pepitas
¼ cup chopped green onions
1 tablespoon lemon juice
salt to taste

Instructions

1. Pour water in the Instant Pot and place a steamer basket or trivet on top.
2. Cut the squash lengthwise and scoop out the seeds. Set aside.
3. Prepare the filling by mixing in a bowl the quinoa, cranberries, pepitas, green onions, and lemon juice. Season with salt to taste.
4. Scoop the filling inside the hollowed part of the acorn squash. Do this on all squash halves.
5. Place the squash on the trivet.
6. Close the lid and set the vent to the Sealing position.
7. Press the Steam button and cook for 20 minutes.
8. Do natural pressure release.

Nutrition Facts Per Serving

Calories 277, Total Fat 12g, Saturated Fat 2g, Total Carbs 40g, Net Carbs 35g, Protein 7g, Sugar: 2g, Fiber: 5g, Sodium: 10mg, Potassium: 939mg, Phosphorus: 263mg

Lacto-Vegetarian Caramelized Veggies

Prep time: 5 minutes, cook time: 5 hours; Serves 4

Ingredients:

1-pound small potatoes
½ pounds frozen mixed vegetables
3 tablespoons olive oil
A sprig of rosemary
A sprig of sage
A sprig of thyme
5 tablespoons butter
salt and pepper to taste

Instructions

1. Place all ingredients in the Instant Pot.

2. Stir to combine.
3. Close the lid but do not Seal the vent.
4. Press the Slow Cook function and adjust the cooking time to 5 hours.
5. Stir halfway through the cooking time for even browning.

Nutrition Facts Per Serving
Calories 341, Total Fat 25g, Saturated Fat 11g, Total Carbs 27g, Net Carbs 22g, Protein 4g, Sugar: 3g, Fiber: 5g, Sodium: 141mg, Potassium: 578mg, Phosphorus: 98mg

One-Pot Spicy Tomato Spaghetti

Prep time: 5 minutes, cook time: 15 minutes; Serves 4

Ingredients:
1 tablespoon olive oil
2 cloves garlic, minced
1 fresh red chili, chopped
salt and pepper to taste
4 plum tomatoes, chopped
6 ounces dry spaghetti
4 tablespoons nutritional yeast
1 cup water
1 bunch fresh basil leaf, chopped

Instructions
1. Press the Sauté button on the Instant Pot and heat the oil. Sauté the garlic and red chili until fragrant.
2. Stir in the tomatoes and season with salt and pepper to taste. Sauté for 3 minutes until the tomatoes are wilted.
3. Add in the spaghetti, nutritional yeast, and water. Stir to combine.
4. Close the lid and set the vent to the Sealing position.
5. Press the Pressure Cook or Manual button and adjust the cooking time to 10 minutes.
6. Do natural pressure release.
7. Once the lid is open, stir in the basil leaves last.

Nutrition Facts Per Serving
Calories 264, Total Fat 4g, Saturated Fat 0.5g, Total Carbs 47g, Net Carbs 44g, Protein 10g, Sugar: 12g, Fiber: 3g, Sodium: 545mg, Potassium: 521mg, Phosphorus: 107mg

Aubergine And Tomato Rogan Josh

Prep time: 5 minutes, cook time: 15 minutes; Serves 2

Ingredients:
1 tablespoon olive oil
1 shallot, chopped
2 cloves garlic, minced
2 teaspoons Rogan Josh spice paste or garam masala
2 big ripe tomatoes, chopped
1 large aubergine, chopped
½ cup water
salt and pepper to taste
Juice from ½ lemon
½ cup pistachios, shelled
1 bunch fresh coriander

Instructions
1. Press the Sauté button on the Instant Pot and heat the olive oil.
2. Sauté the shallot and garlic for 30 seconds or until fragrant.
3. Toast the garam masala or Rogan Josh spice paste for a minute until fragrant.
4. Add in the tomatoes and stir for 3 minutes.
5. Stir in the aubergine and water. Season with salt and pepper to taste. Drizzle with lemon juice.
6. Close the lid and set the vent to the Sealing position.
7. Press the Pressure Cook or Manual button and adjust the cooking time to 8 minutes.
8. Do natural pressure release.
9. Once the lid is open, stir in the pistachios and coriander.

Nutrition Facts Per Serving
Calories 281, Total Fat 22g, Saturated Fat 3g, Total Carbs 19g, Net Carbs 14g, Protein 9g, Sugar: 3g, Fiber: 5g, Sodium: 53mg, Potassium :915mg, Phosphorus: 238mg

Instant Pot Roasted Root Vegetables

Prep time: 5 minutes, cook time: 5 hours; Serves 6

Ingredients:

1-pound medium-sized potatoes, scrubbed and quartered

2 large carrots, peeled and roughly chopped

1 large parsnips, peeled and roughly chopped

1 bulb garlic, smashed

½ bunch fresh rosemary

3 tablespoons olive oil

salt and pepper to taste

Instructions

1. Place all ingredients in a mixing pot and toss to coat all ingredients with the oil and seasoning.

2. Place into the Instant Pot.

3. Close the lid but do not seal the vent.

4. Press the Slow Cook function and adjust the cooking time to 5 hours.

5. Halfway through the cooking time, carefully stir the vegetables for even browning.

6. Cook until done.

Nutrition Facts Per Serving

Calories 144, Total Fat 7g, Saturated Fat 1g, Total Carbs 19g, Net Carbs 16g, Protein 2g, Sugar: 3g, Fiber: 3g, Sodium: 23mg, Potassium: 478mg, Phosphorus: 67mg

Tomato Curry

Prep time: 5 minutes, cook time: 15 minutes; Serves 4

Ingredients:

2 tablespoons olive oil

4 cloves garlic, minced

1 1-inch ginger, sliced thinly

1 ½ pounds mixed tomatoes

A pinch of saffron

½ cup almond meal

2 fresh red chilis, chopped

5 curry leaves

1 tablespoon garam masala

1 14-ounce can coconut milk

2 teaspoon mango chutney (optional)

salt and pepper to taste

Instructions

1. Press the Sauté button on the Instant Pot and heat the oil.

2. Sauté the garlic and ginger until fragrant.

3. Stir in the tomatoes and saffron for 2 minutes.

4. Add in the rest of the ingredients.

5. Close the lid and set the vent to the Sealing position.

6. Press the Manual button and adjust the cooking time to 10 minutes.

7. Do natural pressure release.

Nutrition Facts Per Serving

Calories 113, Total Fat 7g, Saturated Fat 1g, Total Carbs 11g, Net Carbs 8g, Protein 3g, Sugar: 3g, Fiber: 3g, Sodium: 176mg, Potassium: 625mg, Phosphorus:75 mg

Potato and Artichoke Al Forno

Prep time: 5 minutes, cook time: 5 hours; Serves 5

Ingredients:

½ pound baby potatoes, scrubbed clean

2 large fennel bulbs, peeled and sliced thinly

1 14-ounce artichoke hearts in oil

1 cup double cream

Salt and pepper to taste

Instructions

1. Place all ingredients in the Instant Pot and give a good stir.

2. Close the lid and do not seal the vent.

3. Press the Slow Cook button and adjust the cooking time to 5 hours.

Nutrition Facts Per Serving

Calories 258, Total Fat 16g, Saturated Fat 7g, Total Carbs 26g, Net Carbs 16g, Protein 6g, Sugar: 7g, Fiber: 10g, Sodium: 115mg, Potassium: 876mg, Phosphorus: 168mg

Mushroom Bourguignon

Prep time: 5 minutes, cook time: 5 minutes; Serves 6

Ingredients:

2 tablespoons olive oil

2 cloves garlic, minced

12 shallots, chopped

16 ounces dried porcini mushrooms, soaked in water overnight then drained

4 portobello mushrooms, sliced

16 ounces shiitake mushrooms, sliced

16 ounces chestnut mushrooms, sliced

1 medium carrot, sliced

1 sprig fresh thyme

2 bay leaves

1 cup red wine

2 tablespoons tomato paste

Salt and pepper to taste

Instructions

1. Press the Sauté button on the Instant Pot and heat the oil.
2. Sauté the garlic and shallots until fragrant. Stir in the mushrooms and sauté for 3 minutes.
3. Add in the rest of the ingredients.
4. Close the lid and set the vent to the Sealing position.
5. Press the Pressure Cook or Manual button and adjust the cooking time to 5 minutes.
6. Do natural pressure release.

Nutrition Facts Per Serving

Calories 346, Total Fat 6g, Saturated Fat 0.8g, Total Carbs 76g, Net Carbs 64g, Protein 12g, Sugar: 9g, Fiber: 12g, Sodium: 26mg, Potassium: 1662mg, Phosphorus: 337mg

Aubergine Penne Arrabbiata

Prep time: 5 minutes, cook time: 15 minutes; Serves 6

Ingredients:

2 tablespoons olive oil

4 cloves garlic, minced

12 fresh mixed color chilis, chopped

2 aubergines, sliced

6 ounces dried whole wheat penne

1 14-ounce can plum tomatoes

3 tablespoons nutritional yeast

½ cup water

salt and pepper to taste

Instructions

1. Press the Sauté button on the Instant Pot and heat the olive oil.
2. Sauté the garlic and chilis for 1 minute until lightly toasted.
3. Stir in the aubergines for 2 minutes.
4. Add in the rest of the ingredients and scrape the bottom to remove the brown bits at the bottom.
5. Close the lid and set the vent to the Sealing position.
6. Press the Pressure Cook or Manual button and adjust the cooking time to 10 minutes,
7. Do natural pressure release.

Nutrition Facts Per Serving

Calories 291, Total Fat 8g, Saturated Fat 2g, Total Carbs 40g, Net Carbs 35g, Protein 17g, Sugar: 16g, Fiber: 5g, Sodium: 1044mg, Potassium: 579mg, Phosphorus: 290mg

Green Beans Ala Trapanese

Prep time: 5 minutes, cook time: 14 minutes; Serves 4

Ingredients:

1 cup blanched almond

2 tablespoons olive oil

1 clove of garlic, minced

2 cups ripe cherry tomatoes, chopped

2 cups green beans

salt and pepper to taste

½ cup pecorino cheese

1 bunch fresh basil

1 cup rocket arugula

Instructions

1. Press the Sauté button on the Instant Pot and toast the almond for 3 minutes until lightly golden. Set aside to cool. Once cool, place in a plastic bag and crush with a rolling pan.
2. With the Sauté button still on, heat the oil and sauté the garlic until fragrant.

3. Stir in the tomatoes for 3 minutes or until wilted.
4. Add in the green beans and season with salt and pepper to taste.
5. Close the lid and set the vent to the Sealing position.
6. Press the Pressure Cook or Manual button and adjust the cooking time to 6 minutes.
7. Do quick pressure release.
8. Once the lid is open, press the Sauté button and stir in the pecorino cheese, basil, arugula, and ground almond. Cook for another 3 minutes.

Nutrition Facts Per Serving
Calories 128, Total Fat 11g, Saturated Fat 3g, Total Carbs 5g, Net Carbs 3g, Protein 4g, Sugar: 1g, Fiber: 2g, Sodium: 118mg, Potassium: 137mg, Phosphorus: 81mg

Indian Spinach

Prep time: 5 minutes, cook time: 7 minutes; Serves 2

Ingredients:
1 tablespoon olive oil
1 teaspoon black mustard seed
1 teaspoon cumin seeds
1 onion, chopped
1 1-inch ginger, sliced
1 teaspoon curry powder
½ cup coconut cream
1-pound baby spinach
Juice from ½ lemon
salt and pepper to taste

Instructions
1. Press the Sauté button on the Instant Pot and heat the oil. Toast the mustard seeds and cumin seeds. Stir in the onion and ginger until fragrant.
2. Add in the rest of the ingredients.
3. Close the lid and set the vent to the Sealing position.
4. Press the Pressure Cook or Manual button and adjust the cooking time to 5 minutes.
5. Do natural pressure release.

Nutrition Facts Per Serving
Calories 348, Total Fat 29g, Saturated Fat 19g, Total Carbs 20g, Net Carbs 12g, Protein 10g, Sugar: 4g, Fiber: 8g, Sodium: 187mg, Potassium: 1596mg, Phosphorus: 219mg

Veggie Feijoada

Prep time: 5 minutes, cook time: 30 minutes; Serves 5

Ingredients:
2 tablespoons olive oil
2 red onions, chopped
3 cloves garlic, minced
1 teaspoon ground coriander
1 teaspoon smoked paprika
4 ripe tomatoes, chopped
1 cup brown rice
1 cup diced sweet potatoes
1 red bell pepper, seeded and sliced
½ zucchini, diced
Juice from ½ lemon
A bunch of chopped corianders for garnish
salt and pepper to taste
2 cups water

Instructions
1. Press the Sauté button on the Instant Pot and heat the oil. Sauté the onions and garlic until fragrant.
2. Add in the coriander and paprika and stir for another minute until fragrant.
3. Stir in the tomatoes and brown rice. Stir for another minute.
4. Add in the rest of the ingredients.
5. Close the lid and set the vent to the Sealing position.
6. Press the Pressure Cook or Manual button and adjust the cooking time to 25 minutes.
7. Do natural pressure release.

Nutrition Facts Per Serving
Calories 95, Total Fat 6g, Saturated Fat 0.8g, Total Carbs 11g, Net Carbs 8g, Protein 2g, Sugar: 5g, Fiber: 3g, Sodium: 9mg, Potassium: 390mg, Phosphorus: 52mg

Mushroom, Vegetable, And Rice Curry

Prep time: 5 minutes, cook time: 33 minutes; Serves 6

Ingredients:

1 tablespoon olive oil
2 cloves garlic, minced
1 onion, chopped
1 fresh chili, chopped
1 teaspoon turmeric powder
1 teaspoon fenugreek seeds
1 teaspoon black mustard seeds
1 teaspoon curry powder
½ pounds mixed mushrooms sliced
½ pounds mixed vegetables
½ cup brown basmati rice
1 14-ounce coconut milk
salt and pepper to taste
½ cup water
A bunch of fresh coriander, chopped

Instructions

1. Press the Sauté button on the Instant Pot and heat the oil. Sauté the garlic and onion for a minute. Stir in the chili, turmeric powder, fenugreek seeds, mustard seeds, and curry powder. Stir for another minute or until toasted.
2. Stir in the mushrooms and stir for 3 minutes or until wilted.
3. Stir in the rest of the ingredients except for the coriander.
4. Close the lid and do not seal the vent.
5. Press the Rice button and cook using the pre-set cooking time.
6. Once cooked, stir in the coriander last.

Nutrition Facts Per Serving

Calories 174, Total Fat 10g, Saturated Fat 2g, Total Carbs 23g, Net Carbs 15g, Protein 7g, Sugar: 7g, Fiber: 8g, Sodium: 147mg, Potassium: 968mg, Phosphorus: 450mg

Smoky Veggie Chili

Prep time: 5 minutes, cook time: 37 minutes; Serves 5

Ingredients:

1 tablespoon olive oil
2 onions, chopped
1 teaspoon cumin seeds
2 teaspoons smoked paprika
2 teaspoons cocoa powder
1 tablespoon peanut butter
1 fresh chili, chopped
3 mixed color peppers, seeded and chopped
3 large tomatoes, chopped
2 sweet potatoes, peeled and cubed
8 small jacket potatoes
1 bunch fresh coriander, chopped
salt and pepper to taste
1 cup water

Instructions

1. Press the Sauté button on the Instant Pot and heat the oil.
2. Sauté the onions and cumin until fragrant.
3. Stir in the paprika, cocoa powder, peanut butter, chili, peppers, tomatoes, and potatoes.
4. Season with salt and pepper and pour in water.
5. Close the lid and set the vent to the Sealing position.
6. Press the Meat/Stew button and cook using the preset cooking time.
7. Do natural pressure release.

Nutrition Facts Per Serving

Calories 586, Total Fat 4g, Saturated Fat 0.7g, Total Carbs 126g, Net Carbs 108g, Protein 15g, Sugar: 14g, Fiber: 18g, Sodium: 123mg, Potassium: 3131mg, Phosphorus: 426mg

Cauliflower Dhal

Prep time: 5 minutes, cook time: 22 minutes; Serves 3

Ingredients:

2 tablespoons olive oil
4 shallots, chopped
1 clove of garlic, minced
2 teaspoons mustard seeds
½ of dried chili, chopped

A handful of curry leaves
½ pound yellow split peas
salt and pepper to taste
1 small cauliflower head, cut into florets

2 14-ounces coconut milk

Instructions

1. Press the Sauté button on the Instant Pot and heat the oil. Sauté the shallots and garlic for 1 minute until translucent.
2. Add in the mustard seeds and toast for 1 minute.
3. Add the chili, curry leaves, and split peas.
4. Stir in the rest of the ingredients and season with salt and pepper to taste.

5. Close the lid and set the vent to the Sealing position.
6. Press the Bean button and adjust the cooking time to 20 minutes.
7. Do natural pressure release.

Nutrition Facts Per Serving
Calories 223, Total Fat 11g, Saturated Fat 2g, Total Carbs 26g, Net Carbs 18g, Protein 8g, Sugar: 14g, Fiber: 8g, Sodium: 432mg, Potassium: 1122mg, Phosphorus: 153mg

Spiced Aubergine And Coconut Curry

Prep time: 5 minutes, cook time:7 minutes; Serves 3

Ingredients:

3 tablespoons coconut oil
6 Asian aubergines, sliced into round pieces
1 1-inch piece ginger, sliced thinly
2 cloves garlic, minced
1 white onion, chopped
2 teaspoons cumin seeds
1 tablespoon black mustard seed
12 fresh curry leaves
2 dried chilis, chopped
1 tablespoon tomato puree
2 teaspoons garam masala
1 14-ounces coconut milk
salt and pepper to taste
½ bunch coriander, chopped

Instructions

1. Press the Sauté button and heat the oil. Sear the aubergine on all sides until lightly golden. This will take about 3 minutes on each side.

2. Stir in the ginger, garlic, and onion. Cook for another 1 minute.
3. Add the cumin seeds, mustard seeds, curry leaves, and chilis. Toast for another minute.
4. Add the rest of the ingredients except for the coriander leaves.
5. Close the lid and set the vent to the Sealing position.
6. Press the Pressure Cook or Manual button and adjust the cooking time to 5 minutes.
7. Do natural pressure release.
8. Once opened, stir in coriander.
9. Serve and enjoy.

Nutrition Facts Per Serving
Calories 178, Total Fat 15g, Saturated Fat 12g, Total Carbs 11g, Net Carbs 8g, Protein 2g, Sugar: 5g, Fiber: 3g, Sodium: 145mg, Potassium: 459mg, Phosphorus: 67mg

Creamy Lacto-Vegetarian Tomato Soup

Prep time: 5 minutes, cook time: 25 minutes; Serves 6

Ingredients:

1 tablespoon butter
½ onion, diced
4 cloves garlic, minced
3 teaspoon Italian seasoning
½ teaspoon red pepper flakes
3 tablespoons flour
3 cups vegetable broth
1 28-ounce can dice tomatoes
3 tablespoons tomato paste
4 cups cheese tortellini
1/3 cup cream
salt and pressure to taste
3 cups spinach

½ cup grated Parmesan cheese
basil leaves for garnish

Instructions

1. Press the Sauté button on the Instant Pot and heat the butter.
2. Add the onion, garlic, Italian seasoning, and red pepper flakes until fragrant.
3. While stirring constantly, add the flour until a roux is formed.
4. Add in the broth and stir vigorously until the flour roux is dissolved.

5. Stir in the tomatoes, tomato paste, tortellini, and cream. Season with salt and pepper to taste.
6. Close the lid and set the vent to the Sealing position.
7. Press the Soup/Broth button and cook for 20 minutes.
8. Do quick pressure release.

9. Once the lid is open, press the Sauté button and stir in the spinach. Cook for 3 minutes.
10. Serve with parmesan cheese and basil leaves.

Nutrition Facts Per Serving
Calories 300, Total Fat 21g, Saturated Fat 13g, Total Carbs 14g, Net Carbs 10g, Protein 16g, Sugar: 6g, Fiber: 4g, Sodium: 708mg, Potassium: 538mg, Phosphorus: 307mg

Sicilian Aubergine Stew

Prep time: 5 minutes, cook time: 25 minutes; Serves 5

Ingredients:
2 tablespoons olive oil
1 small onion, chopped
3 cloves garlic, minced
1 large aubergine, chopped
2 large tomatoes, chopped
1 tablespoons caper
8 green olives, pitted
1 tablespoon red wine vinegar
½ cup couscous
salt and pepper to taste
3 cups water
1 tablespoon flaked almonds

Instructions
1. Press the Sauté button and heat the olive oil. Sauté the onion and garlic until fragrant.
2. Stir in the aubergine and tomatoes for three minutes until slightly wilted.

3. Add the capers, olives, red wine vinegar, and couscous. Season with salt and pepper to taste. Pour water.
4. Close the lid and set the vent to the Sealing position.
5. Press the Meat/Stew button and adjust the cooking time to 20 minutes.
6. Do natural pressure release.
7. Once the lid is open, sprinkle with flaked almonds.

Nutrition Facts Per Serving
Calories 161, Total Fat 10g, Saturated Fat 1g, Total Carbs 9g, Net Carbs 7g, Protein 10g, Sugar: 3g, Fiber: 2g, Sodium: 131mg, Potassium: 323mg, Phosphorus: 99mg

Aubergine Dip

Prep time: 10 minutes, cook time: 10 minutes; Serves 2

Ingredients:
1 large aubergine
1 clove garlic, minced
1 fresh green chili, minced
1 tablespoon extra-virgin olive oil
Juice from ½ lemon
½ teaspoon smoked paprika
salt and pepper to taste

Instructions
1. Pour water into the Instant Pot and place a trivet or steamer basket inside.
2. Place the aubergine inside.
3. Close the lid and set the vent to the Sealing position.
4. Press the Steam button and cook for 10 minutes.

5. Do natural pressure release.
6. Remove the aubergine from the Instant Pot and allow to cool.
7. Once cooled, peel the aubergine and place in a food processor.
8. Add the rest of the ingredients. Pulse until smooth.

Serve with crackers.

Nutrition Facts Per Serving
Calories 102, Total Fat 4g, Saturated Fat 0.5g, Total Carbs 18g, Net Carbs: 9 g, Protein 3g, Sugar: 10g, Fiber: 9g, Sodium: 66mg, Potassium: 662mg, Phosphorus: 72mg

Root Vegetable and Squash Stew

Prep time: 5 minutes, cook time: 25 minutes; Serves 5

Ingredients:

1 tablespoon olive oil

1 red onion

½ small celeriac, sliced

½ butternut squash, seeded and sliced into chunks

1 sweet potato, peeled and cubed

2 carrots, peeled and cubed

1 teaspoon red wine vinegar

1 teaspoon dried thyme

1 bay leaf

1 tablespoon tomato puree

1 cup plum tomatoes, chopped

salt and pepper to taste

1 tablespoon plain flour + 2 tablespoons cold water

Instructions

1. Press the Sauté button on the Instant Pot and heat the oil. Sauté the onion and celeriac. Stir for 3 minutes.

2. Add in the squash, sweet potato, and carrots. Stir for another minute.

3. Stir in the red wine vinegar, thyme, bay leaf, tomato puree, and tomatoes. Season with salt and pepper to taste. Add a cup of water.

4. Close the lid and set the vent to the Sealing position.

5. Press the Meat/Stew button and adjust the cooking time to 20 minutes.

6. Do quick pressure release.

7. Once the lid is open, press the Sauté button and stir in the flour slurry. Cook for another 3 minutes until the sauce thickens.

Nutrition Facts Per Serving

Calories 122, Total Fat 3g, Saturated Fat 1g, Total Carbs 24g, Net Carbs 21g, Protein 1g, Sugar: 15g, Fiber: 3g, Sodium: 53mg, Potassium: 323mg, Phosphorus: 55mg

Veggie Tofu Instant Pot Stir Fry

Prep time: 5 minutes, cook time: 15 minutes; Serves 4

Ingredients:

3 tablespoons olive oil

1 block firm tofu, sliced

2 cloves garlic, minced1 1-inch ginger, sliced thinly

2 fresh red chilis, chopped

½ head broccoli, cut into florets

4 baby corn, sliced

2 tablespoons soy sauce

black pepper to taste

½ cup water

1 tablespoon cornstarch + 2 tablespoons water

3 tablespoons sesame seeds

2 tablespoons cashew nuts

Instructions

1. Press the Sauté button and heat the olive oil. Once the oil is hot, sear the tofu on all edges until lightly golden. This takes about 5 minutes.

2. Once the tofu is golden, sauté the garlic and ginger until fragrant.

3. Add the broccoli and corn. Season with soy sauce and black pepper. Pour in enough water.

4. Close the lid and set the vent to the Sealing position.

5. Press the Pressure Cook or Manual button and adjust the cooking time to 6 minutes.

6. Do quick pressure release.

7. Once the lid is open, press the Sauté button and stir in the cornstarch slurry. Allow to simmer for 3 minutes until the sauce thickens.

8. Sprinkle with sesame seeds and cashew nuts before serving;

Nutrition Facts Per Serving

Calories 296, Total Fat 24g, Saturated Fat 4g, Total Carbs 8g, Net Carbs 5g, Protein 16g, Sugar: 2g, Fiber: 3g, Sodium: 138mg, Potassium: 278mg, Phosphorus: 231mg

Green Dream Noodles

Prep time: 5 minutes, cook time: 25 minutes; Serves 4

Ingredients:

1 tablespoon olive oil
3 cloves garlic, minced
1 1-inch ginger, sliced thinly
½ cup sliced mushrooms
1 sachet miso paste
1 ½ cups vegetable broth
1 cup broccoli florets
1 handful sugar snap peas
2 cup rice noodles
A handful of fresh coriander leaves

Instructions

1. Press the Sauté button on the Instant Pot and heat the oil. Sauté the garlic and ginger for a minute or until fragrant.
2. Stir in the mushrooms and add the miso paste and vegetable broth.
3. Allow to simmer for 3 minutes.
4. Stir in the broccoli florets, peas, and noodles.
5. Close the lid and set the vent to the Sealing position.
6. Press the Soup/Broth button and cook for 20 minutes.
7. Do natural pressure release.
8. Garnish with coriander leaves before serving.

Nutrition Facts Per Serving

Calories 131, Total Fat 4g, Saturated Fat 0.5g, Total Carbs 22g, Net Carbs 21g, Protein 2g, Sugar: 0.1g, Fiber: 1g, Sodium: 21mg, Potassium: 39mg, Phosphorus: 30mg

Slow Cook Glazed Carrots and Parsnips

Prep time: 5 minutes, cook time: 5 hours; Serves 4

Ingredients:

2 large carrots, peeled and cut into thick strips
1 large parsnip, peeled and cut into thick strips
¼ cup maple syrup
salt and pepper to taste

Instructions

1. Place all ingredients in the Instant Pot and give a good stir.
2. Close the lid but do not seal the vent.
3. Press he Slow Cook button and adjust the cooking time to 5 hours.
4. Halfway through the cooking time, give the vegetables a stir.

Nutrition Facts Per Serving

Calories 102, Total Fat 0.2g, Saturated Fat 0g, Total Carbs 25g, Net Carbs 22g, Protein 0.8g, Sugar: 15g, Fiber: 3g, Sodium: 10mg, Potassium: 298mg, Phosphorus: 48mg

Sweet Potato, Squash, Coconut, And Cardamom

Prep time: 10 minutes, cook time: 12 minutes; Serves 4

Ingredients:

2 tablespoons coconut oil

3 cloves garlic, minced

1 onion, chopped

1 1-inch thick ginger

3 cardamom pods

1 cup diced sweet potatoes

1 cup diced kabocha squash

1 14-ounce coconut milk

salt and pepper to taste

Instructions

1. Press the Sauté button on the Instant Pot. Heat the oil and sauté the garlic and onion for 1 minute or until translucent.

2. Add the ginger and cardamom pods until fragrant.

3. Stir in the rest of the ingredients.

4. Close the lid and set the vent to the Sealing position.

5. Press the Pressure Cook or Manual button and adjust the cooking time to 10 minutes.

6. Do natural pressure release.

Nutrition Facts Per Serving

Calories 102, Total Fat 7g, Saturated Fat 6g, Total Carbs 9g, Net Carbs 6g, Protein 2g, Sugar: 4g, Fiber: 3g, Sodium: 109mg, Potassium: 392mg, Phosphorus: 49mg

Jersey Royals with Wild Garlic

Prep time: 5 minutes, cook time: 5 hours; Serves 2

Ingredients:

5 tablespoons olive oil

½ pound Jersey royal potatoes, scrubbed clean and cut into wedges

A handful of garlic leaves

A few sprigs of rosemary

salt and pepper to taste

Instructions

1. Place all ingredients in the Instant Pot. Stir to combine everything.

2. Close the lid but do not seal the vent.

3. Press the Slow Cook button and adjust the cooking time to 5 hours.

4. Give the potatoes a stir halfway through the cooking time.

Nutrition Facts Per Serving

Calories 386, Total Fat 34g, Saturated Fat 5g, Total Carbs 20g, Net Carbs 17g, Protein 2g, Sugar: 0.8g, Fiber: 3g, Sodium: 7mg, Potassium: 478mg, Phosphorus: 65mg

Chapter 3 Legumes and Bean Recipes

Vegetarian Chili

Prep time: 5 minutes, cook time: 35 minutes; Serves 6

Ingredients:

1 tablespoon olive oil
1 medium onion, diced
4 cloves garlic, minced
1 tablespoon chili powder
1 teaspoon ground cumin
2 medium sweet potatoes, scrubbed and diced
2 medium red bell peppers, seeded and chopped
2 ½ cups vegetable broth
1 8-ounce tomato sauce
½ cup uncooked quinoa
1 15-ounce can black beans, rinsed and drained
1 15-ounce can red kidney beans, rinsed and drained
salt and pepper to taste
½ teaspoon granulated sugar

Instructions

1. Press the Sauté button on the Instant Pot and heat the oil. Sauté the onion and garlic for 1 minute until fragrant.
2. Stir in the chili powder and ground cumin. Toast for 30 seconds before adding sweet potatoes and red bell pepper.
3. Add the rest of the ingredients. Give a good stir.
4. Close the lid and set the vent to the Sealing position.
5. Press the Bean/Chili button and cook using the pre-set cooking time.
6. Do natural pressure release.
7. Serve with lime wedges, cilantro, and avocado slices if desired.

Nutrition Facts Per Serving

Calories 197, Total Fat 6g, Saturated Fat 1g, Total Carbs 31g, Net Carbs 25g, Protein 6g, Sugar: 7g, Fiber: 6g, Sodium: 296mg, Potassium: 801mg, Phosphorus: 195mg

Costa Rican Black Bean Soup

Prep time: 5 minutes, cook time: 35 minutes; Serves 4

Ingredients:

2 tablespoons olive oil
2 cloves garlic, minced
3 red onions, chopped
2 celery stalks, chopped
1 green bell pepper, seeded and chopped
2 fresh chilis, chopped
½ bunch fresh thyme
2 14-ounces black beans, rinsed and drained
2 bay leaves
1 tablespoon red wine vinegar
4 corn tortillas
½ bunch coriander chopped
3 cups vegetable broth
salt and pepper to taste

Instructions

1. Press the Sauté button on the Instant Pot and heat the oil. Sauté the garlic and onions until fragrant.
2. Stir in the celery stalks and continue stirring for 3 minutes.
3. Add in the green bel pepper, chilis, thyme, black beans, bay leaves, and red wine. Season with salt and pepper to taste. Stir in the vegetable broth.
4. Close the lid and set the vent to the Sealing position.
5. Press the Soup/Broth button and cook using the preset cooking time.
6. Do natural pressure release.

Nutrition Facts Per Serving

Calories 145, Total Fat 8g, Saturated Fat 1g, Total Carbs 18g, Net Carbs 12g, Protein 4g, Sugar: 6g, Fiber: 6g, Sodium: 16mg, Potassium: 379mg, Phosphorus: 73mg

Red Lentil, Sweet Potato, & Coconut Soup

Prep time: 5 minutes, cook time: 25 minutes; Serves 5

Ingredients:

1 tablespoon olive oil

2 red onions, chopped

½ teaspoon cumin seeds

1 fresh red chili, chopped

½ pound sweet potatoes, peeled and cubed 1 ½ cups red lentils

4 cups vegetable stock

1 14-ounce can coconut milk

Juice from ½ lemon

salt and pepper to taste

Instructions

1. Press the Sauté button on the Instant Pot and heat the oil.
2. Sauté the onions for 3 minutes until translucent
3. Add in cumin seeds and chili. Toast for 1 minute.
4. Stir in the rest of the ingredients.
5. Close the lid and set the vent to the Sealing position.
6. Press the Soup/Broth button and cook for 20 minutes.
7. Do natural pressure release.

Nutrition Facts Per Serving

Calories 97, Total Fat 3g, Saturated Fat 0.5g, Total Carbs 17g, Net Carbs 14g, Protein 2g, Sugar: 6g, Fiber: 3g, Sodium: 111mg, Potassium: 424mg, Phosphorus: 51mg

Farro, Cauliflower, And Asparagus Salad

Prep time: 40 minutes, cook time: 33 minutes; Serves 4

Ingredients:

1 cup faro bean

1 cauliflower, cut into florets

1 cup asparagus stems, trimmed

2 tablespoons pine nuts

3 tablespoons raisins

1 handful beetroot leaves

¼ cup extra virgin olive oil

2 tablespoons red wine vinegar

salt and pepper to taste

Instructions

1. Pour water in the Instant Pot. Place the faro beans. Close the lid and set the vent to the Sealing position.
2. Press the Bean/Chili button and cook using the preset cooking time.
3. Do quick pressure release.
4. Once the lid is open, press the Sauté button and stir in the cauliflower and asparagus. Allow to blanch for 3 minutes.
5. Drain the vegetables and soak in cold water. After 10 minutes, drain the liquid.
6. In a bowl, place the vegetables and add the pine nuts, raisins, and beetroot leaves. Allow to cool in the fridge for 30 minutes.
7. While cooling, mix the olive oil, vinegar, salt and pepper.
8. Pour over the dressing before serving the salad. Toss to coat.

Nutrition Facts Per Serving

Calories 123, Total Fat 7g, Saturated Fat 1g, Total Carbs 14g, Net Carbs 5g, Protein 5g, Sugar: 5g, Fiber:9 g, Sodium: 181mg, Potassium: 743mg, Phosphorus: 121mg

Slow Cooked Lentil Tabbouleh

Prep time: 5 minutes, cook time: 8 hours; Serves 4

Ingredients:

¼ pound lentils, soaked overnight then drained

1 bunch spring onions, chopped

1 cup ripe cherry tomatoes, halved

1 bunch flat-leaf parsley

1 bunch fresh mint

1 red onion, chopped

½ cup vegetable broth

4 tablespoons olive oil

Juice from 1 lemon

salt and pepper to taste

Instructions

1. Place all ingredients in the Instant Pot and stir to combine everything.
2. Close the lid but do not seal the vent.
3. Press the Slow Cook button and adjust the cooking time to 8 hours.
4. Give the beans a mix halfway through the cooking time.

Nutrition Facts Per Serving
Calories 212, Total Fat 15g, Saturated Fat 3g, Total Carbs 19g, Net Carbs 17g, Protein 3g, Sugar: 9g, Fiber: 2g, Sodium: 64mg, Potassium: 165mg, Phosphorus: 60mg

Instant Pot Hummus

Prep time: 5 minutes, cook time: 30 minutes; Serves 6
Ingredients:
½ pound dry chickpeas, soaked overnight then drained
2 cups water
1 small clove of garlic
1 tablespoon tahini
Juice from 1 lemon
1 cup extra virgin olive oil
1 tablespoon paprika
Salt to taste
Instructions
1. Pour the chickpeas and water in the Instant Pot.
2. Close the lid and set the vent to the Sealing position.
3. Press the Bean/Chili button and cook using the preset cooking time. Cook on high pressure.
4. Do natural pressure release.
5. Drain the beans and place in a blender or food processor.
6. Put the remaining ingredients.
7. Pulse until smooth.
8. Serve with cracker or vegetable sticks.

Nutrition Facts Per Serving
Calories 249, Total Fat 21g, Saturated Fat 3g, Total Carbs 12g, Net Carbs 8g, Protein 4g, Sugar: 2g, Fiber: 4g, Sodium: 405mg, Potassium: 164mg, Phosphorus: 82mg

Sweet Potato and White Bean Chili

Prep time: 5 minutes, cook time: 4 hours 5 minutes; Serves 4
Ingredients:
2 tablespoons olive oil
1 large onion, chopped
2 teaspoons ground cinnamon
1 tablespoon ground cumin
1 teaspoon smoked paprika
1 red chili, chopped
1 yellow pepper, seeded and chopped
2 medium sweet potatoes, cubed
1 14-ounce can white cannellini beans
1 14-ounce can tomato
salt and pepper to taste
Instructions
1. Press the Sauté button on the Instant Pot and heat the oil.
2. Sauté the onion for 2 minutes before adding the cinnamon, cumin, and paprika. Toast for 1 minute.
3. Stir in the rest of the ingredients and season with salt and pepper to taste.
4. Press the Cancel button.
5. Close the lid but do not seal the vent.
6. Press the Slow Cook button and adjust the cooking time to 4 hours.

Nutrition Facts Per Serving
Calories 501, Total Fat 9g, Saturated Fat 1g, Total Carbs 86g, Net Carbs 65g, Protein 26g, Sugar: 11g, Fiber: 21g, Sodium: 156mg, Potassium: 2343mg, Phosphorus: 372mg

Tofu Chickpea Curry with Spring Greens

Prep time: 5 minutes, cook time: 30 minutes; Serves 4
Ingredients:
2 tablespoons olive oil
1 block firm tofu, cubed
1 red onion, chopped
3 cloves garlic, minced
1 fresh red chili, chopped
1 tablespoon garam masala

1 14-ounce chopped tomatoes
1 14-ounce chickpeas, drained
Juice from ½ lemon
1 cup vegetable broth
salt and pepper to taste

Instructions
1. Press the Sauté button and heat the oil. Sear the tofu on all sides until lightly golden. This may take between 3 and 5 minutes.
2. Once golden, stir in the onion, garlic, and chili and sauté for another minute.
3. Stir in the rest of the ingredients.
4. Close the lid and set the vent to the Sealing position.
5. Press the Bean/Chili button and cook using the preset cooking time.
6. Do natural pressure release.

Nutrition Facts Per Serving
Calories 369, Total Fat 17g, Saturated Fat 2g, Total Carbs 37g, Net Carbs 28g, Protein 23g, Sugar: 6g, Fiber: 9g, Sodium: 65mg, Potassium: 763mg, Phosphorus: 302mg

Curried Cauliflower, Potatoes, And Chickpeas

Prep time: 5 minutes, cook time: 17 minutes; Serves 4

Ingredients:
2 tablespoons olive oil
2 cloves garlic, minced
1 onion, chopped
1 long green chili, chopped
1 teaspoon turmeric powder
1 teaspoon ground cumin
1 teaspoon mustard seed
1 teaspoon curry powder
1 head cauliflower, cut into florets
1 14-ounce can chickpeas
Juice from 1 lime
½ cup vegetable broth
salt and pepper to taste

Instructions
1. Press the Sauté button on the Instant Pot and heat the olive oil
2. Sauté the garlic and onions until fragrant.
3. Add the chilis, turmeric, cumin, mustard seed, and curry powder. Toast for another minute.
4. Stir in the rest of the ingredients.
5. Close the lid and set the vent to the Sealing position.
6. Press the Pressure Cook or Manual button and adjust the cooking time to 15 minutes.
7. Do natural pressure release.

Nutrition Facts Per Serving
Calories 240, Total Fat 10g, Saturated Fat 1g, Total Carbs 31g, Net Carbs 22g, Protein 9g, Sugar: 7g, Fiber: 9g, Sodium: 336mg, Potassium: 417mg, Phosphorus: 136mg

Curried Chickpea

Prep time: 5 minutes, cook time: 18 minutes; Serves 4

Ingredients:
2 tablespoons olive oil
1 teaspoon garlic paste
1 teaspoon green chili paste
2 onions, chopped
1 fresh green chili, chopped
½ teaspoon mustard seed
1 tablespoon garam masala
1 teaspoon sugar
1 14-ounce can chickpeas
1 14-ounce can tomato
½ cup vegetable broth
salt and pepper to taste

Instructions
1. Press the Sauté button on the Instant Pot and heat the oil.
2. Sauté the garlic pasta, chili pasta, onions, and green chili. Keep stirring for 2 minutes.
3. Stir in the mustard seed and garam masala. Toast for 1 minute.
4. Stir in the rest of the ingredients.
5. Close the lid and set the vent to the Sealing position.
6. Press the Pressure Cook or Manual button and adjust the cooking time to 15 minutes.
7. Do natural pressure release.

Nutrition Facts Per Serving
Calories 242, Total Fat 10g, Saturated Fat 1g, Total Carbs 32g, Net Carbs 23g, Protein 9g, Sugar: 10g, Fiber: 9g, Sodium: 432mg, Potassium: 400mg, Phosphorus: 120mg

Brown Rice Bowl

Prep time: 10 minutes, cook time: 20 minutes; Serves 4

Ingredients:

2 cups brown sushi rice, uncooked

3 cups water

1 cup edamame beans, removed from the pod

2 nori sheets, shredded

2 tablespoons black sesame seeds

A bunch of coriander leaves

Juice from 1 lemon

Juice from 1 orange

2 tablespoons soy sauce

2 tablespoons honey

2 tablespoons rice vinegar

Instructions

1. Place the sushi rice and water in the Instant Pot.
2. Close the lid and do not seal the vent.
3. Press the Rice button and cook until the rice is done.
4. Once the rice is cooked, open the lid and fluff the rice using fork.
5. Place in a bowl and allow to cool.
6. Top with edamame beans, nori sheets, sesame seeds, and coriander leaves. Set aside.
7. Prepare the sauce by mixing in a bowl the lemon juice, orange juice, soy sauce, honey, and vinegar.
8. Drizzle over the salad.

Nutrition Facts Per Serving

Calories 474, Total Fat 9g, Saturated Fat 1g, Total Carbs 87g, Net Carbs 81g, Protein 13g, Sugar: 12g, Fiber: 6g, Sodium: 132mg, Potassium: 434mg, Phosphorus: 412mg

Helen's Chickpea, Leek, And Carrot Stew

Prep time: 5 minutes, cook time: 30 minutes; Serves 4

Ingredients:

1 small leek, chopped

1 small carrots, peeled and diced

1 14-ounce canned chickpeas

2 tablespoons lemon juice

3 cups vegetable broth

Salt and pepper to taste

Instructions

1. Place all ingredients in the Instant Pot. Give a good stir.
2. Close the lid and set the vent to the Sealing position.
3. Press the Soup/Broth button and cook using the preset cooking time.
4. Do natural pressure release.

Nutrition Facts Per Serving

Calories 158, Total Fat 3g, Saturated Fat 0.2g, Total Carbs 27g, Net Carbs 20g, Protein 7g, Sugar: 6g, Fiber: 7g, Sodium: 257mg, Potassium: 214mg, Phosphorus: 97mg

Basic Black Beans

Prep time: 5 minutes, cook time: 32 minutes; Serves 4

Ingredients:

1 tablespoon vegetable oil

1 yellow onion, chopped

4 cloves garlic, minced

1 tablespoon taco seasoning

1-pound dried black beans, soaked overnight and rinse

3 ½ cups vegetable broth

salt and pepper to taste

Instructions

1. Press the Sauté button on the Instant Pot.
2. Heat the oil and sauté the onion and garlic until fragrant.
3. Stir in the rest of the ingredients.
4. Close the lid and set the vent to the Sealing position.
5. Press the Soup/Broth button and cook using the preset cooking time.
6. Do natural pressure release.

Nutrition Facts Per Serving

Calories 159, Total Fat 3g, Saturated Fat 1g, Total Carbs 37g, Net Carbs 17g, Protein 13g, Sugar: 3g, Fiber: 20g, Sodium: 562mg, Potassium: 393mg, Phosphorus: 142mg

Red Bean and Rice

Prep time: 5 minutes, cook time: 30 minutes; Serves 4

Ingredients:

2 tablespoons olive oil
1 yellow onion, sliced
5 cloves garlic, minced
1 green bell pepper, seeded and chopped
3 celery stalks, chopped
1 tablespoon Cajun seasoning
1 teaspoon mixed herbs (oregano, thyme, and smoked paprika)
1 teaspoon hot sauce
1-pound red beans or kidney beans, soaked overnight and drain
2 cups brown rice
3 bay leaves
4 cups vegetable broth
salt and pepper to taste

Instructions

1. Press the Sauté button on the Instant Pot and heat the oil.
2. Sauté the onion, garlic, bell pepper, and celery for 3 minutes until translucent.
3. Stir in the rest of the ingredients. Give a good stir to remove the browning at the bottom of the pot.
4. Close the lid but do not seal the vent.
5. Press the Rice button and wait until the rice is cooked.

Nutrition Facts Per Serving

Calories 464, Total Fat 8g, Saturated Fat 1g, Total Carbs 76g, Net Carbs 58g, Protein 26g, Sugar: 3g, Fiber: 18g, Sodium: 190mg, Potassium: 1660mg, Phosphorus: 476mg

Pumpkin, Chickpea, And Coconut Curry

Prep time: 5 minutes, cook time: 35 minutes; Serves 5

Ingredients:

2 tablespoons olive oil
1 1-inch ginger, peeled and smashed
4 shallots, chopped
4 cloves garlic, minced
1 fresh red chili, chopped
1 teaspoon mustard seeds
20 curry leaves
¾ pound kabocha squash, seeded and diced
1 14-ounce canned chickpeas, drained and rinsed
1 14-ounce canned tomatoes
2 14-ounce canned coconut milk
salt and pepper to taste

Instructions

1. Press the Sauté button on the Instant Pot and heat the oil.
2. Sauté the ginger, shallots, garlic, red chili, mustard seeds, and curry leaves. Stir for 3 minutes.
3. Add the remaining ingredients.
4. Close the lid and set the vent to the Sealing position.
5. Press the Stew/Broth button and cook using the preset cooking time.
6. Do natural pressure release.

Nutrition Facts Per Serving

Calories 479, Total Fat 23g, Saturated Fat 13g, Total Carbs 48g, Net Carbs 34g, Protein 19g, Sugar: 14g, Fiber: 14g, Sodium: 342mg, Potassium: 641mg, Phosphorus: 231mg

Instant Pot Pinto Beans

Prep time: 5 minutes, cook time: 42 minutes; Serves 6

Ingredients:

1 tablespoon cooking oil
1 yellow onion, chopped
3 cloves garlic, minced
2 cups dry pinto beans
2 bay leaves
3 cups vegetable broth
1 15-ounce canned tomatoes
salt and pepper to taste

Instructions

1. Press the Sauté button on the Instant Pot and heat the oil. Stir in the onion and garlic. Sauté for 2 minutes or until the onions become translucent.

2. Stir in the rest of the ingredients then season with salt and pepper to taste.
3. Close the lid and set the vent to the Sealing position.
4. Press the Bean/Chili button and cook on high for 40 minutes.

5. Do natural pressure release.
Nutrition Facts Per Serving
Calories 276, Total Fat 5g, Saturated Fat g, Total Carbs 44g, Net Carbs g, Protein 15g, Sugar: 4g, Fiber: 12g, Sodium: 92mg, Potassium: 1057 mg, Phosphorus: 284mg

Instant Pot Lentil Gumbo

Prep time: 5 minutes, cook time: 40 minutes; Serves 6
Ingredients:
1 tablespoon olive oil
2 cloves garlic, minced
1 large onion, chopped
2 celery stalks, chopped
1 tablespoon fresh thyme
½ tablespoon fresh oregano
½ teaspoon Cajun mix spice
1 cup lentils, soaked overnight and drained
3 cups vegetable broth
1 13-ounces diced tomatoes
2 tablespoons apple cider vinegar
salt and pepper to taste
2 cups frozen okras
1 cup cauliflower florets
2 cups cornstarch + 3 cups cold water
Instructions
1. Press the Sauté button on the Instant Pot and heat the oil. Sauté the garlic, onion, and celery stalks for 3 minutes. Stir in the thyme, oregano, and Cajun mix. Toast for 1 minute.

2. Stir in the lentils and vegetable broth. Pour in the tomatoes and apple cider vinegar. Season with salt and pepper to taste.
3. Close the lid and set the vent to the Sealing position.
4. Press the Bean/Chili button and cook using the preset cooking time.
5. Do quick pressure release.
6. Once the lid is open, press the Sauté button and stir in the okra and cauliflower. Allow to simmer for 5 minutes.
7. Stir in the cornstarch slurry and cook for another 3 minutes until the sauce has thickened.
Nutrition Facts Per Serving
Calories 80, Total Fat 3g, Saturated Fat 0.4g, Total Carbs 13g, Net Carbs 10g, Protein 4g, Sugar: 3g, Fiber: 3g, Sodium: 42mg, Potassium: 399mg, Phosphorus: 82mg

Instant Pot Baked Beans

Prep time:5 minutes, cook time: 42 minutes; Serves 6
Ingredients:
1 tablespoon olive oil
1 yellow onion, chopped
1-pound small dry white beans, soaked overnight and drain
1-pound kidney beans, soaked overnight and drain
1 cup ketchup
2 tablespoons Dijon mustard
2 tablespoons Worcestershire sauce
½ cup candied jalapenos, chopped
½ cup brown sugar
6 cups water
Salt and pepper to taste
Instructions

1. Press the Sauté button on the Instant Pot and heat the oil. Sauté the onion for 2 minutes until translucent.
2. Stir in the rest of the ingredients.
3. Close the lid and set the vent to the Sealing position.
4. Press the Bean/Chili and cook on 1high for 40 minutes.
5. Do natural pressure release.
Nutrition Facts Per Serving
Calories 446, Total Fat 7g, Saturated Fat 2g, Total Carbs 77g, Net Carbs 65g, Protein 20g, Sugar: 29g, Fiber: 12g, Sodium: 1495mg, Potassium: 1883mg, Phosphorus: 321mg

Instant Pot Lentils and Rice

Prep time: 5 minutes, cook time: 30 minutes; Serves 6

Ingredients:

4 cups vegetable broth
2 cups long grain brown rice
2 cups green lentils, soaked overnight and drained
2 tablespoons paprika
2 teaspoons fennel seeds
2 teaspoons onion powder
2 teaspoon garlic powder
1 tablespoon apple cider vinegar
salt and pepper to taste

Instructions

1. Place all ingredients in the Instant Pot and give a good stir.
2. Close the lid but do not seal the vent.
3. Press the Rice button and cook until the timer sets off.

Nutrition Facts Per Serving

Calories 271, Total Fat 2g, Saturated Fat 0.4g, Total Carbs 56g, Net Carbs 52g, Protein 8g, Sugar: 0.8g, Fiber: 4g, Sodium: 11mg, Potassium: 305mg, Phosphorus: 267mg

Italian Chickpea Stew with Basil

Prep time: 5 minutes, cook time: 45 minutes; Serves 4

Ingredients:

3 tablespoons olive oil
4 cloves garlic, minced
1 onion, chopped
12 ounces dried chickpeas, soaked overnight then drained
1 14-ounce diced tomatoes
¼ cup grated parmesan cheese
1 ½ packed fresh basil leaves
salt and pepper to taste
4 cups water

Instructions

1. Press the Sauté button on the Instant Pot and heat the olive oil.
2. Sauté the garlic and onion until fragrant.
3. Add in the chickpeas and tomatoes. Season with salt and pepper to taste. Pour in water.
4. Close the lid and set the vent to the Sealing position.
5. Press the Bean/Chili button and cook on high for 40 minutes.
6. Do quick pressure release.
7. Once the lid is open, press the Sauté button and stir in the parmesan cheese and basil. Allow to simmer for 3 minutes.

Nutrition Facts Per Serving

Calories 469, Total Fat 17g, Saturated Fat 3g, Total Carbs 61g, Net Carbs 49g, Protein 21g, Sugar: 10g, Fiber:12 g, Sodium: 177mg, Potassium: 885mg, Phosphorus: 295mg

Instant Pot Spicy Black Bean Soup

Prep time: 5 minutes, cook time: 43 minutes; Serves 4

Ingredients:

2 tablespoons olive oil
4 cloves garlic, minced
1 onion, chopped
1 yellow bell pepper, diced
4 teaspoons chili powder
½ teaspoon ground cumin
½ teaspoon dried oregano
6 cups vegetable broth
1-pound dry black beans, soaked overnight then rinsed
1 4-ounce chopped Hatch chili pepper
salt and pepper to taste

Instructions

1. Press the Sauté button on the Instant Pot and heat the oil. Sauté the garlic and onion until fragrant.
2. Stir in the bell pepper, chili powder, cumin, and oregano. Toast for another minute.
3. Stir in the rest of the ingredients.
4. Close the lid and set the vent to the Sealing position.
5. Press the Bean/Chili button and cook on high for 40 minutes , Do natural pressure release.

Nutrition Facts Per Serving

Calories 495, Total Fat 9g, Saturated Fat g1, Total Carbs 91g, Net Carbs 71g, Protein 26g, Sugar: 5g, Fiber: 20g, Sodium: 88mg, Potassium: 1988mg, Phosphorus: 446mg

Instant Pot Chana Masala and Kale

Prep time: 5 minutes, cook time: 45 minutes; Serves 5

Ingredients:

3 tablespoons olive oil
¾ cup chopped onion
1 teaspoon grated garlic
1 teaspoon grated ginger
1 cup dried chickpeas, soaked overnight
1 ½ cup chopped tomatoes
2 tablespoon chana masala powder
¼ teaspoon turmeric powder
¼ teaspoon cumin powder
salt and pepper to taste
1 cup water ¼ cup coconut milk
1 bunch Lacinato kale, torn

Instructions

1. Press the Sauté button on the Instant Pot and heat the oil. Sauté the onion, garlic, and ginger until fragrant.

2. Stir in the chickpeas, tomatoes, chana masala, turmeric, and cumin powder. Season with salt and pepper to taste. Pour in the water and coconut milk.

3. Close the lid and set the vent to the Sealing position.

4. Press the Bean/Chili button and cook on high for 40 minutes.

5. Do quick pressure release.

6. Once the lid is open, press the Sauté button and stir in the kale. Allow to simmer until the kale is wilted.

Nutrition Facts Per Serving

Calories 278, Total Fat 14g, Saturated Fat 3g, Total Carbs 32g, Net Carbs 23g, Protein 10g, Sugar: 7g, Fiber: 9g, Sodium: 151mg, Potassium: 657mg, Phosphorus: 321mg

Instant Pot Hoppin John

Prep time: 5 minutes, cook time: 37 minutes; Serves 6

Ingredients:

2 tablespoons olive oil
1 onion, diced
16 ounces dried black-eyed peas, soaked overnight
1 14-ounce diced tomatoes
1 teaspoon cayenne pepper
1 teaspoon thyme
4 cups vegetable broth
2 cups kale, torn
2 cups cooked rice, fluffed
salt and pepper to taste

Instructions

1. Press the Sauté button and heat the olive oil. Sauté the onion until fragrant.

2. Stir in the peas, tomatoes, cayenne pepper, thyme, and broth. Season with salt and pepper to taste.

3. Close the lid and set the vent to the Sealing position.

4. Press the Soup/Broth button and cook on high for 30 minutes.

5. Do quick pressure release once the timer sets off.

6. Once the lid is open, press the Sauté button and cook kale and cooked rice. Allow to simmer for 5 minutes.

Nutrition Facts Per Serving

Calories 501, Total Fat 13g, Saturated Fat 5g, Total Carbs 72g, Net Carbs 66g, Protein 22g, Sugar: 5g, Fiber: 6g, Sodium: 845mg, Potassium: 806mg, Phosphorus:316 mg

Mexican Black Beans

Prep time: 5 minutes, cook time: 43 minutes; Serves 6

Ingredients:

1 tablespoon grape seed oil
1 cup yellow onion, diced
3 cloves of garlic, minced
1 red bell peppers, seeded and chopped

1-pound dry black beans, soaked overnight then rinsed
1 ½ tablespoon ground cumin
1 teaspoon ancho chili powder

4 cups vegetable broth
1 teaspoon paprika
½ cup salsa verde
Juice from 1 lime
1/3 cup fresh cilantro, chopped
salt and pepper to taste

Instructions

1. Press the Sauté button and heat the oil.
2. Sauté the onion and garlic until fragrant. Stir in the bell pepper, black beans, cumin, and chili powder. Stir for 2 minutes.
3. Pour the broth, paprika, salsa verde, and lime juice. Season with salt and pepper to taste.
4. Close the lid and set the vent to the Sealing position.
5. Press the Bean/Chili button and cook on high for 40 minutes.
6. Do natural pressure release.
7. Once the lid is open, stir in the chopped cilantro before serving.

Nutrition Facts Per Serving

Calories 308, Total Fat 4g, Saturated Fat 0.6g, Total Carbs 53g, Net Carbs 40g, Protein 18g, Sugar: 3.6g, Fiber: 13g, Sodium: 143mg, Potassium: 1287mg, Phosphorus: 312mg

Vegetarian Cacciatore With White Beans

Prep time: 5 minutes, cook time: 45 minutes; Serves 5

Ingredients:

2 tablespoons olive oil
1 cup yellow onion, chopped
1 cup chopped celery
1 tablespoon minced garlic
5 cups sliced mushrooms
1 cup great northern beans, soaked overnight then drain
1 tablespoon tomato paste
1 15-ounce canned tomatoes
½ tablespoons rosemary leaves
2 tablespoons dry red wine
½ cup pitted black olives
Salt and pepper to taste

Instructions

1. Press the Sauté button on the Instant Pot and heat the oil.
2. Sauté the onion, celery, and garlic for 3 minutes until the onions are translucent. Add the mushrooms and cook for another 2 minutes.
3. Stir in the rest of the ingredients. Season with salt and pepper to taste.
4. Close the lid and set the vent to the Sealing position.
5. Press the Bean/Chili button and cook on high for 40 minutes.
6. Do natural pressure release.

Nutrition Facts Per Serving

Calories 258, Total Fat 8g, Saturated Fat 1g, Total Carbs 34g, Net Carbs 22g, Protein 13g, Sugar: 5g, Fiber: 12g, Sodium: 260mg, Potassium: 929mg, Phosphorus: 421mg

Instant Pot Kidney Bean Dal

Prep time: 5 minutes, cook time: 42 minutes; Serves 4

Ingredients:

1 tablespoon coconut oil
1 onion, chopped
3 cloves garlic, minced
1 tablespoon grated ginger
1 tablespoon ground coriander
1 ½ teaspoon ground cumin
1 ½ teaspoon garam masala
1 teaspoon ground turmeric
1 large tomato, chopped
2 whole pitted dates, chopped

1 ½ cup dried red kidney beans, soaked overnight then drained
1 cup water
1 cup coconut milk
Salt and pepper to taste
2 tablespoons chopped cilantro
1 tablespoon lime juice

Instructions

1. Press the Sauté button on the Instant Pot and heat the oil. Sauté the onion and garlic for 1 minute until fragrant. Add in the ginger,

coriander, cumin, garam masala, and turmeric. Stir for another minute.

2. Add in the tomatoes and cook for another minute. Add the dates, kidney beans, water, and coconut milk. Season with salt and pepper to taste.

3. Close the lid and set the vent to the Sealing position.

4. Press the Bean/Chili button and cook on high for 40 minutes.

5. Do quick pressure release.

6. Before serving, garnish with cilantro and drizzle with lemon juice.

Nutrition Facts Per Serving
Calories 184, Total Fat 6g, Saturated Fat 4g, Total Carbs 26g, Net Carbs 19g, Protein 8g, Sugar: 10g, Fiber:7 g, Sodium: 145mg, Potassium: 555mg, Phosphorus: 185mg

Three-Bean Chili

Prep time: 5 minutes, cook time: 45 minutes; Serves 6

Ingredients:
1 teaspoon canola oil
1 green bell pepper, seeded and chopped
1 onion, chopped
1 teaspoon ground cumin
15-ounce canned black beans, rinsed and drained
15-ounce canned pinto beans, rinsed and drained
15-ounce red kidney bean, rinsed and drained
3 cups vegetable stock
6 ounces tomato paste
15-ounce tomato sauce
1 teaspoon apple cider vinegar
3 tablespoon chili powder
2 teaspoon brown sugar
salt and pepper to taste

Instructions

1. Press the Sauté button on the Instant Pot. Heat the oil and sauté the green bell peppers and onions until fragrant. Add the cumin and toast for another minute.

2. Stir in the beans for 1 minute before adding the rest of the ingredients. Give a stir.

3. Close the lid and set the vent to the Sealing position.

4. Press the Bean/Chili button and cook on high for 40 minutes.

5. Do natural pressure release.

Nutrition Facts Per Serving
Calories 24, Total Fat 0.7g, Saturated Fat 0g, Total Carbs 4g Net Carbs 3g, Protein 1g, Sugar: 0.4g, Fiber: 1g, Sodium: 42mg, Potassium: 124mg, Phosphorus: 27mg

Instant Pot Cuban Black Beans

Prep time: 5 minutes, cook time: 42 minutes; Serves 6

Ingredients:
1 tablespoon coconut oil
1 onion, chopped
5 cloves garlic, minced
2 cups green bell peppers, seeded and chopped
½ tablespoon dry oregano
½ tablespoon ground cumin
1 ½ cups dried black beans, soaked overnight then rinsed
¼ cup tomato paste
5 cups vegetable broth
1 bay leaf
salt and pepper to taste

Instructions

1. Press the Sauté button on the Instant Pot and heat the oil. Sauté the onion and garlic for 1 minute until fragrant.

2. Stir in the green bell peppers, oregano and cumin. Sauté for another minute.

3. Add the rest of the ingredients and give a good stir.

4. Close the lid and set the vent to the Sealing position.

5. Press the Bean/Chili button and cook on high for 40 minutes.

6. Do natural pressure release.

Nutrition Facts Per Serving
Calories 305, Total Fat 10g, Saturated Fat 8g, Total Carbs 44g, Net Carbs 34g, Protein 12g, Sugar: 8g, Fiber: 10g, Sodium: 879, Potassium: 1040mg, Phosphorus: 321mg

Instant Pot Red Beans and Rice Soup

Prep time: 5 minutes, cook time: 43 minutes; Serves 6

Ingredients:

2 tablespoons oil
1 large onion, chopped
3 cloves garlic, minced
3 celery stalks, chopped
1 tablespoon smoked paprika
1 tablespoon dried thyme leaves
2 teaspoons dried oregano
½ teaspoon cayenne pepper
1-pound dried red beans, soaked overnight then drained
¾ cup uncooked brown rice
1 10-ounce canned tomatoes
7 cups water
Salt and pepper to taste

Instructions

1. Press the Sauté button on the Instant Pot and heat the oil. Sauté the onions and garlic until fragrant. Stir in the celery stalks and cook for another minute. Season with paprika, thyme, oregano, and cayenne pepper. Stir for another minute.
2. Add in the rest of the ingredients and season with salt and pepper to taste.
3. Close the lid and set the vent to the Sealing position.
4. Press the Bean/Chili button and cook on high for 40 minutes.
5. Do natural pressure release.

Nutrition Facts Per Serving

Calories 83, Total Fat 5g, Saturated Fat 1g, Total Carbs 9g, Net Carbs 5g, Protein 2g, Sugar: 3g, Fiber: 4g, Sodium: 65mg, Potassium: 263mg, Phosphorus: 40mg

Creamy White Bean and Spinach

Prep time: 5 minutes, cook time: 46 minutes; Serves 6

Ingredients:

1 tablespoon oil
1 onion, diced
3 cloves garlic, minced
1 cup diced carrots
1 cup diced celery
1 rosemary sprig
2 tablespoons lemon juice
2 cups dry navy beans, soaked overnight and drained
6 cups vegetable stock
1 cup packed spinach
salt and pepper to taste

Instructions

1. Press the Sauté button on the Instant Pot and heat the oil. Sauté the onion and garlic until fragrant.
2. Add in the carrots and celery and sauté for another 2 minutes until the vegetables have wilted.
3. Stir in the rosemary, lemon juice, navy beans, and vegetable stock. Season with salt and pepper to taste.
4. Close the lid and set the vent to the Sealing position.
5. Press the Bean/Chili button and cook on high for 40 minutes.
6. Do quick pressure release to open the lid.
7. Once the lid is open, press the Sauté button and add in the spinach. Allow to simmer for 3 minutes.

Nutrition Facts Per Serving

Calories 289, Total Fat 4g, Saturated Fat 1g, Total Carbs 47g, Net Carbs 35g, Protein 17g, Sugar: 5g, Fiber:12 g, Sodium: 53mg, Potassium: 1004mg, Phosphorus: 133mg

White Beans with Tomatillos

Prep time: 10 minutes, cook time: 43 minutes; Serves 6

Ingredients:

2 cups tomatillos
1 cup chopped poblano peppers
1 cup chopped onions
1 ½ teaspoons ground cumin
2 teaspoon dried oregano
½ jalapeno, seeds removed then chopped

3 tablespoons coconut oil
1 ½ cups dried Great northern beans, soaked overnight then drained
1 ½ cups water
Salt and pepper to taste

Instructions
1. Put the tomatillos, poblano peppers, onion, cumin, oregano, and jalapeno in a food processor. Pulse until smooth. Set aside.
2. On the Instant Pot, press the Sauté button and heat the oil. Stir in the tomatillo-chili paste and cook for 3 minutes. Stir constantly to avoid browning at the bottom.
3. Add the beans and water. Season with salt and pepper to taste.
4. Close the lid and set the vent to the Sealing position.
5. Press the Bean/Chili button and cook on high for 40 minutes.
6. Do natural pressure release.

Nutrition Facts Per Serving
Calories 241, Total Fat 8g, Saturated Fat 6g, Total Carbs 34 g, Net Carbs 23g, Protein 11g, Sugar: 4g, Fiber: 11g, Sodium: 9mg, Potassium: 820mg, Phosphorus: 234mg

Instant Pot Pinto Beans Vegan Posole

Prep time: 5 minutes, cook time: 47 minutes; Serves 6

Ingredients:
1 tablespoon olive oil
1 onion, chopped
10 cloves garlic, minced
2 yellow bell peppers, seeded and chopped
1 tablespoon ground cumin
1 tablespoon chili powder
1 tablespoon ancho chili powder
1 teaspoon coconut sugar
½ cup tomato paste
1 bay leaf
3 15-ounce canned pinto beans, rinsed and drained
1 15-ounce canned hominy, rinsed and drained
32 ounces vegetable broth
1 cup baby spinach, chopped
salt and pepper to taste

Instructions
1. Press the Sauté button on the Instant Pot and heat the oil. Sauté the onion and garlic for 1 minute until fragrant. Stir in the bell pepper and season with cumin, chili powder, ancho chili, salt and pepper. Stir for another minute.
2. Add in the coconut sugar, tomato paste, bay leaf, beans, and vegetable broth. Adjust the seasoning if needed.
3. Close the lid and set the vent to the Sealing position.
4. Press the Bean/Chili button and cook on high for 40 minutes.
5. Do quick pressure release to open the lid.
6. Once the lid is open, press the Sauté button and add in the spinach. Allow to simmer for 5 minutes.

Nutrition Facts Per Serving
Calories 207, Total Fat 4g, Saturated Fat1 g, Total Carbs 37g, Net Carbs 29g, Protein 8g, Sugar: 8g, Fiber: 8g, Sodium: 1667mg, Potassium: 827mg, Phosphorus: 213mg

Baked Great Northern Beans

Prep time: 5 minutes, cook time: 51 minutes; Serves 4

Ingredients:
2 cups water
1 cup dried great northern bean, soaked overnight then drained
1 teaspoon olive oil
1 onion, chopped
½ cup ketchup
¼ cup molasses
¼ cup dark brown sugar
1 teaspoon smoked paprika
1 teaspoon salt
½ teaspoon ground black pepper

Instructions
1. Place the beans and 2 cups of water in the Instant Pot. Close the lid and set the vent to the Sealing position.
2. Press the Bean/Chili button and cook on high for 40 minutes.

3. Do natural pressure release to open the lid. Drain and discard the liquid. Set the cooked beans aside.
4. Into your clean Instant Pot, press the Sauté button and heat the oil.
5. Sauté the onion for 1 minute until fragrant.
6. Add the cooked beans and the remaining ingredients.

7. Close the lid and set the vent to the Sealing position.
8. Press the Pressure Cook or Manual button and adjust the cooking time to 10 minutes.

Nutrition Facts Per Serving
Calories 293, Total Fat 2g, Saturated Fat 0.4g, Total Carbs 62g, Net Carbs52 g, Protein 11g, Sugar: 31g, Fiber: 10g, Sodium: 288mg, Potassium :1081 mg, Phosphorus: 229mg

Instant Pot Refried Beans

Prep time: 5 minutes, cook time: 32 minutes; Serves 4
Ingredients:
1 tablespoon olive oil
1 onion, chopped
4 cloves of garlic, minced
2 teaspoon ground cumin
1 teaspoon oregano
2 teaspoons chili powder
1-pound dry pinto beans, soaked overnight then drained
3 cups vegetable broth
salt and pepper to taste
Instructions
1. Press the Sauté button on the Instant Pot and heat the oil. Sauté the onion and garlic until fragrant.

2. Stir in the cumin, oregano, and chili powder. Toast for 1 minute.
3. Stir in the rest of the ingredients.
4. Close the lid and set the vent to the Sealing position.
5. Press the Bean/Chili button and cook using the preset cooking time.
6. Do natural pressure release.

Nutrition Facts Per Serving
Calories 315, Total Fat 4g, Saturated Fat 1g, Total Carbs51 g, Net Carbs 38g, Protein 21g, Sugar: 2g, Fiber: 13g, Sodium:461 mg, Potassium: 1113mg, Phosphorus: 231mg

Instant Pot Indian Rajma Kidney Beans

Prep time: 5 minutes, cook time: 45 minutes; Serves 6
Ingredients:
1 tablespoon oil
1 ½ cup diced onion
1 tablespoon minced ginger
1 tablespoon garlic, minced
1 cup canned tomatoes
1 teaspoon cayenne pepper
1 teaspoon turmeric powder
1 teaspoon ground cumin
1 teaspoon ground coriander
1 cup dry red kidney beans, soaked overnight then rinsed
2 cups vegetable broth
salt and pepper to taste
Instructions
1. Press the Sauté button on the Instant Pot and heat the oil. Sauté the onion, ginger, and

garlic until fragrant. Add in the tomatoes and season with tomatoes, cayenne pepper, turmeric, cumin, and coriander. Add in salt and pepper to taste.
2. Stir in the beans and broth. Adjust the seasoning if desired.
3. Close the lid and set the vent to the Sealing position.
4. Press the Chili/Bean button and cook on high for 40 minutes.
5. Do natural pressure release.

Nutrition Facts Per Serving
Calories 161, Total Fat 3g, Saturated Fat 1g, Total Carbs 27g, Net Carbs 21g, Protein 8g, Sugar: 4g, Fiber: 6g, Sodium: 45mg, Potassium: 614mg, Phosphorus: 217mg

Fiasco Beans

Prep time: 5 minutes, cook time: 46 minutes; Serves 6

Ingredients:

¼ cup olive oil

5 cloves garlic, minced

5 medium sage leaves

½ teaspoon crushed red pepper flakes

1-pound dry cannellini beans, soaked overnight and drained

5 big handfuls of kale, torn

6 cups water

Salt and pepper to taste

Instructions

1. Press the Sauté button on the Instant Pot. Heat the oil and sauté the garlic for 1 minute until fragrant. Stir in the sage leaves and red pepper flakes.
2. Add in the cannellini beans and water. Season with salt and pepper to taste.
3. Close the lid and set the vent to the Sealing position.
4. Press the Bean/Chili button and cook on high for 40 minutes.
5. Do quick pressure release.
6. Once the lid is open, press the Sauté button and stir in the kale. Allow to simmer for 5 minutes before serving.

Nutrition Facts Per Serving

Calories 201, Total Fat 12g, Saturated Fat 2g, Total Carbs 17g, Net Carbs 14g, Protein 8g, Sugar: 5g, Fiber: 3g, Sodium: 329mg, Potassium: 289mg, Phosphorus: 82mg

Vegetarian One Pot Barbecued Beans

Prep time: 5 minutes, cook time: 40 minutes; Serves 5

Ingredients:

1 ½ cups white beans, soaked overnight and drained

1 cup tomato sauce

1 cup commercial barbecue sauce

1 cup diced onion

½ jalapeno, chopped

2 teaspoons dried oregano

1 ½ cups vegetable broth

salt and pepper to taste

Instructions

1. Place all ingredients in the Instant Pot. Give a good stir.
2. Close the lid and set the vent to the Sealing position.
3. Press the Bean/Chili button and cook on high for 40 minutes.
4. Do natural pressure release.

Nutrition Facts Per Serving

Calories 371, Total Fat 1g, Saturated Fat 0g, Total Carbs 74g, Net Carbs 60g, Protein 16g, Sugar: 28g, Fiber: 14g, Sodium: 1494mg, Potassium: 1461mg, Phosphorus: 230mg

Butter Beans in Tomato Sauce

Prep time: 5 minutes, cook time: 34 minutes; Serves 3

Ingredients:

1 tablespoon coconut oil

1 onion chopped

2 cloves garlic, minced

1 tablespoon ginger paste

1 large tomato, diced

1 cup tomato sauce

1 teaspoon cumin

1 teaspoon garam masala

½ teaspoon paprika

2 bay leaves

1 cup dried butter beans, soaked overnight then drained

1 cup chopped coriander leaves

½ cup water

salt and pepper to taste

Instructions

1. Press the Sauté button on the Instant Pot and heat the oil. Sauté the onion and garlic until fragrant. Stir in the ginger paste and tomatoes. Sauté for 3 minutes until the tomatoes are wilted.

2. Add in the tomato sauce and season with cumin, garam masala, paprika, and bay leaves. Add in water and beans. Season with salt and pepper to taste.
3. Close the lid and set the vent to the Sealing position.
4. Press the Bean/Chili button and cook using the present cooking time.
5. Do natural pressure release.
6. Once the lid is open, stir in the coriander leaves.

Nutrition Facts Per Serving
Calories 180, Total Fat 5g, Saturated Fat 4g, Total Carbs 28g, Net Carbs 20g, Protein 4g, Sugar: 13g, Fiber: 8g, Sodium: 1228mg, Potassium: 649mg, Phosphorus: 94mg

Instant Pot Ranch-Style Beans

Prep time: 5 minutes, cook time: 40 minutes; Serves 6
Ingredients:
1-pound dried pinto beans, soaked overnight and drained
3 cups vegetable broth
½ cup tomato puree
1 tablespoon chili powder
2 teaspoons onion powder
2 teaspoons garlic powder
1 teaspoon brown sugar
1 teaspoon apple cider vinegar
1 teaspoon paprika
1 teaspoon cumin
½ teaspoon oregano
2 drops liquid smoke seasoning
3 cups water
Salt and pepper to taste

Instructions
1. Place all ingredients in the Instant Pot. Give a good stir.
2. Close the lid and set the vent to the Sealing position.
3. Press the Bean/Chili button and cook on high for 40 minutes.
4. Do natural pressure release.
5. Garnish with coriander if desired.

Nutrition Facts Per Serving
Calories 39, Total Fat 0.7g, Saturated Fat 0g, Total Carbs 8g, Net Carbs 6g, Protein 2g, Sugar: 2g, Fiber: 2g, Sodium: 48mg, Potassium: 227mg, Phosphorus: 37mg

Tuscan White Beans with Tomatoes, Mushrooms, And Artichokes

Prep time: 5 minutes, cook time: 45 minutes; Serves 4
Ingredients:
2 tablespoons olive oil
½ cup diced onions
3 cloves garlic, minced
1 ½ cup brown mushrooms, diced
2/3 cup fire-roasted tomatoes
2 14-ounce cans diced tomatoes
2 14-ounce cans Cannellini beans, drained and rinsed
1 teaspoon dried oregano leaf
½ teaspoon dried thyme leaves
1 teaspoon sugar
1 cup vegetable broth
salt and pepper to taste
Instructions

1. Press the Sauté button on the Instant Pot and heat the oil. Sauté the onions and garlic until fragrant.
2. Stir in the mushrooms and cook for another 3 minutes until wilted.
3. Add in the rest of the ingredients.
4. Close the lid and set the vent to the Sealing position.
5. Press the Bean/Chili button and cook on high for 40 minutes.
6. Do natural pressure release.

Nutrition Facts Per Serving
Calories 178, Total Fat 9g, Saturated Fat 1g, Total Carbs 25g, Net Carbs 16g, Protein 6g, Sugar: 12g, Fiber: 9g, Sodium: 258mg, Potassium: 1060mg, Phosphorus: 153mg

Rice and Bean Casserole

Prep time: 5 minutes, cook time: 30 minutes; Serves 8

Ingredients:

1 onion, chopped
3 cloves garlic, minced
1 green pepper, chopped
1 can pinto beans, drained
1 can black beans, drained
1 cup uncooked brown rice
1 can whole corn kernel
2 cups vegetable stock
1 teaspoon dried oregano
1 teaspoon cumin
Salt and pepper to taste

Instructions

1. Place all ingredients in the Instant Pot and give a good stir.
2. Close the lid and set the vent to the Sealing position.
3. Press the Rice button and cook on low until the timer sets off.
4. Open the lid and fluff the rice before serving.

Nutrition Facts Per Serving

Calories 446, Total Fat 7g, Saturated Fat 2g, Total Carbs 82g, Net Carbs 66g, Protein 21g, Sugar: 5g, Fiber: 16g, Sodium: 480mg, Potassium: 793mg, Phosphorus: 195mg

Vegetarian Louisiana-Style Red Beans and Rice

Prep time: 5 minutes, cook time: 42 minutes; Serves 5

Ingredients:

2 tablespoons olive oil
4 cloves garlic, chopped
1 large onion, chopped
4 celery stalks, chopped
1 green bell pepper, seeded and chopped
3 bay leaves
2 teaspoons thyme
1 teaspoon oregano
½ tablespoon hot sauce
2 tablespoons liquid smoke seasoning
1-pound dry red kidney beans
1 32-ounce vegetable broth
salt and pepper to taste
4 cups water

Instructions

1. Press the Sauté button on the Instant Pot and heat the oil.
2. Sauté the garlic, onion, and celery stalks. Stir for 2 minutes until the vegetables become translucent.
3. Stir the rest of the ingredients.
4. Close the lid and set the vent to the Sealing position.
5. Press the Bean/Chili button and cook on high for 40 minutes.
6. Do natural pressure release.

Nutrition Facts Per Serving

Calories 155, Total Fat 6g, Saturated Fat 0.8g, Total Carbs 21g, Net Carbs 18g, Protein 6g, Sugar: 4g, Fiber: 3g, Sodium: 404mg, Potassium: 396mg, Phosphorus: 117mg

Vegetarian Borracho Beans

Prep time: 5 minutes, cook time: 42 minutes; Serves 6

Ingredients:

2 tablespoons extra virgin olive oil
1 cup diced onions
3 cloves garlic, minced
3 large tomatoes, chopped
2 jalapenos, chopped
2 teaspoons paprika
1 teaspoon cumin seeds
1 teaspoon adobo chili powder
2 pounds dry pinto beans, soaked overnight and drained

6 cups vegetable broth
salt and pepper to taste

Instructions

1. Press the Sauté button on the Instant Pot and heat the oil. Sauté the onions and garlic for 1 minute until fragrant.
2. Stir in the tomatoes, jalapenos, paprika, cumin, and adobo chili powder and toast for 1 minute.
3. Add in the rest of the ingredients.

4. Close the lid and set the vent to the Sealing position.
5. Press the Bean/Chili button and cook on high for 40 minutes.
6. Do natural pressure release.

Nutrition Facts Per Serving
Calories 265, Total Fat 3g, Saturated Fat 0.5g, Total Carbs 46g, Net Carbs 30g, Protein 15g, Sugar: 4g, Fiber: 16g, Sodium: 61mg, Potassium: 943mg, Phosphorus: 258mg

Black Bean, Zucchini, And Rice

Prep time: 5 minutes, cook time: 30 minutes; Serves 4
Ingredients:
1 tablespoon canola oil
½ cup chopped onions
½ cup diced green bell peppers
1 15-ounce canned black beans
1 15-ounce canned fire-roasted tomatoes
1 cup uncooked white rice
1 zucchini, quartered then sliced thickly
¾ cup water
Salt and pepper to taste
Instructions
1. Press the Sauté button on the Instant Pot and heat the oil

2. Sauté the onions and bell pepper for 1 minute until fragrant and translucent.
3. Stir in the rest of the ingredients then season with salt and pepper to taste.
4. Close the lid and set the vent to the Sealing position.
5. Press the Rice button and cook on low until the timer sets off.

Nutrition Facts Per Serving
Calories 251, Total Fat 5g, Saturated Fat 0.4g, Total Carbs 48g, Net Carbs 42g, Protein 5g, Sugar: 6g, Fiber: 6g, Sodium: 129mg, Potassium: 387mg, Phosphorus:80 mg

Vegetarian Navy Bean Soup

Prep time: minutes, cook time: minutes; Serves 8
Ingredients:
1 tablespoon olive oil
6 cloves garlic, minced
1 large onion, chopped
2 carrots, peeled and sliced
4 celery stalks, chopped
1 tablespoon fresh thyme leaves
1 tablespoon ground cumin
2 bay leaves
10 cups vegetable broth
1-pound dried navy beans, soaked overnight and drained
salt and pepper to taste
Instructions
1. Press the Sauté button on the Instant Pot and heat the oil. Sauté the garlic and onion for 1 minute until fragrant.

2. Stir in the carrots and celery and cook for 3 minutes until the vegetables have wilted.
3. Add in thyme leaves, cumin, and bay leaves.
4. Stir in the rest of the ingredients.
5. Close the lid and set the vent to the Sealing position.
6. Press the Bean/Chili button and cook on high for 40 minutes. Do natural pressure release.

Nutrition Facts Per Serving
Calories 222, Total Fat 3g, Saturated Fat 0.3g, Total Carbs 38g, Net Carbs 29g, Protein 13g, Sugar: 3g, Fiber: 9g, Sodium: 13mg, Potassium: 748mg, Phosphorus: 246mg

Mediterranean White Bean Soup

Prep time: 5 minutes, cook time: 47 minutes; Serves 6
Ingredients:
1 tablespoon olive oil
1 onion, chopped
2 cloves garlic, minced

1 large carrot, chopped
1 celery rib, chopped
6 cups vegetable broth

1 teaspoon dried thyme
½ teaspoon oregano
3 15-ounce can white beans, rinsed and drained
salt and pepper to taste
2 cups baby spinach

Instructions

1. Press the Sauté button on the Instant Pot and heat the oil. Sauté the onion and garlic for 1 minute. Stir in the carrots and celery and cook for 3 more minutes until the vegetables are wilted.
2. Stir in the broth, thyme, oregano, and beans. Season with salt and pepper to taste.
3. Close the lid and set the vent to the Sealing position.
4. Press the Bean/Chili button and cook on high for 40 minutes.
5. Do quick pressure release.
6. Once the lid is open, press the Sauté button and put the spinach. Allow to simmer for 3 minutes.

Nutrition Facts Per Serving

Calories 249, Total Fat 3g, Saturated Fat 1g, Total Carbs 60g, Net Carbs 44g, Protein 15g, Sugar: 4g, Fiber: 14g, Sodium: 962mg, Potassium: 1307mg, Phosphorus: 216mg

Smoky Barbecue Baked Beans

Prep time: 5 minutes, cook time: 42 minutes; Serves 6

Ingredients:

2 tablespoons coconut oil
2 cloves garlic, minced
1 onion, chopped
1/8 teaspoon red chili flakes
1 teaspoon ground cumin
2 cups diced carrots
1 ¼ cups fire-roasted tomatoes
1 cup commercial barbecue sauce
1 cup dry pinto beans, soaked overnight and rinsed
¼ cup vegetable broth
salt and pepper to taste

Instructions

1. Press the Sauté button and heat the oil. Sauté the garlic and onion until fragrant.
2. Stir in the rest of the ingredients.
3. Close the lid and set the vent to the Sealing position.
4. Press the Bean/Chili and cook on high for 40 minutes.
5. Do natural pressure release.

Nutrition Facts Per Serving

Calories 322, Total Fat 7g, Saturated Fat 5g, Total Carbs 57g, Net Carbs 48g, Protein 10g, Sugar: 25g, Fiber: 9g, Sodium: 1253mg, Potassium: 830mg, Phosphorus: 423mg

One-Pot Cajun-Style Vegan Red Beans and Rice

Prep time: 5 minutes, cook time: 40 minutes; Serves 6

Ingredients:

1 yellow onion, diced
6 cloves garlic, minced
2 celery stalks, chopped
1 green bell peppers, seeded and diced
1-pound dry red kidney beans, soaked overnight and drained
1 tablespoon hot sauce
1 teaspoon dried thyme
1 teaspoon paprika
2 bay leaves
1 32-ounce vegetable broth
1 ½ cups dry brown rice
½ teaspoon liquid smoke seasoning
salt and pepper to taste

Instructions

1. Place all ingredients in the Instant Pot. Give a good stir to combine everything.
2. Close the lid and set the vent to the Sealing position.
3. Press the Bean/Chili button and cook on high for 40 minutes.
4. Do natural pressure release.
5. Open the lid and fluff the rice before serving.

Nutrition Facts Per Serving

Calories 244, Total Fat 2g, Saturated Fat 0.4g, Total Carbs 49g, Net Carbs 43g, Protein 8g, Sugar: 2g, Fiber: 6g, Sodium: 135mg, Potassium: 372mg, Phosphorus: 246mg

Vegetarian Bean and Barley Soup

Prep time: 5 minutes, cook time: 46 minutes; Serves 6

Ingredients:

2 tablespoons olive oil
½ onion, diced
2 celery stalks, chopped
2 carrots, diced
½ cup frozen vegetables
1 cup pearled barley uncooked
¼ teaspoon paprika
¼ teaspoon basil
½ teaspoon thyme
salt and pepper to taste
8 cups water
1 cup chopped kale

Instructions

1. Press the Sauté button on the Instant Pot and heat the olive oil.
2. Sauté the onion, celery, carrots, and frozen vegetables. Stir for 3 minutes until the vegetables have wilted
3. Stir in the rest of the ingredients except for the kale.
4. Close the lid and set the vent to the Sealing position.
5. Press the Bean/Chili button and cook on high for 40 minutes.
6. Do natural pressure release.
7. Once the lid is open, press the Sauté button and stir in the kale. Simmer for 3 minutes.

Nutrition Facts Per Serving

Calories 182, Total Fat 5g, Saturated Fat 0.7g, Total Carbs 31g, Net Carbs 24g, Protein 4g, Sugar: 2g, Fiber: 7g, Sodium: 28mg, Potassium: 229mg, Phosphorus: 95mg

Three Bean Curry

Prep time: 5 minutes, cook time: 42 minutes; Serves 3

Ingredients:

2 tablespoons olive oil
1 onion, chopped
3 cloves garlic, minced
2 teaspoons grated ginger
1 teaspoon cumin
2 teaspoons paprika
½ teaspoon turmeric
1 14-ounce can fire-roasted tomatoes
1 6-ounce can tomato paste
1 14-ounce can coconut milk
1 14-ounce can black beans, rinsed and drained
1 14-ounce can pinto beans, rinsed and drained
1 14-ounce can chickpea beans, rinsed and drained
3 teaspoons coriander, chopped
salt and pepper to taste

Instructions

1. Press the Sauté button on the Instant Pot and heat the oil.
2. Sauté the onion and garlic for 1 minute until fragrant.
3. Add in the ginger, paprika, and turmeric. Stir for another minute.
4. Pour in the tomatoes, tomato paste, coconut milk, black beans, pinto beans, and chickpea beans.
5. Season with salt and pepper to taste.
6. Close the lid and set the vent to the Sealing position.
7. Press the Bean/Chili button and cook on high for 40 minutes.
8. Do natural pressure release.
9. Once the lid is open, stir in the coriander as garnish.

Nutrition Facts Per Serving

Calories 565, Total Fat 16g, Saturated Fat 2g, Total Carbs 89g, Net Carbs 63g, Protein 25g, Sugar: 23g, Fiber: 26g, Sodium: 974mg, Potassium: 1945mg, Phosphorus: 394mg

Chapter 4 Soup & Stew Recipes

Farmers1 Market Vegetable Soup

Prep time: 5 minutes, cook time: 23 minutes; Serves 8

Ingredients:
2 tablespoons olive oil
1 onion, diced
4 cloves garlic, minced
2 cups diced celery stalks
2 cups diced fennel bulb
2 cups diced carrots
1 tablespoon fresh thyme
2 tablespoons white wine
2 cups diced zucchini
½ cup corn kernels
4 cups vegetable stock
2 bay leaves
2 cups water
salt and pepper to taste

Instructions

1. Press the Sauté button on the Instant Pot and heat the oil. Sauté the onion, garlic, celery, and fennel for 3 minutes until translucent and fragrant.
2. Add the rest of the ingredients. Give a good stir to remove the browning on the pan.
3. Close the lid and set the vent to the Sealing position.
4. Press the Soup/Broth button and cook on high for 20 minutes.
5. Do natural pressure release.

Nutrition Facts Per Serving
Calories, Total Fat g, Saturated Fat g, Total Carbs g, Net Carbs g, Protein g, Sugar: g, Fiber: g, Sodium: mg, Potassium: mg, Phosphorus: mg

Vegetarian Tortilla Soup

Prep time: 5 minutes, cook time: 22 minutes; Serves 5

Ingredients:
1 tablespoon olive oil
1 onion, chopped
4 garlic cloves, minced
1 green bell pepper, chopped
2 15-ounce canned black beans, rinsed and drained
2 teaspoons dried oregano
1 teaspoon cumin
1 28-ounce crushed tomatoes
1 ½ cups frozen corn
1 tablespoon adobo sauce
4 cups vegetable broth
salt and pepper to taste
6 6-inch corn tortillas, toasted

Instructions

1. Press the Sauté button on the Instant Pot and heat the oil.
2. Sauté the onion and garlic until fragrant.
3. Stir in the rest of the ingredients, except for tortillas.
4. Close the lid and set the vent to the Sealing position.
5. Press the Soup/Broth button and adjust the cooking time to 20 minutes.
6. Do natural pressure release.
7. Serve with tortillas on the side.

Nutrition Facts Per Serving
Calories, Total Fat g, Saturated Fat g, Total Carbs g, Net Carbs g, Protein g, Sugar: g, Fiber: g, Sodium: mg, Potassium: mg, Phosphorus: mg

Tomato Basil Soup

Prep time: minutes, cook time: minutes; Serves

Ingredients:
2 tablespoons olive oil
3 cloves garlic, minced
1 onion, chopped
2 tablespoons white wine vinegar

1 28-ounce can fire-roasted crushed tomatoes
4 cups vegetable broth
salt and pepper to taste
1 cup basil leaves

Instructions

1. Press the Sauté button on the Instant Pot. Heat the oil and sauté the garlic and onion for 1 minute until fragrant.
2. Stir in the white wine vinegar, tomatoes, and broth. Season with salt and pepper to taste.
3. Close the lid and set the vent to the Sealing position.
4. Press the Pressure Cook or Manual button. Adjust the cooking time to 15 minutes.
5. Do quick pressure release.
6. Once the lid is open, stir in the basil leaves last.

Nutrition Facts Per Serving
Calories 155, Total Fat 10g, Saturated Fat 2g, Total Carbs 17g, Net Carbs 13g, Protein 3g, Sugar: 9g, Fiber: 4g, Sodium:482mg, Potassium: 474mg, Phosphorus: 132mg

Farro And Brussels Sprouts Soup

Prep time: 10 minutes, cook time: 22 minutes; Serves 4

Ingredients:
¼ cup olive oil
2 shallots, chopped
4 cloves garlic, minced
1 1-inch ginger, grated
2 carrots, peeled and chopped
8 ounces mushrooms, chopped
16 Brussels sprouts, halved
1 teaspoon dried thyme
2 tablespoons Worcestershire sauce
1 tablespoon soy sauce
1 15-ounce can cannellini beans
½ cup dry farro beans, soaked overnight and drained
8 cups vegetable broth
salt and pepper to taste
4 cups baby spinach

Instructions

1. Press the Sauté button on the Instant Pot and heat the oil.
2. Sauté the shallots and garlic until fragrant.
3. Add in the ginger, carrots, and mushrooms. Stir for another 2 minutes.
4. Stir in the Brussels sprouts and thyme. Season with Worcestershire sauce, soy sauce, salt and pepper.
5. Stir in the beans and vegetable broth.
6. Close the lid and set the vent to the Sealing position.
7. Press the Pressure Cook or Manual button and adjust the cooking time to 15 minutes.
8. Do quick pressure release.
9. Once the lid is open, press the Sauté button and add in the spinach. Allow to simmer for 3 minutes.

Nutrition Facts Per Serving
Calories 269, Total Fat 16g, Saturated Fat 2g, Total Carbs 28g, Net Carbs 19g, Protein 10g, Sugar: 7g, Fiber: 9g, Sodium: 289mg, Potassium: 1003mg, Phosphorus: 197mg

Sweet Potato Kale Soup

Prep time: 5 minutes, cook time: 25 minutes; Serves 4

Ingredients:
2 tablespoons olive oil
4 cloves garlic, minced
1 yellow onion, chopped
1-pound cubed sweet potatoes
2 teaspoons dried oregano
1 ½ teaspoons cumin
1 teaspoon garlic powder
4 cups vegetable broth
2 radishes sliced thinly
1 tablespoon lime juice
salt and pepper to taste
2 cups chopped kale

Instructions

1. Press the Sauté button on the Instant Pot and heat the oil.
2. Sauté the garlic and onion for 1 minute until fragrant.
3. Add in the sweet potatoes and season with oregano, cumin, and garlic powder.
4. Pour in the broth, radish, and lime juice. Season with salt and pepper to taste.

5. Close the lid and set the vent to the Sealing position.
6. Press the Soup/Broth button and cook for 20 minutes.
7. Do quick pressure release to open the lid.
8. Once the lid is open, press the Sauté button and stir in the kale. Simmer for 3 minutes before serving.

Nutrition Facts Per Serving
Calories 192, Total Fat 10g, Saturated Fat 1g, Total Carbs 25g, Net Carbs g21, Protein 4g, Sugar: 2g, Fiber: 4g, Sodium: 15mg, Potassium: 593mg, Phosphorus: 92mg

Creamy Coconut Curry Soup

Prep time: 5 minutes, cook time: 16 minutes; Serves 4

Ingredients:
2 tablespoons coconut oil
3 cloves garlic, minced
2 shallots, chopped
2 15-ounce cans chickpeas
salt and pepper to taste
3 tablespoons curry powder
1 teaspoon cumin
1 teaspoon coriander
1 pinch cayenne pepper
1 tablespoon white wine vinegar
4 cups vegetable broth
1 tablespoon maple syrup
1 15-ounce can full-fat coconut milk

Instructions
1. Press the Sauté button and heat the oil. Sauté the garlic and shallots until fragrant.
2. Stir in the chickpeas and season with salt, pepper, curry powder, cumin, coriander, and cayenne pepper. Stir for 1 minute.
3. Add in the rest of the ingredients.
4. Close the lid and set the vent to the Sealing position.
5. Press the Manual button and adjust the cooking time to 15 minutes.
6. Do natural pressure release.

Nutrition Facts Per Serving
Calories 637, Total Fat 38g, Saturated Fat 29g, Total Carbs 62g, Net Carbs 42g, Protein 18g, Sugar: 16g, Fiber: 20g, Sodium: 544mg, Potassium: 650mg, Phosphorus: 314mg

Easy Lentil Stew

Prep time: 5 minutes, cook time: 45 minutes; Serves 5

Ingredients:
2 tablespoons olive oil
1 large onion, chopped
3 cloves garlic, minced
1 tablespoon oregano
1 tablespoon dried basil
1 cup red lentils, soaked overnight and drained
2 28-ounce cans fire-roasted tomatoes
2 cups water
salt and pepper to taste
3 cups kale, torn

Instructions
1. Press the Sauté button on the Instant Pot and heat the oil.
2. Sauté the onion and garlic until fragrant. Stir in the oregano and basil.
3. Add the lentils and tomatoes. Pour in water and season with salt and pepper to taste.
4. Close the lid and set the vent to the Sealing position.
5. Press the Bean/ Chili button and cook on high for 40 minutes.
6. Do quick pressure release.
7. Once the lid is open, press the Sauté button and stir in the kale.
8. Allow to simmer for 3 minutes before serving.

Nutrition Facts Per Serving
Calories 256, Total Fat 7g, Saturated Fat 1g, Total Carbs 40g, Net Carbs 29g, Protein 13g, Sugar: 10g, Fiber: 11g, Sodium: 373mg, Potassium: 963mg, Phosphorus: 187mg

Vegan Butternut Squash

Prep time: 5 minutes, cook time: 22 minutes; Serves 5

Ingredients:

3 tablespoons olive oil

1 onion, chopped

1 teaspoon cumin

1 medium butternut squash, seeded and diced

3 carrots, peeled and diced

2 medium sweet potatoes, peeled and diced

4 cups vegetable broth

Salt and pepper to taste

2 tablespoons sesame seeds

Instructions

1. Press the Sauté button on the Instant Pot and heat the oil. Sauté the onion for 1 minute until translucent. Stir in the cumin and toast for another minute.

2. Add the squash, carrots, and sweet potatoes. Pour in the broth and season with salt and pepper to taste.

3. Close the lid and set the vent to the Sealing position.

4. Press the Soup/Broth button and cook for 20 minutes.

5. Do natural pressure release.

6. Garnish with sesame seeds before serving.

Nutrition Facts Per Serving

Calories 164, Total Fat 10g, Saturated Fat 1g, Total Carbs 17g, Net Carbs 13g, Protein 2g, Sugar: 6g, Fiber: 4g, Sodium: 36mg, Potassium: 358mg, Phosphorus: 72mg

Easy Instant Pot Veggie Ramen

Prep time: 5 minutes, cook time: 36 minutes; Serves 4

Ingredients:

1 tablespoon coconut oil

1 onion, chopped

3 cloves garlic, minced

2 carrots, chopped

2 tablespoons gochujang (Korean chili paste)

1 tablespoon miso paste

½ cup commercial kimchi

½ tablespoon soy sauce

1 large kombu seaweed, broken into two pieces

1 block firm tofu, cubed

9 ounces ramen noodles

6 cups water

2 tablespoons sesame seed oil

2 tablespoons sesame seeds

Instructions

1. Press the Sauté button on the Instant Pot and heat the oil. Sauté the onion and garlic for 1 minute.

2. Stir in the carrots, gochujang, miso paste, kimchi, soy sauce, and kombu. Pour in water.

3. Close the lid and set the vent to the Sealing position.

4. Press the Broth/ Soup button and cook using the preset cooking time.

5. Do quick pressure release.

6. Once the lid is open, remove and discard the kombu.

7. Press the Sauté button and stir in the tofu and ramen noodles. Allow to simmer for 5 minutes or until the noodles are cooked.

8. Drizzle with sesame oil and sesame seeds before serving.

Nutrition Facts Per Serving

Calories 363, Total Fat 20g, Saturated Fat 5g, Total Carbs 33g, Net Carbs 26g, Protein 19g, Sugar: 3g, Fiber: 7g, Sodium: 445mg, Potassium: 570mg, Phosphorus: 277mg

Classic Corn Chowder

Prep time: 5 minutes, cook time: 33 minutes; Serves 5

Ingredients:

1 tablespoon olive oil

3 tablespoons butter

1 onion, chopped

3 cloves garlic, minced

3 celery stalks, chopped

2 carrots, chopped

2 pounds russet potatoes

3 cups corn kernels

2 cups vegetable broth
2 tablespoons soy sauce
1 teaspoon smoked paprika
1 teaspoon thyme
1 teaspoon onion powder
1 teaspoon garlic powder
salt and pepper to taste

Instructions

1. Press the Sauté button on the Instant Pot and heat the oil and butter.
2. Add the onion, garlic, and celery. Stir for 3 minutes until the vegetables have wilted.

3. Stir in the rest of the ingredients.
4. Close the lid and set the vent to the Sealing position.
5. Press the Broth/Soup button and cook using the present cooking button.
6. Do natural pressure release.

Nutrition Facts Per Serving
Calories 346, Total Fat 9g, Saturated Fat 3g, Total Carbs 59g, Net Carbs 53g, Protein 13g, Sugar: 18g, Fiber: 6g, Sodium: 325mg, Potassium: 1337mg, Phosphorus: 364mg

Golden Cauliflower Soup

Prep time: 5 minutes, cook time: 12 minutes; Serves 4

Ingredients:
6 tablespoons extra virgin olive oil
6 cloves garlic, minced
1 onion, minced
1 carrot, diced
1 ½ teaspoons cumin
1 ½ teaspoons coriander
1 teaspoon grated ginger
1 teaspoon turmeric
1 teaspoon cinnamon
7 cups vegetable broth
3 pounds whole cauliflower, cut into florets
salt and pepper to taste

Instructions

1. Press the Sauté button and heat the oil. Sauté the garlic and onions for 1 minute until fragrant and translucent.

2. Stir in the carrots and season with cumin, coriander, grated ginger, turmeric, and cinnamon.
3. Stir in the rest of the ingredients then give a good stir.
4. Press the Pressure Cook or Manual button and adjust the cooking time to 10 minutes.
5. Do natural pressure release.

Nutrition Facts Per Serving
Calories 322, Total Fat 23g, Saturated Fat 4g, Total Carbs 29g, Net Carbs 19g, Protein 8g, Sugar: 14g, Fiber: 10g, Sodium: 473mg, Potassium: 703mg, Phosphorus: 312mg

Homemade Vegetable Soup

Prep time: 5 minutes, cook time: 16 minutes; Serves 4

Ingredients:
¼ cup olive oil
1 onion, chopped
2 cloves garlic, minced
2 celery stalks, chopped
1 tablespoon garlic powder
2 teaspoons basil
1 teaspoon oregano
1 teaspoon thyme
½ teaspoon turmeric
3 carrots, minced
8 cups vegetable broth

5 ounces spiral pasta
salt and pepper to taste

Instructions

1. Press the Sauté button on the Instant Pot and heat the oil. Sauté the onion and garlic until fragrant. Add in the celery, garlic powder, basil, oregano, thyme, and turmeric. Stir 30 seconds before adding the carrots. Stir for 1 minute.
2. Add in the broth and pasta. Season with salt and pepper to taste.
3. Close the lid and set the vent to the Sealing position.

4. Press the Pressure Cook or Manual button and adjust the cooking time to 15 minutes.
5. Do natural pressure release.

Nutrition Facts Per Serving

Calories 204, Total Fat 9g, Saturated Fat 2g, Total Carbs 28g, Net Carbs 26g, Protein 4g, Sugar: 5g, Fiber: 2g, Sodium: 204mg, Potassium: 215mg, Phosphorus: 103mg

Wonton Soup with Mushroom "Meatballs"

Prep time: 1 hour, cook time: 14 minutes; Serves 6

Ingredients:

1 small zucchini, grated
8 ounces cremini mushrooms, chopped
1 large egg
1 ¼ cups breadcrumbs
salt and pepper to taste
2 tablespoons coconut oil
1 1-inch ginger, grated
6 cloves garlic, minced
2 tablespoons white miso paste
2 tablespoons soy sauce
2 tablespoons sesame oil
8 cups vegetable broth
2 baby bok choy, cut crosswise
12 wonton wrappers, sliced in half
8 ounces snow peas
2 scallions, diced

Instructions

1. In a bowl, combine the grated zucchini, mushrooms, egg, and breadcrumbs. Season with salt and pepper to taste. Form small balls using your hands and place in the fridge to set for at least 1 hour.
2. Press the Sauté button on the Instant Pot and heat the oil. Gently sear the meatballs on all side for 3 minutes until lightly golden. Stir in the ginger and garlic for 1 minute.
3. Add the miso paste, soy sauce, sesame oil, and broth. Season with more salt and pepper to taste.
4. Stir in the rest of the ingredients.
5. Press the Pressure Cook or Manual button and adjust the cooking time to 10 minutes.
6. Do natural pressure release.

Nutrition Facts Per Serving

Calories 455, Total Fat 13g, Saturated Fat 5g, Total Carbs 76g, Net Carbs 69g, Protein 13g, Sugar: 4g, Fiber: 7g, Sodium: 703mg, Potassium: 780mg, Phosphorus: 225mg

Noodles with Tomato Broth

Prep time: 5 minutes, cook time: 34 minutes; Serves 4

Ingredients:

2 tablespoons butter
1 clove garlic, minced
1 ½ pound ripe red tomatoes, chopped
3 tablespoons rice vinegar
1 tablespoon sugar
Salt and pepper to taste
4 cups vegetable broth
10 ounces thin noodles
5 large eggs, beaten
A dash of chili flakes

Instructions

1. Press the Sauté button on the Instant Pot and heat the butter. Sauté the garlic for 30 seconds until fragrant.
2. Stir in the tomatoes and rice vinegar. Season with sugar, salt, and pepper. Stir for 3 minutes until the tomatoes have wilted.
3. Pour in the broth and close the lid. Press the Broth/Soup button and cook on high using the preset cooking time.
4. Do quick pressure release once the timer sets off.
5. Once the lid is open, press the Sauté button and stir in the egg noodles. Allow to simmer for 5 minutes before adding the eggs. Allow the eggs to congeal. Adjust the seasoning.
6. Add a dash of chili flakes before serving.

Nutrition Facts Per Serving

Calories 246, Total Fat 12g, Saturated Fat 6g, Total Carbs 27g, Net Carbs 25g, Protein 8g, Sugar: 5g, Fiber: 2g, Sodium: 179mg, Potassium: 460mg, Phosphorus: 147mg

Tomato Soup with Arugula and Croutons

Prep time: 5 minutes, cook time: 36 minutes; Serves 4

Ingredients:

4 tablespoons olive oil
1 white onion, chopped
2 cloves of garlic, minced
2 tablespoons thyme leaves
1 ½ pounds beefsteak tomatoes, chopped
5 cups vegetable broth
salt and pepper to taste
1 cup arugula
2 thick slices country-style bread, torn into bite-sized pieces

Instructions

1. Press the Sauté button on the Instant Pot and heat the oil. Stir in the onion and garlic until fragrant and translucent.
2. Add the thyme and tomatoes. Sauté for 3 minutes until the tomatoes are soft.
3. Stir in the vegetable broth and season with salt and pepper to taste.
4. Close the lid and set the vent to the Sealing position.
5. Press the Broth/Soup button and cook on high using the standard preset cooking time.
6. Once the timer sets off, do quick pressure release.
7. Open the lid and press the Sauté button. Stir in the arugula and simmer for 3 minutes.
8. Ladle the soup into bowls and top with croutons.

Nutrition Facts Per Serving

Calories 161, Total Fat 14g, Saturated Fat 2g, Total Carbs 9g, Net Carbs 7g, Protein 2g, Sugar: 1g, Fiber: 2g, Sodium: 42mg, Potassium: 511mg, Phosphorus: 75mg

Cauliflower-Cashew Soup

Prep time: 5 minutes, cook time: 30 minutes; Serves 6

Ingredients:

½ cup olive oil
2 cloves garlic, minced
2 teaspoons fresh thyme leaves
2 bay leaves, minced
½ cup dry white wine
1 large head cauliflower, cut into florets
1 cup cashew nut paste
¼ teaspoon cayenne pepper
6 cups vegetable stock
4 shallots, sliced
2 teaspoons fresh lemon juice
salt and pepper to taste

Instructions

1. Press the Sauté button and heat the olive oil. Sauté the garlic and thyme leaves until fragrant. Stir in the rest of the ingredients and season with salt and pepper to taste.
2. Close the lid and set the vent to the Sealing position.
3. Press the Broth/Soup button and cook on high using the preset cooking time.

Nutrition Facts Per Serving

Calories 324, Total Fat 30g, Saturated Fat 5g, Total Carbs 9g, Net Carbs 7g, Protein 7g, Sugar: 2g, Fiber: 2g, Sodium: 226mg, Potassium: 287mg, Phosphorus: 174mg

Miso Tahini Squash Soup

Prep time: 5 minutes, cook time: 21 minutes; Serves 4

Ingredients:

2 tablespoons coconut oil
1 1-inch ginger, peeled and grated
4 cloves garlic, minced
5 cups vegetable broth or water
1 kabocha squash, diced
5 tablespoons miso paste
¼ cup tahini or sesame seed paste
salt and pepper to taste

2 green scallions, chopped
2 tablespoons toasted sesame seeds

Instructions

1. Press the Sauté button on the Instant Pot and heat the oil. Sauté the ginger and garlic for 30 seconds before adding the broth, squash, miso paste, and tahini. Season with salt and pepper to taste.

2. Close the lid and set the vent to the Sealing position.
3. Press the Broth/Soup button and cook on high for 20 minutes.
4. Do natural pressure release to open the lid.
5. Once the lid is open, stir in the scallions and sesame seeds as garnish.

Nutrition Facts Per Serving
Calories 235, Total Fat 18g, Saturated Fat 8g, Total Carbs 15g, Net Carbs 11g, Protein 6g, Sugar: 4g, Fiber: 4g, Sodium: 1506mg, Potassium: 588mg, Phosphorus: 191mg

Maitake Mushrooms in Soy Broth

Prep time: 5 minutes, cook time: 30 minutes; Serves 4

Ingredients:
2 cloves garlic, minced
1 1-inch ginger, sliced thinly
½ pound maitake mushrooms, torn
½ cup low-sodium soy sauce
½ cup dried wakame
4 cups water

Instructions
1. Place all ingredients in the Instant Pot and give a good stir.
2. Close the lid and set the vent to the Sealing position.
3. Press the Soup/Broth button and cook using the preset cooking time.
4. Do natural pressure release.

Nutrition Facts Per Serving
Calories 43, Total Fat 0.3g, Saturated Fat 0.04g, Total Carbs 7g, Net Carbs 5g, Protein 4g, Sugar: 1g, Fiber: 2g, Sodium: 1235mg, Potassium: 241mg, Phosphorus: 105mg

Purple Sweet Potato Soup

Prep time: 5 minutes, cook time: 10 minutes; Serves 4

Ingredients:
1 onion, chopped
4 cups button mushrooms, sliced
½ teaspoon ground cinnamon
½ teaspoon ground cumin
¼ teaspoon chili powder
¼ cup balsamic vinegar
1-pound purple sweet potatoes, cubed
2 cups light coconut milk
2 cups water
salt and pepper to taste
Juice from 1 lemon

Instructions
1. Place the onion, mushrooms, cinnamon, cumin, chili powder, vinegar, sweet potatoes, coconut milk, and water. Season with salt and pepper to taste.
2. Close the lid and set the vent to the Sealing position.
3. Press the Pressure Cook or Manual button and cook on high for 10 minutes.
4. Do natural pressure release.
5. Once the lid is open, drizzle with lemon juice.

Nutrition Facts Per Serving
Calories 355, Total Fat 29g, Saturated Fat 25g, Total Carbs 23g, Net Carbs 13g, Protein 6g, Sugar: 8g, Fiber: 10g, Sodium: 36mg, Potassium: 991mg, Phosphorus: 231mg

Curried Split Pea Soup

Prep time: 5 minutes, cook time: 31 minutes; Serves 4

Ingredients:
2 tablespoons coconut oil
1 onion, chopped
4 large carrots, chopped
1 teaspoon fennel seeds
2 teaspoons curry powder
1 teaspoon mustard seeds
12-ounce yellow split peas
6 cups vegetable broth
salt to taste

Instructions
1. Press the Sauté button on the Instant Pot and heat the oil.

2. Sauté the onion, carrots, fennel seeds, curry powder, and mustard seeds for 1 minute.
3. Stir in the split peas and vegetable broth. Season with salt to taste.
4. Close the lid and set the vent to the Sealing position.
5. Press the Bean/Chili button and cook on high using the preset cooking time.
6. Do natural pressure release.

Nutrition Facts Per Serving
Calories 406, Total Fat 8g, Saturated Fat 6g, Total Carbs 64g, Net Carbs 39g, Protein 22g, Sugar: 11g, Fiber: 25g, Sodium: 65mg, Potassium: 994mg, Phosphorus: 316mg

Beet, Ginger, And Coconut Milk

Prep time: 5 minutes, cook time: 15 minutes; Serves 4

Ingredients:
1 tablespoon olive oil
1 onion, diced
3 cloves garlic, minced
1 tablespoon grated ginger
3 large red beets, peeled and cubed
5 cups vegetable stock
1 14-ounce can coconut milk
salt and pepper to taste

Instructions
1. Press the Sauté button on the Instant Pot. Sauté the onion and garlic until fragrant.
2. Add in the ginger and the rest of the ingredients. Season with salt and pepper to taste.
3. Close the lid and set the vent to the Sealing position.
4. Press the Pressure Cook or Manual button and cook on high for 15 minutes.
5. Do natural pressure release.

Nutrition Facts Per Serving
Calories 91, Total Fat4 g, Saturated Fat 0.6g, Total Carbs 13g, Net Carbs 10g, Protein 2g, Sugar: 8g, Fiber: 3g, Sodium: 154mg, Potassium: 503mg, Phosphorus: 56mg

Thai Coconut, Broccoli, And Coriander Soup

Prep time: 5 minutes, cook time: 10 minutes; Serves 4

Ingredients:
1/3 cup green curry paste
1 14-ounce can coconut milk
1-pound broccoli florets
2 cups baby spinach
2 cups cilantro leaves
2 scallions, shredded
3 cups water
Salt and pepper to taste

Instructions
1. Place the curry paste and coconut milk in the Instant Pot.
2. Give a good stir to combine the curry and coconut milk.
3. Stir the rest of the ingredients.
4. Close the lid and set the vent to the Sealing position.
5. Press the Pressure Cook or Manual button and cook on high for 10 minutes.
6. Do natural pressure release.

Nutrition Facts Per Serving
Calories 52, Total Fat 1g, Saturated Fat 0.3g, Total Carbs 9g, Net Carbs 3g, Protein 4g, Sugar: 2g, Fiber: 6g, Sodium: 108mg, Potassium: 476mg, Phosphorus: 98mg

3-Ingredient Tomato Soup

Prep time: 5 minutes, cook time: 37 minutes; Serves 5

Ingredients:
6 tablespoons olive oil
1 onion, chopped
4 pounds plum tomatoes, halved
2 cups water

salt and pepper to taste
1 cup heavy cream

Instructions

1. Press the Sauté button on the Instant Pot and heat the oil.
2. Sauté the onion until fragrant and stir in the tomatoes. Sauté for another minute.
3. Add in the water and season with salt and pepper to taste.
4. Close the lid and set the vent to the Sealing position.
5. Press the Broth/Soup button and cook on high using the preset cooking time.
6. Do quick pressure release.
7. Once the lid is open, press the Sauté button and stir in the cream.
8. Allow to simmer for 5 minutes.

Nutrition Facts Per Serving
Calories 558, Total Fat 25g, Saturated Fat 8g, Total Carbs 87g, Net Carbs 84g, Protein 2g, Sugar: 82g, Fiber: 3g, Sodium: 79mg, Potassium: 381mg, Phosphorus: 68mg

Celery Root and Carrot Soup

Prep time: 5 minutes, cook time: 30 minutes; Serves 4
Ingredients:
½ large celery stalk, chopped
½ pounds carrots, peeled and chopped
¼ cup plain yogurt
2 tablespoons maple syrup
2 teaspoons ground coriander
1 teaspoon grated ginger
4 cups water
salt and pepper to taste
Celery leaves for garnish

Instructions
1. Place all ingredients except for the celery leaves.
2. Give a good stir.
3. Close the lid and set the vent to the Sealing position.
4. Press the Pressure Cook or Manual button and cook on high using the preset cooking time.
5. Do natural pressure release.
6. Garnish with celery leaves before serving.

Nutrition Facts Per Serving
Calories 56, Total Fat 0.6g, Saturated Fat 0.3g, Total Carbs 12g, Net Carbs 10g, Protein 0.9g, Sugar: 9g, Fiber: 2g, Sodium: 43mg, Potassium: 187mg, Phosphorus: 33mg

Cauliflower Leek Soup

Prep time: 5 minutes, cook time: 16 minutes; Serves 4
Ingredients:
3 tablespoons olive oil
5 cloves garlic, minced
1 large russet potato, peeled and chopped
1 large cauliflower, cut into florets
3 cups vegetable broth
salt and pepper to taste

Instructions
1. Press the Sauté button on the Instant Pot and heat the oil. Sauté the garlic until fragrant.
2. Add in the rest of the ingredients. Give a good stir.
3. Close the lid and set the vent to the Sealing position.
4. Press the Manual button and adjust the cooking time to 15 minutes.
5. Do natural pressure release.

Nutrition Facts Per Serving
Calories 220, Total Fat 11g, Saturated Fat 2g, Total Carbs 28g, Net Carbs 21g, Protein 6g, Sugar: 5g, Fiber: 7g, Sodium: 68mg, Potassium: 1028mg, Phosphorus: 149mg

Roasted Sweet Potato and Ginger Soup

Prep time: 5 minutes, cook time: 16 minutes; Serves 5
Ingredients:
2 tablespoons extra virgin olive oil
1 onion, chopped
2 tablespoons minced ginger
1 jalapeno pepper, seeded and minced
2 teaspoons ground coriander
½ teaspoon ground nutmeg
2 medium sweet potatoes, cubed

4 cups vegetable soup
salt and pepper to taste
Instructions
1. Press the Sauté button on the Instant Pot and heat the oil.
2. Sauté the onion until translucent. Stir in the ginger, jalapeno pepper, coriander, and nutmeg. Toast for 1 minute.
3. Stir in the rest of the ingredients and season with salt and pepper to taste.

4. Press the Pressure Cook or Manual button and adjust the cooking time to 15 minutes.
5. Do natural pressure release.
Nutrition Facts Per Serving
Calories 181, Total Fat 3g, Saturated Fat 0.5g, Total Carbs 33g, Net Carbs 27g, Protein 5g, Sugar: 9g, Fiber: 6g, Sodium: 449mg, Potassium: 191mg, Phosphorus: 29mg

Green Soup with Lemon and Cayenne

Prep time: 5 minutes, cook time: 25 minutes; Serves 6
Ingredients:
2 tablespoons olive oil
2 onion, chopped
¼ cup arborio rice
4 cups vegetable broth
3 cups water
salt and pepper to taste
1 large bunch kale
4 cups spinach
1 tablespoon lemon juice
Instructions
1. Press the Sauté button on the Instant Pot and heat the oil.
2. Sauté the onion until fragrant.

3. Stir in the rice and vegetable broth. Add water and season with salt and pepper to taste.
4. Close the lid and set the vent to the Sealing position.
5. Press the Broth/Soup button and cook on high for 20 minutes.
6. Do quick pressure release to open the lid.
7. Press the Sauté button and stir in the kale, spinach, and lemon juice.
Nutrition Facts Per Serving
Calories 75, Total Fat 6g, Saturated Fat 0.8g, Total Carbs 8g, Net Carbs 6g, Protein 2g, Sugar: 2g, Fiber: 2g, Sodium: 18mg, Potassium: 241mg, Phosphorus: 103mg

Creamy Thai Carrot Sweet Potato Soup

Prep time: 5 minutes, cook time: 21 minutes; Serves 5
Ingredients:
1 teaspoon coconut oil
2 cups sweet onion, chopped
2 cloves garlic, minced
1 tablespoon minced ginger
2 tablespoons red curry paste
4 cups vegetable broth
¼ cup peanut butter
3 cups diced carrots
3 cups diced sweet potatoes
salt and pepper to taste
Instructions
1. Press the Sauté button on the Instant Pot and heat the oil.

2. Press the onion, garlic, and ginger for 1 minute. Stir in the red curry paste for 30 seconds.
3. Add the rest of the ingredients and season with salt and pepper to taste.
4. Close the lid and set the vent to the Sealing position.
5. Press the Broth/Soup button and cook on high for 20 minutes.
6. Do natural pressure release.
Nutrition Facts Per Serving
Calories 305, Total Fat 13g, Saturated Fat 4g, Total Carbs 44g, Net Carbs g, Protein 7g, Sugar: 15g, Fiber: 9g, Sodium: 254mg, Potassium: 543mg, Phosphorus: 193mg

West African Peanut Soup

Prep time: 5 minutes, cook time: 35 minutes; Serves 5

Ingredients:

6 cups vegetable broth
1 red onion, chopped
4 cloves garlic, chopped
2 tablespoons fresh ginger, minced
¾ cup unsalted peanut butter
½ cup tomato sauce
1 bunch collard greens, ribs removed and torn
¼ cup chopped peanuts for garnish
salt and pepper to taste

Instructions

1. Place the broth, onion, garlic, ginger, peanut butter, and tomato sauce in the Instant Pot. Season with salt and pepper to taste. Give a good stir.
2. Close the lid and set the vent to the Sealing position.
3. Press the Broth/Soup button and cook on high for 30 minutes.
4. Do quick pressure release to open the lid.
5. Once the lid is open, press the Sauté button and stir in the collard greens. Allow to simmer for 3 minutes.
6. Garnish with chopped peanuts before serving.

Nutrition Facts Per Serving

Calories 431, Total Fat 30g, Saturated Fat 6g, Total Carbs 33g, Net Carbs 19g, Protein 17g, Sugar: 14g, Fiber: 14g, Sodium: 581mg, Potassium: 467mg, Phosphorus: 321mg

Vegetable Cabbage Soup

Prep time: 5 minutes, cook time: 15 minutes; Serves 4

Ingredients:

2 tablespoons olive oil
1 onion chopped
2 cloves garlic, minced
2 celery stalks, chopped
2 carrots, chopped
½ teaspoon chili powder
1 15-ounce can fire-roasted tomatoes
1 15-ounce can white beans, drained and rinsed
1 teaspoon thyme leaves
½ head of cabbage, chopped
2 cups water
salt and pepper to taste

Instructions

1. Press the Sauté button on the Instant Pot and heat the oil. Stir in the onion, garlic, and celery for 2 minutes until translucent and fragrant.
2. Add the carrots, chili powder, and tomatoes. Stir for another 2 minutes.
3. Stir in the rest of the ingredients and season with salt and pepper to taste.
4. Close the lid and set the vent to the Sealing position.
5. Press the Pressure Cook or Manual button and adjust the cooking time to 10 minutes.
6. Do natural pressure release.

Nutrition Facts Per Serving

Calories 150, Total Fat 8g, Saturated Fat 1g, Total Carbs 20g, Net Carbs 13g, Protein 4g, Sugar: 9g, Fiber: 7g, Sodium: 183mg, Potassium: 651mg, Phosphorus: 85mg

Cream of Asparagus Soup

Prep time: 5 minutes, cook time: 35 minutes; Serves 4

Ingredients:

2 tablespoons butter
1 clove garlic, minced
2 pounds asparagus ends, trimmed and cut into 1-inch pieces
2 cups vegetable broth
salt and pepper to taste
½ cup heavy cream

Instructions

1. Press the Sauté button on the Instant Pot and heat the butter. Sauté the garlic until fragrant.
2. Add in the asparagus and broth. Season with salt and pepper to taste.
3. Close the lid and set the vent to the Sealing position.
4. Press the Broth/Soup button and cook on high for 30 minutes.

5. Do quick pressure release to open the lid.
6. Once the lid is open, press the Sauté button and add the cream.
7. While the cream is simmering, use a hand-held immersion blender and blend until creamy.

Nutrition Facts Per Serving
Calories 149, Total Fat 12g, Saturated Fat 7g, Total Carbs 9g, Net Carbs 4g, Protein 5g, Sugar: 5g, Fiber:5 g, Sodium: 56mg, Potassium: 474mg, Phosphorus: 130mg

Chunky Tomato-Red Pepper Soup

Prep time: 5 minutes, cook time: 40 minutes; Serves 6

Ingredients:
2 tablespoons butter
1 medium onion, chopped
2 cloves garlic, minced
2 medium red bell peppers, seeded and chopped
2 tablespoons smoked paprika
1 14-ounce can whole plum tomatoes
1 teaspoon sugar
Salt and pepper to taste
1 ½ cup vegetable broth
1 cup heavy cream

Instructions
1. Press the Sauté button and heat the butter until slightly melted. Stir in the onion and garlic until fragrant.
2. Add the bell pepper, paprika, and tomatoes. Season with sugar, salt and pepper. Stir for 3 minutes.
3. Pour in the broth.
4. Close the lid and set the vent to the Sealing position.
5. Press the Broth/Soup button and cook on high for 30 minutes.
6. Do quick pressure release to open the lid.
7. Once the lid is open, press the Sauté button and stir in the cream.
8. Allow to simmer for another 5 minutes.

Nutrition Facts Per Serving
Calories 200, Total Fat 13g, Saturated Fat 7g, Total Carbs 18g, Net Carbs 14g, Protein 4g, Sugar:8 g, Fiber: 4g, Sodium: 348mg, Potassium: 297mg, Phosphorus: 78mg

Easy Veggie Soup

Prep time: 5 minutes, cook time: 35 minutes; Serves 6

Ingredients:
2 tablespoons olive oil
1 ½ cups yellow onion, chopped
4 cloves garlic, minced
1 ¼ cups chopped celery
2 cups chopped carrots
4 14-ounce cans vegetable broth
2 14-ounce cans diced tomatoes
1 cup diced tomatoes
2 bay leaves
½ teaspoon dried thyme
1 cup frozen green beans
¼ cup baby corn
salt and pepper to taste

Instructions
1. Press the Sauté button on the Instant Pot and heat the oil.
2. Stir in the onions and garlic. Sauté for 3 minutes until fragrant.
3. Add in the celery and carrots and sauté for another 2 minutes.
4. Stir in the rest of the ingredients and season with salt and pepper to taste.
5. Close the lid and set the vent to the Sealing position.
6. Press the Broth/Soup button and cook on high for 30 minutes.
7. Do natural pressure release.

Nutrition Facts Per Serving
Calories 198, Total Fat 5g, Saturated Fat 1g, Total Carbs 31g, Net Carbs 24g, Protein 7g, Sugar: 8g, Fiber: 6g, Sodium: 259mg, Potassium: 1051mg, Phosphorus: 341mg

Hearty Winter Vegetable Soup

Prep time: 5 minutes, cook time: 35 minutes; Serves 6

Ingredients:

2 tablespoons olive oil
1 onion, chopped
2 celery stalks, chopped
1 rutabaga, peeled and chopped
1 turnip, peeled and chopped
1 carrot, peeled and chopped
1 parsnip, peeled and diced
1 tablespoon rosemary, chopped
2 bay leaves
1 cup pearled barley, soaked overnight then drained
6 cups vegetable stock
salt and pepper to taste

Instructions

1. Press the Sauté button on the Instant Pot and heat the oil. Sauté the onion and celery for 2 minutes until translucent and fragrant.
2. Add the vegetables and season with rosemary.
3. Stir in the rest of the ingredients and season with salt and pepper to taste.
4. Close the lid and set the vent to the Sealing position.
5. Press the Broth/Soup button and cook on high for 30 minutes.
6. Do natural pressure release.

Nutrition Facts Per Serving

Calories 211, Total Fat 5g, Saturated Fat 0.7g, Total Carbs 39g, Net Carbs 31g, Protein 5g, Sugar: 6g, Fiber: 8g, Sodium: 23mg, Potassium :449 mg, Phosphorus: 135mg

Zanzibar Carrot and Tomato Soup

Prep time: 5 minutes, cook time: 28 minutes; Serves 5

Ingredients:

½ tablespoons olive oil
2 carrots, chopped
1 28-ounces whole peeled tomatoes
1 tablespoon lime juice
A dash of cinnamon
A dash of ground cloves
½ cup coconut milk
5 cups vegetable broth
salt and pepper to taste
2 tablespoons cornstarch + 3 tablespoons water
5 green onions, chopped

Instructions

1. Press the Sauté button on the Instant Pot and heat the oil.
2. Sauté the carrots and tomatoes for 2 minutes until wilted.
3. Stir in the lime juice, cinnamon, cloves, coconut milk, and vegetable broth. Season with salt and pepper to taste.
4. Close the lid and set the vent to the Sealing position.
5. Press the Pressure Cook and Manual button. Adjust the cooking time to 20 minutes.
6. Do quick pressure release to open the lid.
7. Press the Sauté button and stir in the cornstarch slurry. Allow to simmer for 3 minutes.
8. Garnish with green onions last.

Nutrition Facts Per Serving

Calories 192, Total Fat 11g, Saturated Fat 6g, Total Carbs 20g, Net Carbs 16g, Protein 7g, Sugar: 7g, Fiber: 4g, Sodium: 269mg, Potassium: 745mg, Phosphorus: 181mg

French Onion Soup

Prep time: 5 minutes, cook time: 20 minutes; Serves 5

Ingredients:

2 pounds onion, chopped
3 tablespoons butter
4 cloves garlic, minced
2 teaspoons brown sugar
2 tablespoons plain white flour
1 cup dry white wine
4 cups vegetable stock
2 teaspoons soy sauce
1 teaspoon marmite
2 bay leaves

salt and pepper to taste

Instructions

1. Place the onion and butter for 8 minutes until the onions are translucent. Stir in the garlic and sauté for 2 minutes.
2. Stir in the sugar and the flour. Stir for another minute.
3. Stir in the rest of the ingredients until the flour is dissolved.

4. Close the lid and set the vent to the Sealing position.
5. Press the Pressure Cook or Manual button and adjust the cooking time to 10 minutes.
6. Do natural pressure release.

Nutrition Facts Per Serving

Calories 224, Total Fat 12g, Saturated Fat 7g, Total Carbs 22g, Net Carbs 19g, Protein 8g, Sugar: 9g, Fiber: 3g, Sodium: 481mg, Potassium: 333mg, Phosphorus: 158mg

Miso Spinach Mushroom Soup

Prep time: 5 minutes, cook time: 35 minutes; Serves 5

Ingredients:

2 tablespoons coconut oil
2 cups fresh shiitake mushrooms, stems removed and sliced thinly
1 tablespoon grated ginger
1 tablespoon grated garlic
4 cups vegetable broth
2 tablespoons miso paste
salt and pepper to taste
5 cups baby spinach leaves

Instructions

1. Press the Sauté button and heat the oil. Sauté the mushrooms, ginger and garlic. Sauté for 3 minutes.
2. Stir in the broth and miso paste. Adjust the seasoning with salt and pepper to taste.

3. Close the lid and set the vent to the sealing position.
4. Press the Broth/Soup button and cook on high for 30 minutes.
5. Do quick pressure release to open the lid.
6. Once the lid is open, press the Sauté button and stir in the spinach leaves. Allow to simmer for 3 minutes until wilted.

Nutrition Facts Per Serving

Calories 75, Total Fat 6g, Saturated Fat 5g, Total Carbs 5g, Net Carbs 4g, Protein 2g, Sugar: 1g, Fiber: 1g, Sodium: 278mg, Potassium: 202mg, Phosphorus: 31mg

Vegan Turmeric Detox Soup

Prep time: 5 minutes, cook time: 35 minutes; Serves 5

Ingredients:

1 tablespoon vegetable oil
½ cup white onion, chopped
2 cloves garlic, minced
1 cup chopped carrots
1 cup chopped celery
½ teaspoon ground turmeric
2 teaspoon grated ginger
1 cup chopped green beans
1 cup chopped kale
4 cups vegetable broth
Juice from 1 lemon
1 teaspoon paprika
salt and pepper to taste

Instructions

1. Press the Sauté button on the Instant Pot and heat the oil.

2. Stir in the onion and garlic for 1 minute until fragrant.
3. Add the carrots and celery and stir for another 2 minutes.
4. Add the rest of the ingredients and season with salt and pepper to taste.
5. Close the lid and set the vent to the Sealing position.
6. Press the Broth/Soup button and cook on high for 30 minutes.
7. Do natural pressure release.

Nutrition Facts Per Serving

Calories 73, Total Fat 4g, Saturated Fat 0.6g, Total Carbs 9g, Net Carbs 7g, Protein 1g, Sugar: 2g, Fiber: 2g, Sodium: 70mg, Potassium: 258mg, Phosphorus: 34mg

Curried Cauliflower and Potato Soup

Prep time: 5 minutes, cook time: 20 minutes; Serves 5

Ingredients:

3 teaspoons olive oil
1 shallot, diced
2 cloves garlic, minced
5 cups diced russet potatoes
1 large head cauliflower, cut into florets
3 teaspoons curry powder
6 cups vegetable stock
salt and pepper to taste

Instructions

1. Press the Sauté button on the Instant Pot and heat the oil.
2. Stir in the shallot and garlic until fragrant.
3. Add the rest of the ingredients.
4. Close the lid and set the vent to the Sealing position.
5. Press the Pressure Cook or Manual button and adjust the cooking time to 15 minutes.
6. Do natural pressure release.

Nutrition Facts Per Serving

Calories 178, Total Fat 4g, Saturated Fat 1g, Total Carbs 31g, Net Carbs 27g, Protein 6g, Sugar: 2g, Fiber: 4g, Sodium: 47mg, Potassium: 820mg, Phosphorus: 122mg

Celery Root Soup

Prep time: 5 minutes, cook time: 40 minutes; Serves 6

Ingredients:

3 tablespoons olive oil
1 onion, chopped
2 cloves garlic, minced
1 large celery root, chopped
4 cups vegetable broth
salt and pepper to taste
½ cup heavy cream
1 tablespoon truffle oil
1 tablespoon chopped parsley

Instructions

1. Press the Sauté button and heat the oil. Stir in the onion, garlic, and celery. Sauté for 4 minutes until fragrant.
2. Pour in the broth and season with salt and pepper to taste.
3. Close the lid and set the vent to the Sealing position.
4. Press the Broth/Soup button and cook on high for 30 minutes.
5. Once the timer sets off, do quick pressure release.
6. Once the lid is open, press the Sauté button and pour in the cream. Allow to simmer for 5 minutes.
7. Drizzle with truffle oil and parsley before serving.

Nutrition Facts Per Serving

Calories 126, Total Fat 13g, Saturated Fat 4g, Total Carbs 3g, Net Carbs 2g, Protein 0.6g, Sugar: 1g, Fiber: 1g, Sodium: 19mg, Potassium: 86mg, Phosphorus: 17mg

Winter Veggie Curry

Prep time: 5 minutes, cook time: 16 minutes; Serves 5

Ingredients:

2 tablespoons extra virgin coconut oil
1 onion, chopped
4 cloves garlic, minced
1 tablespoon Thai red curry paste
1 turnip, chopped
1 parsnip, chopped
1 14-ounce can light coconut milk
4 cups vegetable stock
1 tablespoon ground turmeric
2 tablespoons sugar
salt and pepper to taste

Instructions

1. Press the Sauté button on the Instant Pot and heat the oil. Sauté the onion and garlic until fragrant.
2. Stir in the rest of the ingredients and stir to combine everything.
3. Close the lid and set the vent to the Sealing position.

4. Press the Pressure Cook or Manual button and adjust the cooking time to 15 minutes.
5. Do natural pressure releases.

Nutrition Facts Per Serving
Calories 265, Total Fat 25g, Saturated Fat 18g, Total Carbs 12g, Net Carbs 9g, Protein 3g, Sugar: 7g, Fiber: 3g, Sodium: 14mg, Potassium: 304mg, Phosphorus: 100mg

Spicy Vegetarian Cabbage Soup

Prep time: 5 minutes, cook time: 16 minutes; Serves 6

Ingredients:
1 tablespoon olive oil
1 white onion, chopped
6 cloves garlic, minced
1 celery stalk, sliced
1-pound potatoes, diced
2 carrots, peeled and chopped
2 10-ounce cans fire-roasted potatoes
1 small green cabbage, chopped
½ teaspoon crushed red pepper flakes
salt and pepper to taste

Instructions
1. Press the Sauté button on the Instant Pot and heat the oil.
2. Sauté the onion and garlic for 1 minute until fragrant.
3. Stir in the rest of the ingredients.
4. Close the lid and set the vent to the Sealing position.
5. Press the Pressure Cook or Manual button and adjust the cooking time to 15 minutes.
6. Do natural pressure release.

Nutrition Facts Per Serving
Calories 201, Total Fat 3g, Saturated Fat 0.4g, Total Carbs 42g, Net Carbs 37g, Protein 5g, Sugar: 3g, Fiber: 5g, Sodium: 252mg, Potassium: 872mg, Phosphorus: 164mg

Moroccan Carrot Soup

Prep time: 5 minutes, cook time: 31 minutes; Serves 6

Ingredients:
6 tablespoons olive oil
½ teaspoon ground cumin
½ teaspoon ground coriander
½ teaspoon ground cinnamon
¼ teaspoon cayenne pepper
5 cups vegetable broth
3 cups chopped carrots
¾ cup yogurt
salt and pepper to taste

Instructions
1. Press the Sauté button on the Instant Pot and heat the oil. Toast the cumin, coriander, cinnamon, and cayenne pepper for 1 minute.
2. Pour in the rest of the ingredients.
3. Close the lid and set the vent to the Sealing position.
4. Press the Broth/Soup button and cook on high using the preset cooking time.
5. Do natural pressure release.

Nutrition Facts Per Serving
Calories 162, Total Fat 15g, Saturated Fat 3g, Total Carbs 7g, Net Carbs 5g, Protein 2g, Sugar: 4g, Fiber: 2g, Sodium: 53mg, Potassium: 230mg, Phosphorus: 50mg

Mushroom with Winter Veggies

Prep time: 5 minutes, cook time: 35 minutes; Serves 5

Ingredients:
6 tablespoons unsalted butter
2 large onions, chopped
2 heads garlic, minced
2 celery stalks, chopped
1 ½ pounds assorted mushrooms
1 cup carrots
1 cup butternut squash, chopped
1 bay leaf
¼ cup fresh parsley, chopped
1 cup light red wine
4 cups vegetable broth
2 tablespoons lemon juice

salt and pepper to taste

Instructions

1. Press the Sauté button on the Instant Pot and heat the butter.
2. Stir in the onions, garlic, and celery. Sauté for 3 minutes until fragrant.
3. Stir in the mushrooms and add the carrots, squash, and the rest of the ingredients. Season with salt and pepper to taste.

4. Close the lid and set the vent to the Sealing position.
5. Press the Broth/Soup button and cook on high for 30 minutes.
6. Do natural pressure release.

Nutrition Facts Per Serving

Calories 172, Total Fat 10g, Saturated Fat 6g, Total Carbs 16g, Net Carbs 12g, Protein 6g, Sugar: 7g, Fiber: 4g, Sodium: 43mg, Potassium: 760mg, Phosphorus: 165mg

Fire-Roasted Tomato Soup

Prep time: 5 minutes, cook time: 36 minutes; Serves 5

Ingredients:

3 tablespoons olive oil
½ cup onion, chopped
3 cloves garlic, minced
2 cans roasted tomatoes
¼ cup orange juice
4 cups vegetable broth
salt and pepper to taste
¼ cup heavy cream

Instructions

1. Press the Sauté button and heat the olive oil.
2. Stir in the onion and garlic. Sauté for 3 minutes until the onions are translucent.
3. Stir in the tomatoes and the rest of the ingredients except for the cream.

4. Close the lid and set the vent to the Sealing position.
5. Press the Broth/Soup button and cook on high for 30 minutes.
6. Do quick pressure release to open the lid.
7. Once the lid is open, press the Sauté button and stir in the heavy cream. Allow to simmer for 3 minutes.

Nutrition Facts Per Serving

Calories 118, Total Fat 11g, Saturated Fat 3g, Total Carbs 6g, Net Carbs 4g, Protein 1g, Sugar: 4g, Fiber: 2g, Sodium: 91mg, Potassium: 196mg, Phosphorus: 25mg

Cream of Mushroom Soup

Prep time: 5 minutes, cook time: 36 minutes; Serves 6

Ingredients:

¼ cup butter
2 cloves garlic, minced
1 onion, chopped
2 8-ounce pack cremini mushrooms, sliced
2/3 cup shiitake mushrooms, sliced
1 teaspoon dried thyme
4 cups vegetable stock
salt and pepper to taste
1/3 cup heavy cream

Instructions

1. Press the Sauté button on the Instant Pot and heat the butter.
2. Sauté the garlic and onions until fragrant. Add in the mushrooms and season with thyme, salt, and pepper. Stir for 3 minutes to sweat the mushrooms.

3. Add the stock.
4. Close the lid and set the vent to the Sealing position.
5. Press the Broth/Soup button and cook on high for 30 minutes.
6. Do quick pressure release.
7. Once the lid is open, press the Sauté button and stir in the cream.
8. Allow to simmer for 3 minutes.

Nutrition Facts Per Serving

Calories 325, Total Fat 11g, Saturated Fat 7g, Total Carbs 60g, Net Carbs 51g, Protein 8g, Sugar: 3g, Fiber: 9g, Sodium: 74mg, Potassium: 1201mg, Phosphorus: 236mg

Easy Parsnip Soup

Prep time: 5 minutes, cook time: 33 minutes; Serves 8

Ingredients:

¼ cup extra virgin olive oil
1 onion, chopped
1 celery stalk, chopped
2 pounds parsnips, peeled and chopped
1 bay leaf
5 cups vegetable broth
salt and pepper to taste

Instructions

1. Press the Sauté button and heat the olive oil. Sauté the onion, celery, and parsnips for 3 minutes until wilted.
2. Stir in the rest of the ingredients and season with salt and pepper to taste.
3. Close the lid and set the vent to the Sealing position.
4. Press the Broth/Soup button and cook on high using the preset cooking time.
5. Do natural pressure release.

Nutrition Facts Per Serving

Calories 117, Total Fat 3g, Saturated Fat 0.4g, Total Carbs 22g, Net Carbs 16g, Protein 2g, Sugar: 6g, Fiber: 6g, Sodium: 72mg, Potassium: 453mg, Phosphorus: 86mg

Clear Mushroom Broth

Prep time: 5 minutes, cook time: 30 minutes; Serves 6

Ingredients:

2 cups fresh shiitake mushrooms, chopped
1 cup cremini mushrooms, chopped
2 cloves garlic peeled
1 onion, peeled
2 bay leaves
1 carrot, roughly chopped
5 cups water
salt and pepper to taste

Instructions

1. Place all ingredients in the Instant Pot.
2. Close the lid and set the vent to the Sealing position.
3. Press the Broth/Soup button and cook on high using the preset cooking time.
4. Do natural pressure release.
5. Remove the solids and serve the broth.

Nutrition Facts Per Serving

Calories 18, Total Fat 0.1g, Saturated Fat 0g, Total Carbs 4g, Net Carbs 3g, Protein 1g, Sugar: 1g, Fiber: 1g, Sodium: 10mg, Potassium: 107mg, Phosphorus: 25mg

Instant Pot Loaded Potato Soup

Prep time: 5 minutes, cook time: 35 minutes; Serves 6

Ingredients:

1 tablespoon butter
1 onion, chopped
3 cloves garlic, minced
3 cups vegetable broth
7 russet potatoes, chopped
salt and pepper to taste
1 cup milk + 1 tablespoon flour

Instructions

1. Press the Sauté button on the Instant Pot and heat the butter. Sauté the onion and garlic until fragrant.
2. Stir in the broth and potatoes and season with salt and pepper to taste.
3. Close the lid and set the vent to the Sealing position.
4. Press the Broth/Soup button and cook on high using the preset cooking time.
5. Do natural pressure release to open the lid.
6. Once the lid is open, press the Sauté button and stir in the cream.
7. Simmer for 5 minutes.

Nutrition Facts Per Serving

Calories 387, Total Fat 3g, Saturated Fat 1g, Total Carbs 82g, Net Carbs 76g, Protein 11g, Sugar: 6g, Fiber: 6g, Sodium: 57mg, Potassium: 1885mg, Phosphorus: 282mg

Vegetarian Red Borscht Soup

Prep time: 5 minutes, cook time: 35 minutes; Serves 6

Ingredients:

1 tablespoon olive oil
1 onion, chopped
3 cloves garlic, minced
1 cup fresh shiitake mushrooms, halved
3 beets, peeled and shredded
3 carrots, peeled and shredded
3 potatoes, peeled and cubed
1 6-ounce can tomato paste
1 teaspoon white sugar
4 cups water
salt and pepper to taste
½ cup sour cream for topping

Instructions

1. Press the Sauté button on the Instant Pot and heat the oil. Sauté the onion and garlic for 1 minute before adding the shiitake mushrooms. Stir for 2 minutes until the mushrooms have wilted.

2. Add the beets, carrots, and potatoes. Stir in the tomato paste and sugar.

3. Pour in the water and stir to dissolve the tomato paste. Season with salt and pepper to taste.

4. Close the lid and set the vent to the Sealing position.

5. Press the Broth/Soup button and cook on high using the preset cooking time.

6. Do natural pressure release to open the lid.

7. Once the lid is open, place sour cream on top before serving.

Nutrition Facts Per Serving

Calories 258, Total Fat 5g, Saturated Fat 2g, Total Carbs 48g, Net Carbs 40g, Protein 8g, Sugar: 10g, Fiber: 8g, Sodium: 88mg, Potassium: 1328mg, Phosphorus: 177mg

Green Velvet Soup

Prep time: 5 minutes, cook time: 32 minutes; Serves 4

Ingredients:

2 tablespoons olive oil
1 onion, chopped
2 celery stalks, chopped
2 potatoes, diced
¾ cup dried split peas
2 zucchinis, chopped
2 bay leaves
1 teaspoon dried basil
6 cups vegetable broth
salt and pepper to taste

Instructions

1. Press the Sauté button on the Instant Pot and heat the oil.

2. Sauté the onion and celery. Sauté for 3 minutes until translucent.

3. Stir in the rest of the ingredients. Season with salt and pepper to taste.

4. Close the lid and set the vent to the sealing position.

5. Press the Broth/Soup button and cook using the preset cooking time.

6. Do natural pressure release.

Nutrition Facts Per Serving

Calories 120, Total Fat 0.8g, Saturated Fat 0g, Total Carbs 24g, Net Carbs 18g, Protein 6g, Sugar: 6g, Fiber: 6g, Sodium: 389mg, Potassium: 655mg, Phosphorus: 143mg

Vietnamese-Style Veggie Curry Soup

Prep time: 5 minutes, cook time: 23 minutes; Serves 5

Ingredients:

2 tablespoons olive oil
1 onion, chopped
2 cloves garlic, minced
1 1-inch piece ginger, thinly slices
1 stalk lemon grass
4 tablespoons curry powder

1-pound fried tofu, cubed
8 mushrooms, sliced
8 small potatoes, cubed
4 cups vegetable broth
1 14-ounce can coconut milk
1 bay leaf

2 kaffir lime leaves
Salt and pepper to taste
2 cup bean sprouts
8 sprigs chopped cilantro

Instructions

1. Press the Sauté button on the Instant Pot and heat the oil. Sauté the onion and garlic until fragrant. Stir in the ginger, lemon gras, and curry powder. Stir for 30 seconds before adding the tofu, mushrooms, potatoes, and broth.
2. Give a good stir to remove the brown bits at the bottom of the pan.
3. Add the coconut milk, bay leaf, and kaffir lime leaves. Season with salt and pepper to taste.
4. Close the lid and set the vent to the Sealing position.
5. Press the Broth/Soup button and cook on high for 20 minutes.
6. Do manual pressure release.
7. Serve with bean sprouts and cilantro.

Nutrition Facts Per Serving
Calories 479, Total Fat 27g, Saturated Fat 12g, Total Carbs 51g, Net Carbs 42g, Protein 16g, Sugar: 8g, Fiber: 9g, Sodium: 271mg, Potassium: 1096mg, Phosphorus: 212mg

Delicata Cream Squash Soup

Prep time: 10 minutes, cook time: 6 hours and 35 minutes; Serves 6

Ingredients:
3 delicata squash, seeded and chopped
2 tablespoons butter
1 onion, chopped
3 cups vegetable broth
Salt and pepper to taste
1 ½ cups heavy whipping cream

Instructions

1. The night before preparing the dish, place squash in the Instant Pot. Close the lid but do not seal the vent. Press the Slow Cook button and adjust the time to 4 hours. "Roast" the squash overnight.
2. The following morning take the squash out and place in a baking sheet. Mash until smooth. Set aside.
3. To a clean Instant Pot, heat the butter and sauté the onion. Add the squash and stir for 1 minute.
4. Add in the broth and season with salt and pepper to taste.
5. Close the lid and set the vent to the Sealing position.
6. Press the Broth/Soup button and cook on high for 30 minutes.
7. Do natural pressure release.
8. Once the lid is open, press the Sauté button again and stir in the cream. Simmer for 3 minutes.

Nutrition Facts Per Serving
Calories 417, Total Fat 31g, Saturated Fat 19g, Total Carbs 34g, Net Carbs 29g, Protein 4g, Sugar: 9g, Fiber: 5g, Sodium: 344mg, Potassium: 984mg, Phosphorus: 150mg

Lacto-Vegetarian Tomato Spinach and Basil Soup

Prep time: 35 minutes, cook time: 40 minutes; Serves 5

Ingredients:
2 tablespoons butter
1 onion, chopped
3 cloves garlic, minced
1 14-ounce can tomato
1 28-ounce tomato puree
1 tablespoon parmesan cheese
1 ½ cups milk
2 cups fresh basil leaves
1 tablespoon sugar
4 cups water
Salt and pepper to taste

Instructions

1. Press the Sauté button on the Instant Pot and heat the butter.
2. Sauté the onion and garlic until fragrant.
3. Stir in the tomatoes and tomato puree. Dissolve the puree by mixing thoroughly for 3 minutes.

4. Stir in the sugar and water. Season with salt and pepper to taste.
5. Close the lid and set the vent to the Sealing position.
6. Press the Broth/Soup button and cook on high using the preset cooking time.
7. Do quick pressure release to open the lid.
8. Once the lid is open, press the Sauté button and stir in the cheese and milk. Allow to

simmer for 3 minutes before adding the basil leaves.

Nutrition Facts Per Serving
Calories 208, Total Fat 9g, Saturated Fat 5g, Total Carbs 29g, Net Carbs 24g, Protein 8g, Sugar: 19g, Fiber: 5g, Sodium: 1218mg, Potassium: 1142mg, Phosphorus: 438mg

Carrot Chili and Cilantro

Prep time: 5minutes, cook time: 31 minutes; Serves 5
Ingredients:
1 tablespoon olive oil
1 onion, chopped
2 cloves garlic, crushed
1 teaspoon chili paste
3 large carrots, peeled and sliced
1 potato, peeled and chopped
5 cups broth
salt and pepper to taste
1 tablespoon chopped fresh cilantro
Instructions
1. Press the Sauté button on the Instant Pot and heat the oil.
2. Sauté the onion and garlic until fragrant.
3. Stir in the rest of the ingredients except for the cilantro.

4. Close the lid and set the vent to the Sealing position.
5. Press the Broth/Soup button and cook on high for 30 minutes. Do natural pressure release.
6. Once the timer sets off, do quick pressure release to open the lid.
7. Garnish with cilantro before serving.

Nutrition Facts Per Serving
Calories 140, Total Fat 4g, Saturated Fat 0g, Total Carbs 25g, Net Carbs 21g, Protein 3g, Sugar: 8g, Fiber: 4g, Sodium: 487mg, Potassium: 390mg, Phosphorus: 241mg

Cabbage, Potato, And Tomato Soup

Prep time: 5 minutes, cook time: 35 minutes; Serves 5
Ingredients:
¼ cup margarine
1 onion, chopped
4 cloves garlic, minced
3 celery stalks, chopped
2 potatoes, peeled and chopped
1 14-ounce can tomato
1 head small cabbage, chopped
½ cup ketchup
1 teaspoon Italian seasoning
4 cups water
Salt and pepper to taste
Instructions
1. Press the Sauté button on the Instant Pot and heat the margarine.

2. Sauté the onion, garlic, and celery for 3 minutes or until the celery stalks are translucent.
3. Add the potatoes, tomatoes, and cabbages.
4. Stir in the rest of the ingredients.
5. Close the lid and set the vent to the Sealing position.
6. Press the Broth/Soup button and cook on high for 30 minutes.
7. Do natural pressure release.

Nutrition Facts Per Serving
Calories 144, Total Fat 5g, Saturated Fat 3g, Total Carbs 24g, Net Carbs 19g, Protein 4g, Sugar: 8g, Fiber: 5g, Sodium: 549mg, Potassium: 640mg, Phosphorus: 104mg

Calming Winter Soup

Prep time: 5 minutes, cook time: 36 minutes; Serves 5

Ingredients:

¼ cup olive oil
1 onion, chopped
1 celery stalk, chopped
2 cups butternut squash, chopped
1 cup celery root, peeled and chopped
1 sweet potato, peeled and chopped
5 cups vegetable broth
salt and pepper to taste
½ cup half-and-half
3 tablespoons butter

Instructions

1. Press the Sauté button on the Instant Pot and heat the oil. Sauté the onion and celery. Sauté for 3 minutes until translucent.

2. Add in the squash, celery root, and potatoes. Add the broth and season with salt and pepper to taste.

3. Close the lid and set the vent to the Sealing position.

4. Press the Broth/Soup button and cook on high using the preset cooking time.

5. Do quick pressure release to open the lid.

6. Once the lid is open, press the Sauté button and stir in the half-and-half and butter. Allow to simmer for 3 minutes.

Nutrition Facts Per Serving

Calories 324, Total Fat 6g, Saturated Fat g6, Total Carbs 41g, Net Carbs 31g, Protein 5g, Sugar: 9g, Fiber: 10g, Sodium: 1786mg, Potassium: 1036mg, Phosphorus: 321mg

Chunky Creamy Asparagus Soup

Prep time: 5 minutes, cook time: 16 minutes; Serves 5

Ingredients:

6 tablespoons butter
1 ½ cups onion, chopped
1 ½ pounds fresh asparagus, trimmed and cut into 1-inch thick
3 cups water
2 tablespoons tamari
salt and pepper to taste
6 tablespoons all-purpose flour dissolved in 2 cups milk

Instructions

1. Press the Sauté button on the Instant Pot and heat the butter.

2. Stir in the onion until fragrant.

3. Add asparagus and water. Season with tamari, salt and pepper to taste.

4. Close the lid and set the vent to the Sealing position.

5. Press the Pressure Cook or Manual button and adjust the cooking time to 10 minutes.

6. Do quick pressure release.

7. Once the lid is open, press the Sauté button and stir in the flour dissolved in milk.

8. Allow to simmer for 5 minutes until the liquid thickens.

Nutrition Facts Per Serving

Calories 255, Total Fat 15g, Saturated Fat 9g, Total Carbs 22g, Net Carbs 19g, Protein 10g, Sugar: 12g, Fiber: 3g, Sodium: 876mg, Potassium: 562mg, Phosphorus: 312mg

Vegetarian Potato-Leek Soup

Prep time: 5 minutes, cook time: 33 minutes; Serves 8

Ingredients:

¼ cup olive oil

2 leeks, chopped

1-pound potatoes, cut into cubes

3 cups vegetable broth

1 ¾ cups water

Salt and pepper to taste

Instructions

1. Press the Sauté button on the Instant Pot and heat the oil.
2. Stir in the leeks and sauté for 3 minutes.
3. Add the potatoes and stir or another minute.
4. Stir in the rest of the ingredients and season with salt and pepper to taste.
5. Close the lid and set the vent to the Sealing position.
6. Press the Broth/Soup button and cook on high for 30 minutes.
7. Do natural pressure release.

Nutrition Facts Per Serving

Calories 176, Total Fat 7g, Saturated Fat 1g, Total Carbs 26g, Net Carbs 23g, Protein 3g, Sugar: 3g, Fiber: 3g, Sodium: 316mg, Potassium: 520mg, Phosphorus: 111mg

Persian Barley Soup

Prep time: 5 minutes, cook time: 32 minutes; Serves 8

Ingredients:

2 tablespoons coconut oil

1 onion, chopped

1 cup cooked pearl barley

1 teaspoon turmeric

¼ cup tomato paste

1 cup diced carrots

Juice from 1 lime

4 cups vegetable stock

salt and pepper to taste

Instructions

1. Press the Sauté button on the Instant Pot and heat the oil.
2. Sauté the onion for 2 minutes until translucent.
3. Stir in the rest of the ingredients and season with salt and pepper to taste.
4. Close the lid and set the vent to the Sealing position.
5. Press the Broth/Soup button and cook using the preset cooking time.
6. Do natural pressure release.

Nutrition Facts Per Serving

Calories 193, Total Fat 7g, Saturated Fat 3g, Total Carbs 28g, Net Carbs 24g, Protein 6g, Sugar: 3g, Fiber: 4g, Sodium: 178mg, Potassium: 287mg, Phosphorus: 51mg

Chapter 5 Pasta & Noodle Recipes

Vegetarian Instant Pot Spaghetti

Prep time: 10 minutes, cook time: 10 minutes; Serves 5

Ingredients:
1 can black olives, rinsed and drained
1 can chickpeas, rinsed and drained
1 cup frozen lima beans
1 cup frozen spinach
1 cup water
1 jar spaghetti sauce
1 squash, shredded
1 tablespoon Italian seasoning
1 teaspoon cumin
1 teaspoon garlic powder
1 zucchini, sliced
3 cups dried pasta

Instructions:
1. Mix well all ingredients in pot.
2. Cover pot, press manual button, set to hi pressure, and set time to 5 minutes.
3. Do a complete natural release.
4. Uncover and toss to mix.
5. Serve and enjoy.

Nutrition Facts Per Serving
Calories 169, Total Fat 1g, Saturated Fat 2g, Total Carbs 35g, Net Carbs 28g, Protein 6g, Sugar: 1g, Fiber 7g, Sodium 175mg, Potassium 325mg, Phosphorus 120mg

Simple and Creamy Alfredo Fettuccine

Prep time: 10 minutes, cook time: 10 minutes; Serves 4

Ingredients:
1/8 tsp freshly ground black pepper
½ tsp salt
1 tbsp olive oil
8 oz dried fettuccine, cooked and drained
2 cups vegetable stock
1/4 cup whipping cream
1 cup grated low fat, low sodium parmesan cheese
1 tbsp fresh parsley, chopped

Instructions:
1. Add all ingredients in Instant Pot except for whipping cream, cheese, and parsley. Do not mix.
2. Cover, seal, press manual button, and cook on high for 1 minute.
3. Cover seal with a kitchen towel to avoid splatters and do a quick release pressure.
4. Stir in cream and cheese.
5. Cover and let it sit for 5 minutes to allow flavors to mix. Mix again before ladling on to plates.
6. Serve and enjoy with a sprinkle of parsley.

Nutrition Facts Per Serving
Calories 301, Total Fat 19g, Saturated Fat 9g, Total Carbs 3g, Net Carbs 3g, Protein 29g, Sugar: 2g, Fiber 0g, Sodium 1911mg, Potassium 325mg, Phosphorus 363mg

Rigate Penne Pasta

Prep time: 10 minutes, cook time: 25 minutes; Serves +

Ingredients:
1 tablespoon olive oil
3 cloves garlic, minced
1 onion, sliced
1 shallot, diced
12 white mushrooms sliced
1 zucchini, sliced
A pinch of dried basil
A pinch of oregano
A dash of sherry wine
1 cup vegetable stock
1 tablespoon coconut aminos
1 tablespoon Worcestershire sauce
2 cups water
2 tablespoon soy sauce
3 tablespoon tomato paste
1-lb penne pasta

Salt and pepper to taste

Instructions:

1. Press sauté button and heat oil.
2. Sauté the garlic, onion and shallot. Stir constantly for two minutes. Add the mushrooms, zucchini, oregano and dried basil.
3. Pour in the sherry wine and deglaze the bottom of the pot. Add the vegetable stock and the rest of the ingredients.
4. Season with salt and pepper to taste.
5. Press cancel, cover pot, press manual button, set to hi pressure, and set time to 10 minutes.
6. Do a natural release for 10 minutes, and then do a QPR.
7. Uncover.
8. Serve and enjoy.

Nutrition Facts Per Serving
Calories 152, Total Fat 4g, Saturated Fat 1g, Total Carbs 26g, Net Carbs 22g, Protein 4g, Sugar: 3g, Fiber 4g, Sodium 179mg, Potassium 258mg, Phosphorus 109mg

Tomato and Capers on Pasta

Prep time: 10 minutes, cook time: 15 minutes; Serves 6

Ingredients:
2 tablespoon olive oil
2 garlic cloves, sliced
1 ½ cups diced tomatoes
2 cups pasta of your choice
A dash of chili pepper
A dash of oregano
¾ cup red wine
2 cups water
Salt and pepper to taste
2 tablespoon capers
Grated vegan parmesan for garnish

Instructions:
1. Press sauté button and heat oil.
2. Sauté the garlic until fragrant.
3. Add the tomatoes and pasta. Season with oregano and chilis.
4. Add the red wine and water. Season with salt and pepper to taste.
5. Press cancel, cover pot, press manual button, set to hi pressure, and set time to 6 minutes.
6. Do a QPR. Uncover and stir in capers. Cover and let it sit for 10 minutes to allow flavors to infuse.
7. Serve and enjoy with parmesan cheese.

Nutrition Facts Per Serving
Calories 152, Total Fat 5g, Saturated Fat 1g, Total Carbs 26g, Net Carbs 22g, Protein 4g, Sugar: 3g, Fiber 4g, Sodium 179mg, Potassium 258mg, Phosphorus 109mg

Stuffed Vegetarian Pasta Shells

Prep time: 10 minutes, cook time: 30 minutes; Serves 10

Ingredients:
20 jumbo pasta shells, cooked and drained
Water
1 8-oz can no salt added tomato sauce
1 28-oz can fire roasted crushed tomatoes with added puree
¼ cup chopped pepperoncini peppers
1 tsp dried oregano
2 garlic cloves, minced
5 oz frozen chopped spinach, thawed, drained and squeezed dry
1 9oz package frozen artichoke hearts, thawed and chopped
¼ tsp freshly ground black pepper
½ cup fat free cream cheese softened
1 cup crumbled feta cheese
1 cup shredded provolone cheese

Instructions:
1. In Instant Pot, add pasta shells. Add water until shells are just submerged.
2. Cover, seal, press manual button, and cook on high for 1 minute.
3. Cover seal with a kitchen towel to avoid splatters and do a quick release pressure.
4. Drain pasta shells and run under cold water to stop cooking process and set aside.
5. In a bowl, mix well tomato sauce, crushed tomatoes, peppers, and oregano.
6. In another bowl, mix well the remaining ingredients and stuff into the pasta shells.

7. Place stuffed pasta shells on a lightly greased baking pan and top with tomato sauce.
8. Bake for 25 minutes in a preheated 375°F oven.
9. Serve and enjoy.

Nutrition Facts Per Serving
Calories 153, Total Fat 7g, Saturated Fat 5g, Total Carbs 14g, Net Carbs 10g, Protein 11g, Sugar: 7g, Fiber 4g, Sodium 555mg, Potassium 604mg, Phosphorus 259mg

Fusilli with Spinach and Garlic

Prep time: 10 minutes, cook time: 15 minutes; Serves 8
Ingredients:
1-pound fusilli pasta
5 cups water
4 cloves garlic, minced
4 cups spinach, chopped
4 tablespoons vegan butter
Salt and pepper to taste
½ cup vegan parmesan cheese
Instructions:
1. Place the pasta in the Instant Pot. Pour in water to cover the pasta.
2. Add the garlic and spinach.
3. Cover pot, press manual button, set to hi pressure, and set time to 6 minutes.
4. Do a QPR. Uncover and stir in remaining ingredients. Season with pepper and salt. Mix well. Let pasta rest for 5 to 10 minutes to allow flavors to mix.
5. Serve and enjoy.

Nutrition Facts Per Serving
Calories 128, Total Fat 6g, Saturated Fat 4g, Total Carbs 17g, Net Carbs 14g, Protein 2g, Sugar: 0g, Fiber 3g, Sodium 61mg, Potassium 109mg, Phosphorus 54mg

Italian Pasta and Beans

Prep time: 10 minutes, cook time: 10 minutes; Serves 6
Ingredients:
2 tbsp olive oil
3 cloves garlic, minced
1 cup onion, chopped
¼ tsp ground black pepper
1 tsp dried basil leaves
¼ cup chopped parsley
1 can or 15 oz cannelli beans, drained and rinsed well
3 cups vegetable broth
2 cans of 14.5 oz stewed tomatoes, undrained
1/2 lb. seashell pasta, whole wheat
Instructions:
1. Press sauté button on Instant Pot and heat for 3 minutes. Add oil and heat for another 3 minutes. Add garlic and onion. Sauté until tender or for five minutes.
2. Stir in remaining ingredients.
3. Press cancel, cover pot, press pressure cook button, choose high settings, and cook for 5 minutes. Do a 5-minute natural release, and then do a QPR.
4. Serve while hot.

Nutrition Facts Per Serving
Calories 121, Total Fat 6g, Saturated Fat 1g, Total Carbs 14g, Net Carbs 11g, Protein 4g, Sugar: 1g, Fiber 3g, Sodium 402mg, Potassium 194mg, Phosphorus 78mg

Pasta Mediterranean Style

Prep time: 10 minutes, cook time: 10 minutes; Serves 6
Ingredients:
8 oz whole wheat linguine or spaghetti
¼ cup extra virgin olive oil
2 large cloves garlic, chopped
1 can of 15 oz crushed tomatoes with basil
Big pinch of saffron threads soaked in 2 tbsps of water
Big pinch of crushed red pepper
Freshly ground pepper to taste
¼ tsp salt
1 tbsp finely grated lemon zest
¼ cup chopped fresh parsley
Instructions:

1. Cook your pasta following the package label, drain and set aside while covering it to keep it warm.
2. Press sauté button on Instant Pot and heat oil for 5 minutes.
3. Sauté for two to three minutes the garlic and add the saffron plus liquid and the crushed tomatoes. Let it simmer for five minutes.
4. Add the red pepper and continue for a minute to simmer the sauce. Lastly, season with pepper and salt.
5. Then transfer half of the sauce into the pasta bowl and toss to mix. Then ladle the pasta into 4 medium sized serving bowls, top with remaining sauce, lemon zest and parsley in that order before serving.

Nutrition Facts Per Serving
Calories 100, Total Fat 6g, Saturated Fat 1g, Total Carbs 12g, Net Carbs 10g, Protein 3g, Sugar: 2g, Fiber 2g, Sodium 291mg, Potassium 112mg, Phosphorus 44mg

Penne Pesto

Prep time: 10 minutes, cook time: 10 minutes; Serves 4

Ingredients:
1 16-oz package penne pasta
4 cups cold water
4 tbsp olive oil, divided
6 cloves garlic, minced
4 tbsp grated Parmesan cheese
¼ cup pesto
1 ¼ cups cottage cheese
¼ tsp pepper
½ tsp salt

Instructions:
1. Add pasta in Instant Pot. Add water, 1 tbsp oil, and garlic.
2. Cover, seal, press manual button, and cook on high for 1 minute.
3. Do a quick release pressure and cover seal with a kitchen towel to avoid splatters.
4. Add remaining ingredients and toss well to mix.
5. Cover and let it sit for 5 minutes to allow flavors to mix.
6. Serve and enjoy.

Nutrition Facts Per Serving
Calories 438, Total Fat 27g, Saturated Fat 5g, Total Carbs 37g, Net Carbs 31g, Protein 14g, Sugar: 6g, Fiber 6g, Sodium 765mg, Potassium 168mg, Phosphorus 267mg

Lemon-Avocado Sauce on Spaghetti

Prep time: 10 minutes, cook time: 10 minutes; Serves 4

Ingredients:
12-oz whole wheat spaghetti
3 cups cold water + 4 tbsp water, divided
1 large onion, finely sliced
1 tbsp olive oil
2 avocados, pitted and peeled
Pepper to taste
Freshly ground black pepper
Zest and juice of 1 large lemon

Instructions:
1. Add pasta in Instant Pot. Add 3 cups water, 1 tbsp oil, and onion.
2. Cover, seal, press manual button, and cook on high for 1 minute.
3. Do a quick release pressure and cover seal with a kitchen towel to avoid splatters.
4. In a blender, until smooth, puree the lemon juice, 2 tbsp water, and avocado. Pour into the fry pan of pasta.
5. Cover and let it sit for 5 minutes to allow flavors to mix.
6. Serve and enjoy with pepper and lemon zest.

Nutrition Facts Per Serving
Calories 341, Total Fat 22g, Saturated Fat g, Total Carbs 36g, Net Carbs 25g, Protein 7g, Sugar: 4g, Fiber 11g, Sodium 186mg, Potassium 652mg, Phosphorus 142mg

Pasta and Beans, Modern Style

Prep time: 10 minutes, cook time: 10 minutes; Serves 6

Ingredients:

1 box Barilla medium shells, 12-oz
1 cup water
2 tbsp olive oil
1 ½ cup vegetable stock
6 cloves garlic peeled, thinly sliced
1 onion diced
½ cup tomato sauce
1 can Borlotti Bean, drained and rinsed
2 cups collard greens chopped
¼ cup fresh parsley chopped

Instructions:

1. Add pasta in Instant Pot. Add water, oil, vegetable stock, garlic, onion, tomato sauce.
2. Cover, seal, press manual button and cook on high for 1 minute.
3. Do a quick release pressure and cover seal with a kitchen towel to avoid splatters.
4. Stir in remaining ingredients, except for fresh parsley.
5. Cover and let it sit for 5 minutes to allow flavors to mix.
6. Serve and enjoy with parsley on top.

Nutrition Facts Per Serving

Calories 100, Total Fat 6g, Saturated Fat 1g, Total Carbs 9g, Net Carbs 7g, Protein 3g, Sugar: 3g, Fiber 2g, Sodium 408mg, Potassium 252mg, Phosphorus 64mg

Creamy Roasted Red Pepper Pasta

Prep time: 10 minutes, cook time: 20 minutes; Serves 6

Ingredients:

12 oz pasta, cooked and drained
3 cups cold water
¼ tsp crushed red pepper
6 cloves garlic, minced
1/3 cup finely chopped onion
1 tbsp olive oil
1 cup finely shredded Parmesan Cheese
¼ cup snipped fresh basil
½ cup whipping cream
1 12oz jar roasted red sweet peppers, drained and chopped

Instructions:

1. Add pasta, water, crushed red pepper, garlic, onion, and oil in Instant Pot.
2. Cover, seal, press manual button, and cook on high for 1 minute.
3. Cover seal with a kitchen towel to avoid splatters and do a quick release pressure.
4. Stir in remaining ingredients.
5. Cover and let it sit for 5 minutes to allow flavors to mix.
6. Serve and enjoy with parsley on top.

Nutrition Facts Per Serving

Calories 196, Total Fat 9g, Saturated Fat 4g, Total Carbs 24g, Net Carbs 20g, Protein 7g, Sugar: 3g, Fiber 4g, Sodium 439mg, Potassium 174mg, Phosphorus 169mg

Easy Red Sauce-Mushroom Pasta

Prep time: 10 minutes, cook time: 10 minutes; Serves 4

Ingredients:

16-oz whole wheat pasta
2 cups vegetable soup
24-oz can pasta sauce
1 medium onion, chopped
6 cloves garlic, smashed and peeled
4-oz can sliced mushroom, drained
1 tsp salt
1 tsp freshly cracked pepper
1 tbsp sugar
4 tbsp parmesan cheese

Instructions:

1. Evenly spread pasta on bottom of Instant pot. Add soup.
2. Evenly spread pasta sauce on top.
3. Sprinkle remaining ingredients on top, except for cheese. Do not mix.
4. Cover, seal, press manual button, and cook on high for 1 minute.
5. Cover seal with a kitchen towel to avoid splatters and do a quick release pressure.

6. Open pot and mix well. Allow to sit in pot for 3 minutes or so.
7. Ladle into plates and top with 1 tbsp of cheese per plate.
8. Enjoy.

Nutrition Facts Per Serving
Calories 546, Total Fat 4g, Saturated Fat 1g, Total Carbs 117g, Net Carbs 96g, Protein 20g, Sugar: 15g, Fiber 21g, Sodium 2118mg, Potassium 1127mg, Phosphorus 500mg

Sun-Dried Tomato Alfredo

Prep time: 10 minutes, cook time: 10 minutes; Serves 3

Ingredients:
8 oz dried fettuccine
1 cup vegetable stock
½ tsp salt
1 tsp freshly cracked pepper
1 tbsp olive oil
4 tbsp low fat butter
½ cup chopped dried tomatoes
1 ¼ cups almond milk
8 fresh mushrooms, sliced
1 ½ cups fresh broccoli florets
4 oz fresh trimmed and quartered Brussels sprouts
4 oz trimmed fresh asparagus spears
2 tsp finely shredded lemon peel
½ cup finely shredded Parmesan cheese

Instructions:

1. Add all ingredients in Instant Pot except for lemon peel and cheese. Do not mix.
2. Cover, seal, press manual button, and cook on high for 1 minute.
3. Cover seal with a kitchen towel to avoid splatters and do a quick release pressure.
4. Stir in remaining ingredients.
5. Cover and let it sit for 5 minutes to allow flavors to mix.
6. Serve and enjoy with.

Nutrition Facts Per Serving
Calories 403, Total Fat 8g, Saturated Fat 2g, Total Carbs 79g, Net Carbs 88g, Protein 12g, Sugar: 56g, Fiber 11g, Sodium 899mg, Potassium 1033mg, Phosphorus 272mg

Mushroom Bolognese

Prep time: 30 minutes, cook time: 10 minutes; Serves 4

Ingredients:
1 cup boiling water
½-oz dried porcini mushrooms
12-oz whole wheat spaghetti, cut to fit in pot
2 cups water
¼ cup almond milk
1 14-oz can whole peeled tomatoes
½ cup white wine
2 tbsp tomato paste
1 tbsp minced garlic
8 cups finely chopped cremini mushrooms
½ tsp freshly ground black pepper, divided
2 ½ cups chopped onion
1 tbsp olive oil
¼ cup low fat Parmigiano-Reggiano cheese, grated
¼ cup chopped fresh parsley

Instructions:

1. Let porcini stand in a boiling bowl of water for twenty minutes, drain, rinse and chop.
2. Add all ingredients in pot except for parsley and cheese. Mix.
3. Cover, seal, press manual button, and cook on high for 1 minute.
4. Cover seal with a kitchen towel to avoid splatters and do a quick release pressure.
5. Stir in cheese.
6. Cover and let it sit for 5 minutes to allow flavors to mix. Mix again before ladling on to plates.
7. Serve and enjoy with a sprinkle of parsley.

Nutrition Facts Per Serving
Calories 298, Total Fat 10g, Saturated Fat 2g, Total Carbs 45g, Net Carbs 30g, Protein 15g, Sugar: 13g, Fiber 10g, Sodium 388mg, Potassium 1149mg, Phosphorus 342mg

Penne Anti-Pasto

Prep time: 10 minutes, cook time: 10 minutes; Serves 4

Ingredients:

8-oz penne pasta

1 1/2 cups vegetable stock

1 7-oz jar drained and chopped sun-dried tomato halves packed in oil

1/3 cup pesto

½ cup grated low fat Parmigiana-Reggiano cheese, divided

1 6-oz jar drained, sliced, marinated and quartered artichoke hearts

1/4 cup pitted and chopped Kalamata olives

1 medium red bell pepper, diced

¼ cup pine nuts, toasted

Instructions:

1. Add pasta, stock, sun-dried tomato and its oil, and pesto.

2. Cover, seal, press manual button, and cook on high for 1 minute.

3. Cover seal with a kitchen towel to avoid splatters and do a quick release pressure.

4. Stir in cheese, artichoke, olive, and bell pepper.

5. Cover and let it sit for 5 minutes to allow flavors to mix. Mix again before ladling on to plates.

6. Serve and enjoy with a sprinkle of pine nuts.

Nutrition Facts Per Serving

Calories 432, Total Fat 29g, Saturated Fat 5g, Total Carbs 37g, Net Carbs g, Protein 13g, Sugar: 2g, Fiber 11g, Sodium 732mg, Potassium 1208mg, Phosphorus 388mg

Wild Mushroom Pastitsio

Prep time: 10 minutes, cook time: 6 minutes; Serves 4

Ingredients:

12-oz fusilli pasta

2 cups almond milk

1/2 cup vegetable stock

1 8oz can tomato sauce

1/8 tsp ground nutmeg

¼ tsp black pepper

¼ tsp salt

2 8-oz packages pre-sliced exotic mushroom blend, chopped

2 garlic cloves, minced

1 cup chopped onion

4 tsp olive oil

1 ½ cups shredded low fat mozzarella cheese

3 tbsp chopped fresh parsley

1 tbsp chopped fresh oregano

Instructions:

1. Add all ingredients in pot except for cheese, parsley, and oregano. Mix.

2. Cover, seal, press manual button, and cook on high for 1 minute.

3. Cover seal with a kitchen towel to avoid splatters and do a quick release pressure.

4. Stir in cheese, parsley, and oregano.

5. Cover and let it sit for 5 minutes to allow flavors to mix. Mix again before ladling on to plates.

6. Serve and enjoy.

Nutrition Facts Per Serving

Calories 661, Total Fat 48g, Saturated Fat 33g, Total Carbs 39g, Net Carbs 22g, Protein 25g, Sugar: 12g, Fiber 7g, Sodium 658mg, Potassium 763mg, Phosphorus 507mg

Eggplant and Feta Penne

Prep time: 10 minutes, cook time: 1 minute; Serves 6

Ingredients:

12-oz penne

2 1/2 cups vegetable stock

1 14.5-oz can dice tomatoes

1/2 tsp ground black pepper

¼ tsp salt

1 tsp dried oregano

2 tbsp tomato paste

4 garlic cloves, minced

4 ½ cups cubed peeled eggplant

¼ cup chopped fresh parsley

½ cup crumbled feta cheese

Instructions:

1. Add all ingredients in pot except for parsley and cheese. Mix.

2. Cover, seal, press manual button, and cook on high for 1 minute.
3. Cover seal with a kitchen towel to avoid splatters and do a quick release pressure.
4. Mix before ladling on to plates.
5. Serve and enjoy with a sprinkle of feta and parsley.

Nutrition Facts Per Serving
Calories 156, Total Fat 6g, Saturated Fat 4g, Total Carbs 18g, Net Carbs 13g, Protein 9g, Sugar: 7g, Fiber 5g, Sodium 594mg, Potassium 597mg, Phosphorus 200mg

Fresh Tomato and Basil Pasta

Prep time: 10 minutes, cook time: 6 minutes; Serves 2
Ingredients:
1 ¼ lbs. tomatoes, chopped
8-oz uncooked penne
2 cups vegetable stock
1/8 tsp black pepper
¼ tsp salt
2 tsp minced garlic
1 cup vertically sliced onions
2 tsp olive oil
6 tbsp grated fresh low sodium pecorino Romano cheese
¼ cup torn fresh basil leaves
Instructions:
1. Evenly spread tomatoes on bottom of pot.
2. Add remaining ingredients except for cheese and basil. Don't Mix.
3. Cover, seal, press manual button, and cook on high for 1 minute.
4. Cover seal with a kitchen towel to avoid splatters and do a quick release pressure.
5. Stir in cheese and basil.
6. Cover and let it sit for 5 minutes to allow flavors to mix. Mix again before ladling on to plates.
7. Serve and enjoy.

Nutrition Facts Per Serving
Calories 491, Total Fat 12g, Saturated Fat 4g, Total Carbs 87g, Net Carbs 75g, Protein 20g, Sugar: 87g, Fiber 12g, Sodium 797mg, Potassium 436mg, Phosphorus 436mg

Mushroom Stroganoff

Prep time: 10 minutes, cook time: 6 minutes; Serves 6
Ingredients:
1 can cream of mushroom soup
16-oz whole wheat pasta
3 cups vegetable stock
1-lb mushrooms, chopped
½ tsp salt
1 tsp freshly ground pepper
1 tbsp butter
2 cloves garlic, minced
1 medium onion, chopped
Instructions:
1. Add all ingredients in Instant Pot.
2. Cover, seal, press manual button, and cook on high for 1 minute.
3. Cover seal with a kitchen towel to avoid splatters and do a quick release pressure.
4. Serve and enjoy.

Nutrition Facts Per Serving
Calories 365, Total Fat 7g, Saturated Fat 3g, Total Carbs 71g, Net Carbs 58g, Protein 13g, Sugar: 6g, Fiber 13g, Sodium 509mg, Potassium 802mg, Phosphorus 367mg

Easy Lasagna Soup

Prep time: 10 minutes, cook time: 1 minute; Serves 6
Ingredients:
1 tablespoon olive oil
1 onion, chopped
½ green pepper, chopped
2 carrots, peeled and chopped
1 small zucchini, chopped
1 can diced tomatoes
4 cups vegetable stock
2 cups water

½ box of lasagna noodles, broken into small pieces
½ teaspoon onion powder
1 teaspoon oregano
Pepper

Instructions:
1. Add all ingredients in Instant Pot.
2. Cover, seal, press manual button, and cook on high for 1 minute.
3. Allow for natural pressure release.
4. Serve and enjoy.

Nutrition Facts Per Serving
Calories 69, Total Fat 4g, Saturated Fat 1g, Total Carbs 6g, Net Carbs 4g, Protein 5g, Sugar: 3g, Fiber 2g, Sodium 291mg, Potassium 398mg, Phosphorus 110mg

Pasta with Escarole and Cannellini

Prep time: 10 minutes, cook time: 10 minutes; Serves 5

Ingredients:
1 ½ cups canned cannellini beans, rinsed well and drained
2 carrots, chopped into large pieces
2 celery stalks, chopped
1 bulb of garlic, minced
1 sprig of rosemary
2 bay leaves
1 onion, chopped
3 roma tomatoes, chopped
1 cup vegetable stock
3 ounces pasta of your choice
Pepper to taste
1 tablespoon olive oil
½ small head of escarole, torn
6 sprigs of parsley

Instructions:
1. Add all ingredients in Instant Pot.
2. Cover, seal, press manual button, and cook on high for 1 minute.
3. Allow for natural pressure release for 5 minutes then do a QPR.
4. Serve and enjoy with escarole and parsley on top.

Nutrition Facts Per Serving
Calories 109, Total Fat 4g, Saturated Fat 1g, Total Carbs 17g, Net Carbs 14g, Protein 4g, Sugar: 5g, Fiber 3g, Sodium 105mg, Potassium 514mg, Phosphorus 97mg

Fresh Tomato 'n Pesto Pasta

Prep time: 10 minutes, cook time: 10 minutes; Serves 6

Ingredients:
Pepper to taste
2 tsp olive oil
1 cup cherry tomatoes, halved
4 cups vegetable stock
½ tsp salt
¾ cups prepared pesto
16-oz whole wheat pasta
¼ cup fresh Basil, chopped
¼ cup parmesan cheese, grated

Instructions:
1. Evenly spread halved tomatoes on bottom of pot.
2. Add remaining ingredients on top, except for basil and cheese. Do not mix.
3. Cover, seal, press manual button, and cook on high for 1 minute.
4. Cover seal with a kitchen towel to avoid splatters and do a quick release pressure.
5. Stir in cheese and basil.
6. Cover and let it sit for 5 minutes to allow flavors to mix. Mix again before ladling on to plates.
7. Serve and enjoy.

Nutrition Facts Per Serving
Calories 491, Total Fat 23g, Saturated Fat 4g, Total Carbs 63g, Net Carbs 52g, Protein 16g, Sugar: 5g, Fiber 11g, Sodium 796mg, Potassium 650mg, Phosphorus 438mg

Creamy Mac and Cheese

Prep time: 10 minutes, cook time: 10 minutes; Serves 6

Ingredients:

1 ½ cups almond milk
8-oz cream cheese fat free
6-oz sharp cheddar, grated, low sodium
½ tsp salt
3 cups vegetable stock
1 tsp ground mustard
1 tsp Sriracha, optional
Pepper to taste
16-oz elbow macaroni

Instructions:

1. In a blender puree all ingredients except for macaroni.
2. Evenly spread macaroni on bottom of pot and pour pureed cheese sauce on top.
3. Cover, seal, press manual button, and cook on high for 1 minute.
4. Cover seal with a kitchen towel to avoid splatters and do a quick release pressure.
5. Serve and enjoy.

Nutrition Facts Per Serving

Calories 491, Total Fat 14g, Saturated Fat 6g, Total Carbs 66g, Net Carbs 63g, Protein 26g, Sugar: 10g, Fiber 3g, Sodium 871mg, Potassium 534mg, Phosphorus 557mg

Creole Pasta

Prep time: 10 minutes, cook time: 6 minutes; Serves 6

Ingredients:

16-oz pasta, whole wheat
2 1/2 cups vegetable stock
1 28-oz jar Pasta sauce, low sodium
1 tsp Cajun seasoning
½ tsp celery seeds
2 bell peppers, sliced
2 medium onions, sliced
1 tbsp olive oil

Instructions:

1. Add all ingredients in Instant Pot.
2. Cover, seal, press manual button, and cook on high for 1 minute.
3. Cover seal with a kitchen towel to avoid splatters and do a quick release pressure.
4. Serve and enjoy.

Nutrition Facts Per Serving

Calories 205, Total Fat 6g, Saturated Fat 0g, Total Carbs 33g, Net Carbs 26g, Protein 7g, Sugar: 9g, Fiber 7g, Sodium 742mg, Potassium 648mg, Phosphorus 165mg

Pasta Florentine

Prep time: 10 minutes, cook time: 6 minutes; Serves 6

Ingredients:

1 tbsp Italian seasoning
4-oz sliced Mozzarella cheese, low sodium
2 cloves garlic minced
16-oz whole wheat pasta
½ tsp salt
1 can of cream of mushroom soup, low sodium
3 cups water
8 cups baby spinach
4 tbsp Parmesan cheese

Instructions:

1. Add all ingredients in pot except for spinach and cheese. Mix.
2. Cover, seal, press manual button, and cook on high for 1 minute.
3. Cover seal with a kitchen towel to avoid splatters and do a quick release pressure.
4. Stir in spinach and cheese. Let it rest for 5 minutes to allow flavors to meld.
5. Mix before ladling on to plates.
6. Serve and enjoy.

Nutrition Facts Per Serving

Calories 360, Total Fat 8g, Saturated Fat 3g, Total Carbs 63g, Net Carbs 52g, Protein 16g, Sugar: 3g, Fiber 11g, Sodium 407mg, Potassium 584mg, Phosphorus 395mg

Kale Pasta Pesto

Prep time: 10 minutes, cook time: 6 minutes; Serves 6

Ingredients:

3 cloves of garlic, minced

3 cups kale, rinsed

¾ cup walnuts

2 tablespoons lemon juice, freshly squeezed

¾ teaspoon salt

¼ teaspoon ground pepper

¼ cup flaxseed oil

1-pound whole grain pasta

3 1/2 cups vegetable broth

Instructions:

1. In blender add all ingredients except for pasta and broth. Puree until smooth and creamy.

2. Add pasta and both in Instant pot and pour in kale sauce.

3. Cover, seal, press manual button, and cook on high for 1 minute.

4. Cover seal with a kitchen towel to avoid splatters and do a quick release pressure.

5. Mix before ladling on to plates.

6. Serve and enjoy.

Nutrition Facts Per Serving

Calories 450, Total Fat 20g, Saturated Fat 2g, Total Carbs 62g, Net Carbs 55g, Protein 11g, Sugar: 2g, Fiber 7g, Sodium 774mg, Potassium 443mg, Phosphorus 273mg

Simple Lemony Pasta

Prep time: 10 minutes, cook time: 6 minutes; Serves 2

Ingredients:

8-oz angel hair whole wheat spaghetti

2 cups vegetable broth

1 lemon, juiced and zested

3 1/2 ounces low-sodium parmesan cheese

Freshly ground black pepper

1 tablespoon olive oil

¼ cup packed fresh basil leaves, torn

Instructions:

1. Add pasta and broth in Instant Pot.

2. Cover, seal, press manual button, and cook on high for 1 minute.

3. Cover seal with a kitchen towel to avoid splatters and do a quick release pressure.

4. Stir in remaining ingredients and cover. Let it rest for 5 minutes to allow flavors to meld.

5. Mix before ladling on to plates.

6. Serve and enjoy.

Nutrition Facts Per Serving

Calories 494, Total Fat 28g, Saturated Fat 12g, Total Carbs 34g, Net Carbs g, Protein 32g, Sugar: 2g, Fiber 5g, Sodium 1038mg, Potassium 335mg, Phosphorus 573mg

Zucchini Pasta Salad

Prep time: 10 minutes, cook time: 10 minutes; Serves 4

Ingredients:

8-oz whole wheat macaroni, uncooked

2 cups vegetable broth

1/3 cup diced onion

¼ cup sliced carrots

½ cup chopped zucchini

¼ cup fat free mayonnaise

¼ cup light sour cream

¼ tsp pepper

Instructions:

1. Add macaroni and vegetable broth in Instant Pot.

2. Cover, seal, press manual button, and cook on high for 1 minute.

3. Cover seal with a kitchen towel to avoid splatters and do a quick release pressure.

4. Drain macaroni and run under cold water to cool and stop the cooking process.

5. Drain pasta well.

6. In a large bowl, mix well remaining ingredients.

7. Add pasta into bowl and toss to coat.

8. Serve and enjoy.

Nutrition Facts Per Serving

Calories 126, Total Fat 3g, Saturated Fat 2g, Total Carbs 21g, Net Carbs 18g, Protein 7g, Sugar: 2g, Fiber 3g, Sodium 412mg, Potassium 207mg, Phosphorus 109mg

Cheesy Broccoli Sauce over Pasta

Prep time: 10 minutes, cook time: 10 minutes; Serves 6

Ingredients:

3 cups vegetable broth

6 ½ cups fresh broccoli florets, no stems

1 tsp olive oil

5 cloves garlic, peeled, smashed and chopped

½ tsp pepper

¼ cup grated fat free Parmesan cheese

12-oz uncooked whole wheat pasta

Instructions:

1. Blend all ingredients, except for pasta until smooth.
2. In Instant Pot, add pasta and pour over broccoli sauce.
3. Cover, seal, press manual button, and cook on high for 1 minute.
4. Cover seal with a kitchen towel to avoid splatters and do a quick release pressure.
5. Mix well, serve and enjoy.

Nutrition Facts Per Serving

Calories 242, Total Fat 3g, Saturated Fat 1g, Total Carbs 46g, Net Carbs 37g, Protein 12g, Sugar: 2g, Fiber 9g, Sodium 489mg, Potassium 469mg, Phosphorus 320mg

Lentil 'n Pasta in Cilantro Sauce

Prep time: 10 minutes, cook time: 10 minutes; Serves 6

Ingredients:

2 cups water

2 small dry red peppers, whole

1 tsp turmeric

1 tsp ground cumin

3 cloves garlic, minced

1 15-ounce can low sodium, diced tomatoes with juice

1 large onion, chopped

½ cup dry lentils, rinsed

½ cup orzo or tiny pasta

¼ cup fresh cilantro, chopped

3 tbsp low fat sour cream

Instructions:

1. Add all ingredients in Instant Pot, except for cilantro and sour cream.
2. Cover, seal, press manual button, and cook on high for 1 minute.
3. Cover seal with a kitchen towel to avoid splatters and do a quick release pressure.
4. Stir in remaining cilantro and cover. Let it rest for 5 minutes to allow flavors to meld.
5. Mix before ladling on to plates.
6. Serve and enjoy with sour cream on top.

Nutrition Facts Per Serving

Calories 151, Total Fat 3g, Saturated Fat 1g, Total Carbs 32g, Net Carbs 29g, Protein 4g, Sugar: 18g, Fiber 3g, Sodium 82mg, Potassium 392mg, Phosphorus 85mg

Veggie-Pasta Soup

Prep time: 15 minutes, cook time: 10 minutes; Serves 6

Ingredients:

1 medium onion, chopped

2 medium carrots, chopped

2 stalks celery, chopped

12 ounces fresh green beans, cut into ½-inch pieces

2 cloves garlic, minced

8 cups low-sodium vegetable broth

1 (15 ounce) cans low-sodium cannellini or other white beans, rinsed

4 cups chopped kale

2 medium zucchinis, chopped

4 Roma tomatoes, seeded and chopped

2 teaspoons red-wine vinegar

¾ teaspoon salt

½ teaspoon ground pepper

1 cup bow tie pasta

8 teaspoons prepared pesto

Instructions:

1. Add all ingredients in Instant Pot, except for pesto.
2. Cover, seal, press manual button, and cook on high for 3 minutes.

3. Cover seal with a kitchen towel to avoid splatters and do a quick pressure release.
4. Adjust seasoning to taste (pepper and salt) if needed. Let it rest for 5 minutes.
5. Mix before ladling on to bowls.
6. Serve and enjoy with pesto on top.

Nutrition Facts Per Serving
Calories 147, Total Fat 2g, Saturated Fat 1g, Total Carbs 31g, Net Carbs 25g, Protein 7g, Sugar: 15g, Fiber 6g, Sodium 506mg, Potassium 1140mg, Phosphorus 144mg

Creamy Orzo Soup

Prep time: 15 minutes, cook time: 10 minutes; Serves 4

Ingredients:
1 1/2 cups diced yellow onion
1 cup diced carrot
1 cup diced celery
2 cloves garlic, minced
1 tablespoon minced parsley
2 cups low-sodium vegetable stock
1 teaspoon fennel seeds, crushed
1 teaspoon ground black pepper
1 15.5 ounce can of white beans, rinsed and drained
½ orzo pasta
1 1/2 cups chopped kale
2 cups almond milk

Instructions:
1. Add all ingredients in Instant Pot, except for kale and milk.
2. Cover, seal, press manual button, and cook on high for 2 minutes.
3. Cover seal with a kitchen towel to avoid splatters and do a quick release pressure.
4. Stir in kale and cover. Let it rest for 5 minutes to cook kale.
5. Mix in almond milk before ladling on to bowls.
6. Serve and enjoy.

Nutrition Facts Per Serving
Calories 192, Total Fat 9g, Saturated Fat 3g, Total Carbs 24g, Net Carbs 19g, Protein 8g, Sugar: 14g, Fiber 5g, Sodium 171mg, Potassium 788mg, Phosphorus 188mg

Spanish Soup with Pasta

Prep time: 10 minutes, cook time: 5 minutes; Serves 6

Ingredients:
1 daikon radish, peeled and cubed
1 turnip, peeled and cubed
2 carrots, peeled and cubed
2 stalks of celery, chopped
A pinch of saffron
6 cups vegetable stock
1 cup pasta shells, small
1 bay leaf
¼ tsp salt
½ tsp pepper

Instructions:
1. Add all ingredients in Instant Pot.
2. Cover, seal, press manual button, and cook on high for 2 minutes.
3. Cover seal with a kitchen towel to avoid splatters and do a quick release pressure.
4. Open pot and discard bay leaf.
5. Ladle into bowls, serve and enjoy.

Nutrition Facts Per Serving
Calories 85, Total Fat 2g, Saturated Fat 1g, Total Carbs 11g, Net Carbs g, Protein 7g, Sugar: 2g, Fiber 3g, Sodium 786mg, Potassium 534mg, Phosphorus 169mg

Creamy Asparagus & Pasta Soup

Prep time: 15 minutes, cook time: 10 minutes; Serves 6

Ingredients:
1 cup peeled and diced potatoes
1/2-pound fresh asparagus, cut into 1/4-inch pieces, divided
1/2 cup chopped onion
1 cup shell pasta, small
2 stalks celery, chopped

2 cups water

¼ tsp salt

2 tablespoons butter

½ tsp cracked black pepper, to taste

1 1/2 cups almond milk

Instructions:

1. Add all ingredients in Instant Pot, except for milk.
2. Cover, seal, press manual button, and cook on high for 2 minutes.
3. Cover seal with a kitchen towel to avoid splatters and do a quick release pressure.
4. Mix in almond milk before ladling on to bowls.
5. Serve and enjoy.

Nutrition Facts Per Serving

Calories 133, Total Fat 6g, Saturated Fat 4g, Total Carbs 17g, Net Carbs 15g, Protein 4g, Sugar: 5g, Fiber 3g, Sodium 162mg, Potassium 303mg, Phosphorus 109mg

Vegetarian Noodle Soup

Prep time: 10 minutes, cook time: 10 minutes; Serves 4

Ingredients:

1 cup chopped onion

3 cloves garlic, minced

1 cup chopped celery

1 cup sliced, peeled carrots (2 medium)

4 ounces dried linguini, broken

1 cup seashell pasta, small

3 cups vegetable soup

1 cup almond milk

½ tsp pepper

¼ tsp salt

2 tablespoons snipped fresh parsley

Instructions:

1. Add all ingredients in Instant Pot, except for parsley and milk.
2. Cover, seal, press manual button, and cook on high for 2 minutes.
3. Cover seal with a kitchen towel to avoid splatters and do a quick release pressure.
4. Stir in milk and cover. Let it rest for 5 minutes to mix flavors.
5. Mix before ladling on to bowls.
6. Serve and enjoy with garnish of parsley.

Nutrition Facts Per Serving

Calories 230, Total Fat 4g, Saturated Fat 2g, Total Carbs 40g, Net Carbs 33g, Protein 10g, Sugar: 9g, Fiber 7g, Sodium 645mg, Potassium 296mg, Phosphorus 138mg

Easy Tom Yum Glass Noodle Soup

Prep time: 10 minutes, cook time: 25 minutes; Serves 4

Ingredients:

1 stalk lemongrass, cut in half then halved lengthwise

4 cloves garlic, minced

1½ tbsp fresh minced ginger

1/2 medium yellow onion, thinly sliced

4 red tomatoes, chopped

¼ cup water

1 Thai red chili pepper

1½ cups thinly sliced shiitake mushrooms

3 tbsp green curry paste

6 cups vegetable broth, low sodium

2 medium limes, juiced

1 tbsp coconut aminos

1 tbsp sugar

6-oz potato starch noodles

1/2 cup light coconut milk

Instructions:

1. Add all ingredients in Instant Pot, except for coconut milk.
2. Cover, seal, press soup button, and cook for 20 minutes.
3. Do a quick release pressure.
4. Stir in coconut milk and let it rest for 5 minutes.
5. Mix before ladling on to bowls.
6. Serve and enjoy.

Nutrition Facts Per Serving

Calories 230, Total Fat 4g, Saturated Fat 2g, Total Carbs 40g, Net Carbs 33g, Protein 10g, Sugar: 9g, Fiber 7g, Sodium 645mg, Potassium 296mg, Phosphorus 138mg

Coconut Thai Noodle Soup

Prep time: 10 minutes, cook time: 10 minutes; Serves 4

Ingredients:

2 cups vegetable stock
1 thumb-size fresh ginger, sliced
1 stalk fresh lemongrass, cut into 1-inch thick
1 cup sliced mushrooms
2 small Thai chilies, chopped
¼ cup fresh cilantro, minced
6-oz glass noodles
Pepper to taste
2 cups coconut milk
1 tablespoon fresh lime juice
¼ cup basil leaves

Instructions:

1. Add all ingredients in Instant Pot, except for coconut milk, lime juice, and basil.
2. Cover, seal, press soup button, and cook for 20 minutes.
3. Do a quick release pressure.
4. Stir in coconut milk, lime juice, and basil leaves. Let it rest for 5 minutes.
5. Mix before ladling on to bowls.
6. Serve and enjoy.

Nutrition Facts Per Serving

Calories 166, Total Fat 6g, Saturated Fat 3g, Total Carbs 21g, Net Carbs 20g, Protein 10g, Sugar: 7g, Fiber 1g, Sodium 312mg, Potassium 485mg, Phosphorus 205mg

Sweet Potato 'n Pasta Cuban Soup

Prep time: 10 minutes, cook time: 10 minutes; Serves 6

Ingredients:

1 onion, chopped
5 cloves of garlic, minced
1/2-pound sweet potatoes, peeled and diced
1 cup pasta of choice
1 red bell pepper, chopped
1 cup tomatoes
1 bay leaf
1 teaspoon ground cumin
2 teaspoons dried oregano
½ tsp pepper
½ tsp salt
4 cups water

Instructions:

1. Add all ingredients in Instant Pot.
2. Cover, seal, press manual button, and cook on high for 2 minutes.
3. Allow for a 5-minute natural release.
4. Then, cover seal with a kitchen towel to avoid splatters and do a quick release pressure.
5. Open pot and discard bay leaf.
6. Ladle into bowls, serve and enjoy.

Nutrition Facts Per Serving

Calories 81, Total Fat 1g, Saturated Fat 0g, Total Carbs 18g, Net Carbs 15g, Protein 3g, Sugar: 3g, Fiber 3g, Sodium 203mg, Potassium 309mg, Phosphorus 62mg

Vegetarian Minestrone

Prep time: 10 minutes, cook time: 6 minutes; Serves 6

Ingredients:

6 cups vegetable stock
½ tsp pepper
¼ tsp salt
1 onion, diced
3 cloves of garlic, minced
2 stalks of celery, minced
1 carrot, diced
1 zucchini, diced
1 cup roma tomatoes, diced
1 cup basil leaves
1 teaspoon dried oregano
1 teaspoon dried basil
1 bay leaf
1 cup orzo pasta
½ cup spinach, shredded

Instructions:

1. Add all ingredients in Instant Pot, except for spinach.
2. Cover, seal, press manual button, and cook on high for 2 minutes.

3. Cover seal with a kitchen towel to avoid splatters and do a quick release pressure.
4. Open pot, discard bay leaf, stir in spinach and let pot rest for 5 minutes.
5. Ladle into bowls, serve and enjoy.

Nutrition Facts Per Serving
Calories 81, Total Fat 1g, Saturated Fat 0g, Total Carbs 18g, Net Carbs 15g, Protein 3g, Sugar: 3g, Fiber 3g, Sodium 203mg, Potassium 309mg, Phosphorus 62mg

Creamy Mushroom Broccoli with Pasta Soup

Prep time: 10 minutes, cook time: 10 minutes; Serves 4
Ingredients:
1 onion, diced
3 cloves of garlic, diced
2 cups mushrooms, chopped
4 cups water
2 heads of broccoli, cut into florets
Pepper to taste
1 cup rotelle pasta
Instructions:
1. Add all ingredients in Instant Pot.
2. Cover, seal, press manual button, and cook on high for 2 minutes.
3. Meanwhile, in a separate pot cook pasta according to manufacturer's instructions minus the salt and oil. Once done, drain well and set aside.
4. Allow Instant Pot to do a 5-minute natural release.
5. Then, cover seal with a kitchen towel to avoid splatters and do a quick release pressure.
6. Open pot and puree with a handheld blender. Stir in pasta.
7. Ladle into bowls, serve and enjoy.

Nutrition Facts Per Serving
Calories 61, Total Fat 1g, Saturated Fat 0g, Total Carbs 13g, Net Carbs 11g, Protein 3g, Sugar: 2g, Fiber 2g, Sodium 8mg, Potassium 198mg, Phosphorus 67mg

Ethiopian Spinach Pasta Soup

Prep time: 10 minutes, cook time: 10 minutes; Serves 4
Ingredients:
1 onion, chopped
1 teaspoon garlic powder
2 teaspoon ground coriander
½ teaspoon cinnamon powder
½ teaspoon turmeric powder
¼ teaspoon clove powder
¼ teaspoon cayenne pepper
¼ teaspoon cardamom powder
¼ teaspoon grated nutmeg
2 cups bow tie pasta
8 cups water
½ tsp pepper to taste
½ tsp salt
2 cups spinach, chopped
Instructions:
1. Add all ingredients in Instant Pot, except for spinach.
2. Cover, seal, press manual button, and cook on high for 2 minutes.
3. Cover seal with a kitchen towel to avoid splatters and do a quick release pressure.
4. Open pot stir in spinach and let pot rest for 5 minutes.
5. Ladle into bowls, serve and enjoy.

Nutrition Facts Per Serving
Calories 122, Total Fat 1g, Saturated Fat 1g, Total Carbs 25g, Net Carbs g, Protein 3g, Sugar: 2g, Fiber 5g, Sodium 314mg, Potassium 190mg, Phosphorus 77mg

Pho Noodle Soup

Prep time: 10 minutes, cook time: 20 minutes; Serves 6
Ingredients:
6 cups vegetable stock
1 tsp ground cardamom
4 whole star anise
1 tsp whole black peppercorns
1 tsp ground coriander
1 tsp ground cinnamon

1 tbsp apple cider vinegar
2 knobs of ginger, sliced in half
2 cloves garlic, peeled
2 medium onions, sliced in half
1 tbsp fish sauce
1 tsp sugar
1 box rice noodles, cooked according to package instructions
1 bunch cilantro
1 bunch basil
1 cup bean sprouts
1 lime, cut into wedges

Instructions:
1. Add the first 12 ingredients in Instant Pot.
2. Cover, seal, press soup button, and cook for 20 minutes.
3. Do a quick release pressure.
4. Meanwhile, cook rice noodles according to package instructions, drain, and run in cold water to stop cooking process, and set aside.
5. Evenly divide rice noodles on to 6 bowls. Top with cilantro, basil, bean sprouts, and lime wedges on the side.
6. Open pot, ladle soup into prepared bowls, while piping hot.
7. Serve and enjoy.

Nutrition Facts Per Serving
Calories 62, Total Fat 3g, Saturated Fat 1g, Total Carbs 5g, Net Carbs g, Protein 7g, Sugar: 1g, Fiber 1g, Sodium 602mg, Potassium 450mg, Phosphorus 154mg

Rotini and Veggie Salad

Prep time: 10 minutes, cook time: 3 minutes; Serves 8

Ingredients:
12-oz tricolor rotini pasta
3 cups water
1 ½ cups broccoli florets
1 cup grape tomatoes, halved
1 ½ cups English cucumber, diced
1 1/3 cups Italian salad dressing
1 medium yellow bell pepper, chopped
¾ cup carrots, chopped
1 small red onion, chopped
½ cup parmesan cheese, grated

Instructions:
1. Place pasta and water in Instant Pot.
2. Cover, seal, press manual button, and cook on high for 1 minute.
3. Cover seal with a kitchen towel to avoid splatters and do a quick release pressure.
4. Add broccoli florets, cover and let it rest for 5 minutes.
5. Drain broccoli and pasta well. Transfer to bowl.
6. Mix in salad dressing and let pasta soak in the dressing for 10 minutes.
7. Add remaining ingredients and toss well to coat.
8. Serve and enjoy while warm.

Nutrition Facts Per Serving
Calories 360, Total Fat 30g, Saturated Fat 5g, Total Carbs 20g, Net Carbs 17g, Protein 4g, Sugar: 4g, Fiber 3g, Sodium 356mg, Potassium 208mg, Phosphorus 105mg

Orzo Salad Greek Style

Prep time: 10 minutes, cook time: 10 minutes; Serves 6

Ingredients:
1 1/2 cups uncooked orzo pasta
3 cups water
2 (6 ounce) cans marinated artichoke hearts
1 tomato, seeded and chopped
1 cucumber, seeded and chopped
1 red onion, chopped
1 cup crumbled feta cheese
1 (2 ounce) can black olives, drained
1/4 cup chopped fresh parsley
1 tablespoon lemon juice
1/2 teaspoon dried oregano
1/2 teaspoon lemon pepper

Instructions:
1. Place pasta and water in Instant Pot.
2. Cover, seal, press manual button, and cook on high for 1 minute.
3. Meanwhile, drain artichoke hearts and reserve the marinade for use later.

4. Cover seal with a kitchen towel to avoid splatters and do a quick release pressure.
5. Drain pasta well and transfer to bowl.
6. Add remaining ingredients and toss well to coat. Refrigerate for an hour.
7. Drizzle reserved artichoke marinade before serving.

Nutrition Facts Per Serving
Calories 326, Total Fat 10g, Saturated Fat 4g, Total Carbs 49g, Net Carbs 44g, Protein 13g, Sugar: 5g, Fiber 5g, Sodium 615mg, Potassium 233mg, Phosphorus 76mg

Noodle Salad Thai Style

Prep time: 10 minutes, cook time: 10 minutes; Serves 4
Ingredients:
4 cups water
1 (8 ounce) package dried rice noodles
1 tablespoon olive oil
1/4 head romaine lettuce, chopped
1/4 red bell pepper, diced
1/4 cup chopped red onion
3 green onions, chopped
1/4 cucumber, diced
2 tablespoons chopped fresh basil, or to taste
2 tablespoons chopped fresh cilantro, or to taste
1 (1 inch) piece fresh ginger root, minced
1/4 jalapeno pepper, seeded and minced
2 cloves garlic, minced
Sauce Ingredients:
1/3 cup olive oil
1/4 cup rice vinegar
1/4 cup soy sauce
1/4 cup white sugar
1 lemon, juiced
1 lime, juiced

1 teaspoon salt
1/4 teaspoon ground turmeric
1/4 teaspoon paprika
Instructions:
1. Add 4 cups water in Instant Pot and press sauté button and bring to a boil. Once boiling add noodles and boil for 2 to 3 minutes. Press cancel and drain noodles.
2. Transfer noodles to a bowl and remaining ingredients and toss to mix.
3. Meanwhile, mix all sauce ingredients well. Pour over noodle salad and toss well to coat.
4. Allow to marinate for at least 15 minutes before serving.

Nutrition Facts Per Serving
Calories 472, Total Fat 22g, Saturated Fat 3g, Total Carbs 65g, Net Carbs 63g, Protein 4g, Sugar: 14g, Fiber 2g, Sodium 1592mg, Potassium 226mg, Phosphorus 145mg

Warm Pasta Freda

Prep time: 15 minutes, cook time: 2 minutes; Serves 4
Ingredients:
1 (8 ounce) package farfalle (bow tie) pasta
2 cups water
2 tablespoons olive oil
6 fresh basil leaves, chopped
4 tbsp balsamic vinegar
1 1/2 teaspoons fresh oregano leaves
20 cherry tomatoes, halved
7 ounces bocconcini (small balls of fresh mozzarella cheese)
3/4 cup black olives
Instructions:
1. Place pasta and water in Instant Pot.
2. Cover, seal, press manual button, and cook on high for 1 minute.

3. Meanwhile, in a bowl whisk well olive oil, balsamic, basil and oregano. Set aside.
4. Cover seal with a kitchen towel to avoid splatters and do a quick release pressure.
5. Drain pasta well and transfer to bowl. Stir in tomatoes, bocconcini, and olives. Drizzle dressing and toss well to coat.
6. Serve and enjoy.

Nutrition Facts Per Serving
Calories 451, Total Fat 22g, Saturated Fat 9g, Total Carbs 48g, Net Carbs 44g, Protein 17.3g, Sugar: 3g, Fiber 4g, Sodium 314mg, Potassium 300mg, Phosphorus 250mg

Spicy Mac Salad

Prep time: 15 minutes, cook time: 3 minutes; Serves 2

Ingredients:
1/2 (8 ounce) package elbow macaroni
1 1/2 cups water
1/2 cup mayonnaise
1/2 tablespoon apple cider vinegar
2 teaspoons chile-garlic sauce (such as Sriracha®)
1/2 teaspoon salt
1/4 teaspoon garlic powder
1/8 teaspoon cayenne pepper
freshly ground black pepper to taste
1/3 cup diced red bell pepper
1/3 cup cubed pepper Jack cheese
1/4 cup diced jalapeno pepper, or to taste
1/4 cup sliced celery
2 tablespoons diced onion

Instructions:
1. Place pasta and water in Instant Pot.
2. Cover, seal, press manual button, and cook on high for 1 minute.
3. Meanwhile, in a bowl whisk well mayonnaise, vinegar, Sriracha, salt, garlic powder, cayenne, and black pepper. Set aside.
4. Once pot is done cooking, cover seal with a kitchen towel to avoid splatters and do a quick release pressure.
5. Drain pasta well and transfer to bowl. Stir in bell pepper, cheese, jalapeno, celery, and onion. Drizzle dressing and toss well to coat.
6. Refrigerate for at least an hour.
7. Toss salad well. Serve and enjoy.

Nutrition Facts Per Serving
Calories 642, Total Fat 32g, Saturated Fat 7g, Total Carbs 64g, Net Carbs 60g, Protein 25g, Sugar: 8g, Fiber 4g, Sodium 2158mg, Potassium 392mg, Phosphorus 615mg

Tortellini 'n Spinach Salad

Prep time: 10 minutes, cook time: 1 minute; Serves 4

Ingredients:
1 (9 ounce) package cheese-filled tortellini
1 (10 ounce) package frozen chopped spinach, thawed and drained
1/3 cup grated Parmesan cheese
2 cups cherry tomatoes, halved
1 (2 ounce) can sliced black olives
1 (8 ounce) bottle Italian-style salad dressing
Salt and pepper to taste

Instructions:
1. Place pasta and water in Instant Pot.
2. Cover, seal, press manual button, and cook on high for 1 minute.
3. Once pot is done cooking, cover seal with a kitchen towel to avoid splatters and do a quick release pressure.
4. Drain pasta and run in cold water. Drain well.
5. Transfer pasta to a bowl, add remaining ingredients, season with pepper and salt to taste, and toss well to mix.
6. Serve and enjoy.

Nutrition Facts Per Serving
Calories 377, Total Fat 23.2g, Saturated Fat 5g, Total Carbs 33g, Net Carbs 28g, Protein 13g, Sugar: 6g, Fiber 5g, Sodium 1420mg, Potassium 449mg, Phosphorus 645mg

Bow-Tie Southwest Salad

Prep time: 10 minutes, cook time: 10 minutes; Serves 6

Ingredients:

1 (12 ounce) package bow tie pasta
3 cups cold water
1/4 cup extra-virgin olive oil
1/4 cup fresh lime juice
2 tablespoons chopped fresh cilantro
2 teaspoons garlic powder
1 teaspoon ground cumin
1 teaspoon ground red chile pepper
1/4 teaspoon cayenne pepper
¼ teaspoon salt
¼ teaspoon ground black pepper
1 (9 ounce) can whole kernel corn, drained
1/2 (15 ounce) can black beans, drained
1/2 (15 ounce) can diced tomatoes and green chiles, drained
2 green onions, sliced
2 avocados - peeled, pitted, and diced

Instructions:

1. Place pasta and water in Instant Pot.
2. Cover, seal, press manual button, and cook on high for 1 minute.
3. Meanwhile, whisk olive oil, lime juice, cilantro, garlic powder, cumin, ground chile pepper, cayenne pepper, salt, and black pepper together in a large bowl. Stir corn, black beans, diced tomatoes and green chiles, and green onions into the dressing to coat.
4. Once pot is done cooking, cover seal with a kitchen towel to avoid splatters and do a quick release pressure.
5. Drain pasta well and transfer to bowl of salad. Toss well to coat.
6. Slowly fold in diced avocadoes.
7. Refrigerate for an hour.
8. Serve and enjoy.

Nutrition Facts Per Serving

Calories 475, Total Fat 21.2g, Saturated Fat 3g, Total Carbs 64g, Net Carbs 53g, Protein 13g, Sugar: 4g, Fiber 11g, Sodium 415mg, Potassium 694mg, Phosphorus 854mg

Pasta 'n Arugula Italian Salad

Prep time: 10 minutes, cook time: 1 minute; Serves 8

Ingredients:

1 (16 ounce) box penne pasta
5 cups cold water
4 tablespoons olive oil
4 tablespoons balsamic vinegar
3 tablespoons maple syrup
2 cloves garlic, grated
2 teaspoons Dijon mustard
5 tomatoes, chopped
1 (15 ounce) can artichoke hearts, well drained and quartered
1 (8 ounce) package fresh mozzarella cheese, cubed
1/2 bunch basil, chopped
4 cups arugula
sea salt and freshly ground black pepper to taste

Instructions:

1. Place pasta and water in Instant Pot.
2. Cover, seal, press manual button, and cook on high for 1 minute.
3. Once pot is done cooking, cover seal with a kitchen towel to avoid splatters and do a quick release pressure.
4. Drain pasta and run in cold water. Drain well.
5. Transfer pasta to a bowl, add remaining ingredients, season with pepper and salt to taste, and toss well to mix.
6. Serve and enjoy.

Nutrition Facts Per Serving

Calories 407, Total Fat 13g, Saturated Fat 4g, Total Carbs 58g, Net Carbs 53g, Protein 18g, Sugar: 10g, Fiber 5g, Sodium 580mg, Potassium 425mg, Phosphorus 375mg

Chapter 6 Egg and Dairy Recipes

Stewed Peppers and Tomatoes with Eggs

Prep time: 5 minutes, cook time: 4 hours and 3 minutes; Serves 4

Ingredients:

2 teaspoons olive oil
1 onion, chopped
4 cloves garlic, minced
1 28-ounce whole tomatoes
1 orange red bell pepper, seeded and chopped
8 large eggs, unbeaten
A dash of cayenne pepper
salt and pepper to taste

Instructions

1. Press the Sauté button on the Instant Pot and heat the oil. Stir in the onion and garlic until fragrant.
2. Add the tomatoes and bell pepper. Stir for 3 minutes.
3. Press the Cancel button.
4. Make 8 depressions in the mixture and slowly crack the eggs.
5. Close the lid but do not seal the vent.
6. Press the Slow Cook button and adjust the cooking time to 4 hours.
7. Once done, season with pepper and salt to taste.

Nutrition Facts Per Serving

Calories 183, Total Fat 12g, Saturated Fat 4g, Total Carbs 13g, Net Carbs 11g, Protein 8g, Sugar: 3g, Fiber: 2g, Sodium: 278mg, Potassium: 674mg, Phosphorus: 225mg

Slow Cooked Taco Scrambled Eggs

Prep time: 5 minutes, cook time: 5 hours; Serves 4

Ingredients:

2 tablespoons olive oil
1 14-ounce can black beans, rinsed
½ teaspoon cumin seeds
2 cups baby spinach leaves, chopped
8 large eggs, beaten
8 corn tortillas
salt and pepper to taste

Instructions

1. Place the oil, black beans, cumin seeds, spinach, and eggs in the Instant Pot. Give a good stir.
2. Close the lid but do not seal the vent.
3. Press the Slow Cook button and adjust the cooking time to 5 hours.
4. Give a stir halfway through the cooking time.
5. Serve the eggs in tortillas. Season with pepper and salt to taste.

Nutrition Facts Per Serving

Calories 215, Total Fat 17g, Saturated Fat 4g, Total Carbs 9g, Net Carbs 5g, Protein 9g, Sugar: 1g, Fiber: 4g, Sodium: 77mg, Potassium: 407mg, Phosphorus: 192mg

Lacto-Vegetarian Italian Baked Eggs

Prep time: 5 minutes, cook time: 4 hours; Serves 5

Ingredients:

4 large eggs, beaten
6 cherry tomatoes
salt and pepper to taste
14 small mozzarella balls
1 sprig marjoram

Instructions

1. Place the eggs and tomatoes in the Instant Pot and season with salt and pepper to taste.
2. Add the mozzarella cheese balls on top and drizzle with marjoram.
3. Close the lid but do not seal the vent.
4. Press the Slow Cook button and adjust the cooking time to 4 hours.

Nutrition Facts Per Serving

Calories 79, Total Fat 4g, Saturated Fat 1g, Total Carbs 2g, Net Carbs 1.5g, Protein 10g, Sugar: 0.9g, Fiber: 0.5g, Sodium: 175mg, Potassium: 87mg, Phosphorus: 206mg

Pickled Quail Eggs

Prep time: 5 minutes, cook time: 10 minutes; Serves 6

Ingredients:

24 quail eggs, whole
2 shallots, chopped
½ cup white wine vinegar
¼ teaspoon celery seeds
8 cloves
½ teaspoon coriander seeds
2 fresh bay leaves
salt and pepper to taste

Instructions

1. Place a trivet inside the Instant Pot and pour a cup of water.
2. Place the quail eggs on the trivet.
3. Close the lid and set the vent to the Sealing position.
4. Press the Steam button and cook for 10 minutes.
5. Meanwhile, place in a large lidded container the rest of the ingredients. This will be the pickling sauce.
6. Once the timer sets off on the Instant Pot, do quick pressure release.
7. Remove the eggs and place in cold water to stop the cooking process.
8. Once the eggs are cool, peel and place in the pickling sauce.
9. Place in the fridge and allow to pickle for 5 days before serving.

Nutrition Facts Per Serving

Calories 64, Total Fat 4g, Saturated Fat 1g, Total Carbs 1g, Net Carbs 0.7g, Protein 5g, Sugar: 0.5g, Fiber: 0.3g, Sodium: 52mg, Potassium: 76mg, Phosphorus: 86mg

Marinated Eggs

Prep time: 5 minutes, cook time: 10 minutes; Serves 6

Ingredients:

6 large eggs, whole
1 5-cm piece ginger
1 clove garlic, squashed
¼ cup soy sauce
1 tablespoons honey
salt and pepper to taste

Instructions

1. Place a trivet inside the Instant Pot and pour a cup of water.
2. Place the eggs on the trivet.
3. Close the lid and set the vent to the Sealing position.
4. Press the Steam button and cook for 10 minutes.
5. Meanwhile, place in a large lidded container the rest of the ingredients.
6. Once the timer sets off on the Instant Pot, do quick pressure release.
7. Remove the eggs and place in cold water to stop the cooking process.
8. Once the eggs are cool, peel and place in the pickling sauce.
9. Place in the fridge and allow to pickle for 5 days before serving.

Nutrition Facts Per Serving

Calories 97, Total Fat 6g, Saturated Fat 2g, Total Carbs 6g, Net Carbs 5g, Protein 4g, Sugar: 5g, Fiber:1g, Sodium: 169mg, Potassium: 251mg, Phosphorus: 80mg

Mexican Instant Pot Baked Eggs

Prep time: 5 minutes, cook time: 4 hours; Serves 5

Ingredients:

5 large free eggs, beaten
1 red chili, chopped
salt and pepper to taste
½ cup chopped fresh tomatoes
1 ripe avocado, meat scooped out
½ lime, chopped

2 sprigs coriander

Instructions

1. Beat the eggs and season with red chili. Season with salt and pepper to taste.
2. Place in the Instant Pot and close the lid. Do not seal the vent.

3. Press the Slow Cook button and adjust the cooking time to 4 hours.
4. After 4 hours, take the eggs out and top with tomatoes, avocado, lime, and coriander.

Nutrition Facts Per Serving
Calories 158, Total Fat 12g, Saturated Fat 3g, Total Carbs 5g, Net Carbs 2g, Protein 9g, Sugar: 1g, Fiber: 3g, Sodium: 94mg, Potassium: 327mg, Phosphorus: 150mg

Frittata Provencal

Prep time: 5 minutes, cook time: 10 minutes; Serves 8

Ingredients:
1 tablespoon olive oil
1 large potato, peeled and sliced
1 onion, sliced
12 large eggs, beaten
salt and pepper to taste
1 teaspoon fresh thyme, chopped
½ teaspoon paprika
½ cup chopped sun-dried tomatoes
1 log crumbled goat cheese

Instructions
1. Press the Sauté button on the Instant Pot and heat the oil. Sauté the potatoes and onions for 3 minutes. Press the Cancel button and set aside. Clean the Instant Pot.
2. To a clean Instant Pot, place trivet or steamer basket. Pour a cup of water.
3. Arrange the potato slices in a heat-proof casserole dish. Pour in eggs and season with salt and pepper.
4. Add in the thyme, paprika, and tomatoes.
5. Place the dish on the trivet. Close the lid and set the vent to the Sealing position.
6. Press the Steam button and cook for 10 minutes.
7. Do quick pressure release.
8. Top the casserole with goat cheese before serving.

Nutrition Facts Per Serving
Calories 142, Total Fat 9g, Saturated Fat 3g, Total Carbs 11g, Net Carbs 9g, Protein 6g, Sugar: 2g, Fiber: 2g, Sodium: 24mg, Potassium: 343mg, Phosphorus: 139mg

Scrambled Egg Omelet

Prep time: 5 minutes, cook time: 4 hours; Serves 4

Ingredients:
1 cup red ripe tomato
½ bunch fresh basil leaves
1 fresh chili, chopped
salt and pepper to taste
4 large eggs, beaten
¼ cup small mozzarella balls

Instructions
1. Place the tomatoes, basil, and chili. Season with salt and pepper to taste.
2. Add in the beaten eggs and place the mozzarella cheese on top.
3. Close the lid but do not seal the vent.
4. Press the Slow Cook button and adjust the cooking time to 4 hours.

Nutrition Facts Per Serving
Calories 28, Total Fat 2g, Saturated Fat 0.1g, Total Carbs 2g, Net Carbs 1.5g, Protein 2g, Sugar: 1g, Fiber: 0.5g, Sodium: 46mg, Potassium: 94mg, Phosphorus: 34mg

Traditional Baked Eggs in Instant Pot

Prep time: 5 minutes, cook time: 4 hours; Serves 4

Ingredients:
1 small stick unsalted butter
4 large eggs, beaten
salt and pepper to taste

Instructions
1. Mix the butter and eggs. Season.
2. Place in the Instant Pot and give a good stir.
3. Close the lid but do not seal the vent.
4. Press the Slow Cook button and adjust the cooking time to 4 hours.

Nutrition Facts Per Serving
Calories 334, Total Fat 36g, Saturated Fat 20g, Total Carbs 0.6g, Net Carbs 0.6g, Protein 5g, Sugar: 0.1g, Fiber: 0g, Sodium: 28mg, Potassium :58 mg, Phosphorus: 85mg

Instant Pot Yogurt

Prep time: 5 minutes, cook time: 20 hours; Serves 6

Ingredients:

½ gallon pasteurized milk

2 tablespoons yogurt culture

Instructions

1. Place the milk in the Instant Pot and close the lid. Set the vent to the Sealing position. Press the Yogurt button and press the digital readout that says "Boil."
2. Do natural pressure release.
3. Allow the milk to cool to 116^{0}F.
4. Once the milk is cool, stir in the yogurt starter and whisk until dissolved.
5. Place the milk back into the Instant Pot. Close the lid but do not seal the vent.
6. Press the Yogurt button and allow to incubate for 8 hours.
7. After 8 hours, place the yogurt in sterile containers.

Nutrition Facts Per Serving

Calories 251, Total Fat 13g, Saturated Fat 8g, Total Carbs 20g, Net Carbs 20g, Protein 13g, Sugar: 21g, Fiber: 0g, Sodium: 177mg, Potassium: 545mg, Phosphorus: 346mg

Instant Pot Egg Casserole

Prep time: 5 minutes, cook time: 4 hours 3 minutes; Serves 5

Ingredients:

8 large eggs

½ cup milk

1 cup water

salt and pepper to taste

1 teaspoon olive oil

1 cup onion, chopped

1 cup chopped bell pepper

4 ounces mild cheddar cheese

Instructions

1. In a bowl, mix the eggs, milk, water. Season with salt and pepper to taste. Set aside.
2. Press the Sauté button on the Instant Pot and heat the oil.
3. Sauté the onion and bell pepper for 3 minutes until fragrant.
4. Press the Cancel button and pour in the egg mixture.
5. Top with cheddar cheese.
6. Close the lid but do not seal the vent.
7. Press the Slow Cook button and adjust the cooking time to 4 hours.

Nutrition Facts Per Serving

Calories 163, Total Fat 11g, Saturated Fat 4g, Total Carbs 8g, Net Carbs 7.5g, Protein 9g, Sugar: 4g, Fiber: 0.5g, Sodium: 275mg, Potassium: 183mg, Phosphorus: 349mg

Instant Pot Hard-Boiled Eggs

Prep time: 3 minutes, cook time: 6 minutes; Serves 12

Ingredients:

12 eggs

1 cup water

Instructions

1. Place a trivet or steamer rack in the Instant Pot. Pour water inside.
2. Place the eggs on the trivet and close the lid. Set the vent to the Sealing position.
3. Press the Steam button and adjust the cooking time to 6 minutes.
4. Do quick pressure release.

Nutrition Facts Per Serving

Calories 130, Total Fat 10g, Saturated Fat 3g, Total Carbs 1g, Net Carbs 1g, Protein 10g, Sugar: 0.6g, Fiber: 0g, Sodium: 103mg, Potassium: 155mg, Phosphorus: 154mg

Pressure Cooker Egg Bites

Prep time:5 minutes, cook time: 10 minutes; Serves 8

Ingredients:

8 large eggs, beaten

¼ cup milk

½ cup sharp cheddar cheese

salt and pepper to taste

Green onions for garnish

Instructions

1. Place a trivet inside the Instant Pot and pour water.
2. In a bowl, mix the eggs, milk, and cheddar cheese. Season with salt and pepper to taste.
3. Pour into round silicone molds that will fit in the Instant Pot.
4. Close the lid and set the vent to the sealing position.
5. Press the Steam button and adjust the cooking time to 10 minutes.
6. Do quick pressure release.
7. Once cooked, garnish with green onions.

Nutrition Facts Per Serving
Calories 72, Total Fat 5g, Saturated Fat 2g, Total Carbs 1g, Net Carbs 0g, Protein 6g, Sugar: 0.3g, Fiber: 0g, Sodium: 115mg, Potassium: 542mg, Phosphorus: 102mg

Broccoli Frittata

Prep time: 5 minutes, cook time: 4 hours; Serves 5
Ingredients:
4 eggs, beaten
1 cup half-and-half
salt and pepper to taste
2 cups frozen broccoli
1 cup sweet peppers, sliced
1 cup shredded cheddar cheese
Instructions
1. In a bowl, beat together the eggs and half-and-half. Season with salt and pepper to taste.
2. Place the broccoli and sweet peppers in the Instant Pot.
3. Pour the egg mixture.
4. Top with cheddar cheese.
5. Close the lid but do not seal the vent.
6. Press the Slow Cook button and adjust the cooking time to 4 hours.

Nutrition Facts Per Serving
Calories 183, Total Fat 10g, Saturated Fat 3g, Total Carbs 11g, Net Carbs 9g, Protein 13g, Sugar: 6g, Fiber: 2g, Sodium: 331mg, Potassium: 343mg, Phosphorus: 388mg

Quick and Easy Instant Pot Egg Frittata

Prep time: 5 minutes, cook time: 10 minutes; Serves 6
Ingredients:
1 cup water
6 eggs, beaten
1 small onion, chopped
1 green pepper, chopped
salt and pepper to taste
½ cup cheddar cheese
Instructions
1. Pour water in the Instant Pot and place trivet or steamer basket on top.
2. In a bowl, beat the eggs, onion, and pepper. Season with salt and pepper to taste.
3. Place in a heat-proof dish that will fit in the Instant Pot.
4. Place the dish with the egg mixture in the Instant Pot.
5. Close the lid and set the vent to the Sealing position.
6. Press the Steam button and adjust the cooking time to 10 minutes.
7. Do natural pressure release.

Nutrition Facts Per Serving
Calories 182, Total Fat 13g, Saturated Fat 5g, Total Carbs 3g, Net Carbs 2.7g, Protein 12g, Sugar: 2g, Fiber: 0.3g, Sodium: 174mg, Potassium: 206mg, Phosphorus: 213mg

Instant Pot Cauliflower and Cheddar Frittata

Prep time: 5 minutes, cook time: 10 minutes; Serves 5
Ingredients:
1 cup water 2 cups cauliflower
1 cup diced red bell pepper
½ cup grated sharp cheddar cheese
6 eggs, beaten
¼ cup half and half
A pinch of red pepper flakes
salt and pepper to taste
Instructions
1. Place trivet or steamer basket in the Instant Pot and pour water.

2. In a mixing bowl, combine all ingredients until well incorporated.
3. Pour in a silicon dish that will fit inside the Instant Pot.
4. Place on the trivet.
5. Close the lid and set the vent to the Sealing position.

6. Press the Steam button and cook for 10 minutes.
7. Do natural pressure release.

Nutrition Facts Per Serving
Calories 249, Total Fat 17g, Saturated Fat 8g, Total Carbs 7g, Net Carbs g, Protein 17g, Sugar: 3g, Fiber: 2g, Sodium: 332mg, Potassium: 324mg, Phosphorus: 202mg

Spinach Frittata

Prep time: 5 minutes, cook time: 10 minutes; Serves 6
Ingredients:
1 cup water
6 eggs, beaten
2 tomatoes, peeled and chopped
½ onion, chopped
1 cup fresh spinach, chopped
salt and pepper to taste
Instructions
1. Place trivet or steamer basket in the Instant Pot and pour water.
2. In a mixing bowl, combine all ingredients until well incorporated.
3. Pour in a silicon dish that will fit inside the Instant Pot.

4. Place on the trivet.
5. Close the lid and set the vent to the Sealing position.
6. Press the Steam button and cook for 10 minutes.
7. Do natural pressure release

Nutrition Facts Per Serving
Calories 140, Total Fat 10g, Saturated Fat 3g, Total Carbs 3g, Net Carbs 2.4g, Protein 10g, Sugar: 1g, Fiber: 0.6g, Sodium: 122mg, Potassium: 275mg, Phosphorus: 170mg

Overnight Caprese Frittata

Prep time: 5 minutes, cook time: 4 hours minutes; Serves 4
Ingredients:
1 teaspoon olive oil
8 eggs, beaten
1/3 cup heavy whipping cream
salt and pepper to taste
1 cup grape tomatoes, halved
½ cup fresh basil
4 ounces mini mozzarella balls
Grated parmesan cheese for garnish
Instructions
1. Grease the inside of the inner pot with oil.
2. In a bowl, mix the eggs and heavy cream until well incorporated. Season with salt and pepper to taste.

3. Place the tomatoes and basil in the Instant Pot. Pour the egg mixture over.
4. Place the mozzarella balls on top.
5. Close the lid but do not seal the vent.
6. Press the Slow Cook button and adjust the cooking time to 4 hours.
7. Once the eggs are cooked, brush with parmesan cheese.

Nutrition Facts Per Serving
Calories 322, Total Fat 26g, Saturated Fat 11g, Total Carbs 4g, Net Carbs 3.5g, Protein 19g, Sugar: 2g, Fiber: 0.5g, Sodium: 464mg, Potassium: 738mg, Phosphorus: 102mg

Instant Pot One-Pot Mac and Cheese

Prep time: 5 minutes, cook time: 20 minutes; Serves 5
Ingredients:
1-pound elbow macaroni
1 14-ounce can evaporate milk
3 tablespoons unsalted butter
1 ½ cups vegetable broth

3 cups shredded cheddar cheese
salt and pepper to taste
Instructions
1. Put all ingredients in the Instant Pot.

2. Give a good stir to mix everything.
3. Close the lid and set the vent to the Sealing position.
4. Press the Multigrain button and cook on high for 20 minutes.
5. Do natural pressure release.

Nutrition Facts Per Serving
Calories 752, Total Fat 35g, Saturated Fat 20g, Total Carbs 73g, Net Carbs 70g, Protein 34g, Sugar: 8g, Fiber: 3g, Sodium: 718mg, Potassium: 373mg, Phosphorus: 616mg

Instant Pot Soft-Boiled Eggs

Prep time: 2 minutes, cook time: 3 minutes; Serves 4
Ingredients:
4 large eggs
1 cup water
Instructions
1. Place a trivet or steamer basket inside the Instant Pot and pour water over.
2. Place the eggs on top of the trivet.
3. Close the lid and set the vent to the Sealing position
4. Press the Manual button and adjust the cooking time to 3 minutes.
5. Do quick pressure release.
6. Place the eggs in cold water to stop the cooking process.

Nutrition Facts Per Serving
Calories 55, Total Fat 5g, Saturated Fat 2g, Total Carbs 0.6g, Net Carbs 0.6g, Protein 3g, Sugar: 0.1g, Fiber: 0g, Sodium: 8mg, Potassium: 19mg, Phosphorus: 66mg

Instant Pot Broccoli Cheese Soup

Prep time: 5 minutes, cook time: 16 minutes; Serves 6
Ingredients:
2 tablespoons butter
4 cloves garlic, minced
1 onion, chopped
1 ½ cups carrots, chopped
4 cups broccoli florets
1 teaspoon ground nutmeg
3 cups vegetable broth
1 ½ cups shredded cheddar cheese
2 cups heavy cream
salt and pepper to taste
Instructions
1. Press the Sauté button on the Instant Pot and heat the butter. Sauté the garlic and onion until fragrant.
2. Stir in the carrots and broccoli florets. Season with nutmeg and season with salt and pepper to taste.
3. Stir in the broth and adjust the seasoning.
4. Close the lid and set the vent to the Sealing position.
5. Press the Pressure Cook or Manual button and adjust the cooking time to 10 minutes.
6. Do quick pressure release to open the lid.
7. Once the lid is open, press the Sauté button and stir in the cheddar cheese and cream.
8. Allow to simmer for 5 minutes.

Nutrition Facts Per Serving
Calories 335, Total Fat 30g, Saturated Fat 19g, Total Carbs 8g, Net Carbs 6g, Protein 10g, Sugar: 3g, Fiber: 2g, Sodium:287 mg, Potassium: 233mg, Phosphorus: 220mg

Instant Pot Cheese Egg Bake

Prep time: 5 minutes, cook time: 10 minutes; Serves 4
Ingredients:
6 eggs, beaten
salt and pepper to taste
8 ounces broccoli florets, chopped
2 ounces cheddar cheese, shredded
2 green onions, chopped
Instructions
1. Place a trivet in the Instant Pot and pour water.

2. In a bowl, beat the eggs and season with salt and pepper to taste.
3. Place the broccoli in a heat-proof dish. Pour the egg mixture on top. Sprinkle half of the cheddar cheese on top.
4. Place the dish with the egg mixture on the trivet.
5. Close the lid and set the vent to the Sealing position.
6. Press the Steam button and cook for 10 minutes.
7. Do quick pressure release.
8. Once the lid is open, garnish with green onions and cheddar cheese on top.

Nutrition Facts Per Serving
Calories 195, Total Fat 12g, Saturated Fat 5g, Total Carbs 5g, Net Carbs 4g, Protein 14g, Sugar: 14g, Fiber: 1g, Sodium: 491mg, Potassium: 312mg, Phosphorus:167 mg

One-Pot Spanish Omelet

Prep time: 5 minutes, cook time: 4 hours; Serves 5
Ingredients:
1 tablespoon oil
large eggs
salt and pepper to taste
¼ cup chopped red onion
½ cup Mexican cheese blend, divided
2 tablespoon cilantros, chopped
Instructions
1. In a mixing bowl, mix together the oil, eggs, red onion, salt and pepper to taste and cheese blend.
2. Pour the egg mixture into the Instant Pot.
3. Close the lid but do not seal the vent.
4. Press the Slow Cook button on the Instant Pot.
5. Adjust the cooking time to 4 hours.
6. Once the eggs are cooked, garnish with cilantro.

Nutrition Facts Per Serving
Calories 77, Total Fat 7g, Saturated Fat 3g, Total Carbs 1g, Net Carbs 0.9g, Protein 3g, Sugar: 0.4g, Fiber: 0.1g, Sodium: 40mg, Potassium: 24mg, Phosphorus: 64mg

Spinach and Mushroom Omelet

Prep time:5 minutes, cook time: 4 hours; Serves 5
Ingredients:
4 large eggs
1 teaspoon butter, melted
½ cup thinly sliced fresh mushrooms, chopped
½ cup baby spinach, chopped
2 tablespoons shredded provolone cheese
salt and pepper to taste
Instructions
1. Combine all ingredients in a mixing bowl. Stir to combine everything.
2. Pour the egg mixture into the Instant Pot.
3. Close the lid but do not seal the vent.
4. Press the Slow Cook button on the Instant Pot.
5. Adjust the cooking time to 4 hours.

Nutrition Facts Per Serving
Calories 74, Total Fat 6g, Saturated Fat 3g, Total Carbs 2g, Net Carbs 1.5g, Protein 4g, Sugar: 0.8g, Fiber: 0.5g, Sodium: 124mg, Potassium: 106mg, Phosphorus: 120mg

Eggs in Cups

Prep time: 5 minutes, cook time: 15 minutes; Serves 4
Ingredients:
4 eggs
1 cup chopped frozen vegetables of your choice
½ cup cheddar cheese
¼ cup half and half
Salt and pepper to taste
Instructions
1. Place a trivet or steamer basket inside the Instant Pot and pour water over.
2. In a mixing bowl, mix all ingredients until well combined.
3. Pour over greased ramekins until ¾ full.
4. Place aluminum foil over ramekins.

5. Place on the trivet.
6. Close the lid and set the vent to the Sealing position.
7. Press the Steam button and cook for 15 minutes.
8. Do natural pressure release.

Nutrition Facts Per Serving
Calories 205, Total Fat 15g, Saturated Fat 6g, Total Carbs 3g, Net Carbs 3g, Protein 13g, Sugar: 1g, Fiber: 0g, Sodium: 223mg, Potassium: 198mg, Phosphorus: 254mg

Egg Muffins in Instant Pot

Prep time: 5 minutes, cook time: 10 minutes; Serves 4

Ingredients:
4 eggs
¼ teaspoon lemon pepper seasoning
4 tablespoons cheddar cheese, grated
1 green onion, diced
4 slices pre-cooked bacon, crumbled
salt and pepper to taste

Instructions
1. Place a trivet or steamer basket inside the Instant Pot and pour water over.
2. In a mixing bowl, mix all ingredients until well combined.
3. Pour over greased individual muffin cups until ¾ full.
4. Place aluminum foil over the muffin cups.
5. Place on the steamer basket.
6. Close the lid and set the vent to the Sealing position.
7. Press the Steam button and steam for 10 minutes.
8. Do natural pressure release.

Nutrition Facts Per Serving
Calories 256, Total Fat 22g, Saturated Fat 4g, Total Carbs 1g, Net Carbs 1g, Protein 13g, Sugar: 0.8g, Fiber: 0g, Sodium: 257mg, Potassium: 291mg, Phosphorus: 224mg

Egg Salad

Prep time: 5 minutes, cook time: 10 minutes; Serves 12

Ingredients:
12 eggs
½ cup mayonnaise
Salt and pepper to taste

Instructions
1. Place a trivet or steamer basket inside the Instant Pot and pour water over.
2. In a mixing bowl, mix all ingredients until well combined.
3. Grease a baking dish that will fit inside the Instant Pot.
4. Crack eggs into the baking dish. Place aluminum foil over the top of the baking dish.
5. Close the lid and press the Pressure Cook or Manual button.
6. Adjust the cooking time to 10 minutes.
7. Do natural pressure release.
8. Mash the eggs with a fork and add in the mayonnaise. Season with salt and pepper to taste.

Nutrition Facts Per Serving
Calories 162, Total Fat 13g, Saturated Fat 3g, Total Carbs 1g, Net Carbs 0.9g, Protein 10g, Sugar: 0.7g, Fiber: 0.1g, Sodium: 180mg, Potassium: 162mg, Phosphorus: 159mg

Sous Vide Eggs

Prep time: 5 minutes, cook time: 15 minutes; Serves 4

Ingredients:
4 large eggs, lightly beaten
4 cooked bacon strips, crumbled
1 ½ cups cheddar cheese, grated
½ cup cottage cheese
¼ cup heavy cream
A dash of hot sauce

Salt and pepper to taste

Instructions
1. Place a trivet or steamer basket inside the Instant Pot and pour water over.
2. Place bacon in small ramekins.

3. Place in the blender the eggs, cheese, cottage cheese, and cream. Season with salt and pepper to taste. Pulse until well-combined.
4. Pour into the ramekins until ¾ full. Cover with aluminum foil.
5. Close the lid and set the vent to the Sealing position.
6. Press the Steam button.
7. Adjust the cooking time to 15 minutes.
8. Do quick pressure release.
9. Drizzle with a dash of hot sauce.

Nutrition Facts Per Serving
Calories 323, Total Fat 27g, Saturated Fat 14g, Total Carbs 3g, Net Carbs 2.9g, Protein 18g, Sugar: 1g, Fiber: 0.1g, Sodium: 499mg, Potassium: 98mg, Phosphorus: 350mg

Egg Custard

Prep time: 15 minutes, cook time: 10 minutes; Serves 6
Ingredients:
4 cups of milk
6 large eggs, beaten
1 teaspoon vanilla extract
¼ teaspoon ground cinnamon
A pinch of salt
¾ cup white sugar
Instructions
1. Place a trivet or steamer basket inside the Instant Pot and pour water over.
2. In a mixing bowl, combine all ingredients. Whisk until well-combined.
3. Place the egg mixture into a baking dish that will fit inside the Instant Pot. Cover with aluminum foil.
4. Place the baking dish with the egg mixture on the steamer basket.
5. Close the lid and set the vent to the Sealing position.
6. Press the Steam button and cook for 10 minutes.
7. Do natural pressure release.

Nutrition Facts Per Serving
Calories 156, Total Fat 10g, Saturated Fat 5g, Total Carbs 9g, Net Carbs 8.9g, Protein 8g, Sugar: 8g, Fiber: 0.1g, Sodium: 78mg, Potassium: 235mg, Phosphorus: 203mg

Eggs in Marinara Sauce

Prep time: 5 minutes, cook time: 10 minutes; Serves 6
Ingredients:
1 tablespoon coconut oil
2 cloves of garlic, minced
½ onion, diced
1 red bell pepper, diced
1 teaspoon chili powder
½ teaspoon paprika
½ teaspoon ground cumin
Salt and pepper to taste
1 ½ cups commercial marinara sauce
6 eggs
Parsley leaves for garnish
Instructions
1. Press the Sauté button on the Instant Pot.
2. Sauté the garlic and onions until fragrant.
3. Add the bell pepper, chili powder, paprika, and cumin. Season with salt and pepper to taste.
4. Continue stirring for 3 minutes.
5. Pour in the marinara sauce.
6. Gently crack the eggs into the marinara sauce.
7. Close the lid and set the vent to the Sealing position.
8. Press the Steam button and cook for 10 minutes.
9. Do natural pressure release.
10. Once the lid is opened, garnish with parsley

Nutrition Facts Per Serving
Calories 179, Total Fat 12g, Saturated Fat 5g, Total Carbs 8g, Net Carbs 6g, Protein 10g, Sugar: 4g, Fiber: 2g, Sodium: 575mg, Potassium: 399mg, Phosphorus: 186mg

Slow Cooked Curried Scrambled Eggs

Prep time: 5 minutes, cook time: 4 hours; Serves 4

Ingredients:

6 eggs
¼ cup milk
salt and pepper to taste
1 tablespoon cooking oil
1 tablespoon ghee
1 large onion, chopped
2 cloves of garlic, minced
1 tomato, chopped
1 jalapeno pepper, chopped
½ inch ginger, grated
3 scallions, chopped
¼ teaspoon ground turmeric
1 teaspoon garam masala

Instructions

1. In a mixing bowl, combine the eggs and milk. Season and set aside.
2. Press the Sauté button on the Instant Pot.
3. Heat the oil and ghee.
4. Sauté the onion and garlic until fragrant.
5. Add in the tomatoes, pepper, ginger, scallions, turmeric and garam masala. Continue stirring for 3 minutes.
6. Add in the egg mixture and give a good stir.
7. Close the lid but do not seal the vent.
8. Press the Slow Cook button and adjust the cooking time to 4 hours.
9. Once the lid is open, fluff the eggs using two forks.

Nutrition Facts Per Serving

Calories 262, Total Fat 19g, Saturated Fat 5g, Total Carbs 9g, Net Carbs 7g, Protein 15g, Sugar: 5g, Fiber: 2g, Sodium: 165mg, Potassium: 431mg, Phosphorus: 270mg

Asian Scrambled Egg

Prep time: 5 minutes, cook time: 10 minutes; Serves 2

Ingredients:

4 large eggs, beaten
1 tablespoon light soy sauce
½ teaspoon oyster sauce
2 tomatoes, sliced
1 tablespoon oil
½ cup vegetable stock
salt and pepper to taste

Instructions

1. In a mixing bowl, mix all ingredients until well combined.
2. Pour over the Instant Pot.
3. Close the lid and press the Pressure Cook or Manual button.
4. Adjust the cooking time to 10 minutes.
5. Do natural pressure release.
6. Once the lid is open, fluff the eggs using a fork.

Nutrition Facts Per Serving

Calories 196, Total Fat 17g, Saturated Fat 5g, Total Carbs 4g, Net Carbs 3.7g, Protein 6g, Sugar: 2g, Fiber: 0.3g, Sodium: 178mg, Potassium: 95mg, Phosphorus: 146mg

Poblano Cheese Frittata

Prep time: 5 minutes, cook time: 10 minutes; Serves 4

Ingredients:

4 eggs
1 cup half and half
½ teaspoon salt
½ teaspoon cumin
10 ounces canned green chilies, chopped
1 cup Mexican cheese blend, grated
½ cup cilantro, chopped

Instructions

1. Place a trivet or steamer basket inside the Instant Pot and pour water over.
2. In a mixing bowl, combine the eggs and half-and-half. Season with salt and cumin. Whisk until well-combined.
3. Place the egg mixture into a baking dish that will fit inside the Instant Pot.
4. Add in the chilies and top with Mexican cheese blend.
5. Cover the baking dish with aluminum foil.
6. Place the baking dish with the egg mixture on the steamer basket.

7. Close the lid and set the vent to the Sealing position.
8. Press the Manual button and adjust the cooking time to 10 minutes.
9. Do natural pressure release.
10. Garnish with chopped cilantro.

Nutrition Facts Per Serving
Calories 305, Total Fat 21g, Saturated Fat 8g, Total Carbs 14g, Net Carbs 9g, Protein 19g, Sugar: 5g, Fiber: 5g, Sodium: 663mg, Potassium: 590mg, Phosphorus: 409mg

Herbed Quiche

Prep time: 5 minutes, cook time: 15 minutes; Serves 8
Ingredients:
4 eggs
1 cup milk
1/3 cup flour
¼ teaspoon baking soda
½ teaspoon salt
½ teaspoon thyme
1 tablespoon parsley
1/8 teaspoon paprika
A dash of crushed red pepper
½ teaspoon dill
Salt and pepper to taste
1 cup spinach, chopped
2 scallions, chopped
½ cup broccoli, chopped
½ red bell pepper, chopped
½ cup goat cheese, cubed
Instructions
1. Place a trivet or steamer basket inside the Instant Pot and pour water over.
2. In a mixing bowl, combine the eggs, milk, flour, baking soda, salt, thyme, parsley, paprika, crushed red pepper, and dill. Season with salt and pepper to taste.
3. Place the egg mixture into a baking dish that will fit inside the Instant Pot.
4. Stir in the spinach, scallions, broccoli, red bell pepper, and goat cheese.
5. Cover the baking dish with aluminum foil.
6. Place the baking dish with the egg mixture on the steamer basket.
7. Close the lid and set the vent to the Sealing position.
8. Press the Steam button and adjust the cooking time to 15 minutes.
9. Do natural pressure release.

Nutrition Facts Per Serving
Calories 111, Total Fat 6g, Saturated Fat 2g, Total Carbs 8g, Net Carbs 7g, Protein 7g, Sugar: 3g, Fiber: 1g, Sodium: 111mg, Potassium: 213mg, Phosphorus: 121mg

Asparagus and Chive Frittata

Prep time: 5 minutes, cook time: 10 minutes; Serves 6
Ingredients:
6 large eggs
½ cup milk
¼ teaspoon salt
A pinch of black pepper
1 cup cheddar cheese, grated
2 tablespoons chives, chopped
1 cup asparagus heads, trimmed
Instructions
1. Place a trivet or steamer basket inside the Instant Pot and pour water over.
2. In a mixing bowl, combine the eggs and milk. Season with salt and pepper.
3. Place the egg mixture into a baking dish that will fit inside the Instant Pot.
4. Stir in the cheddar cheese, chives, and asparagus heads.
5. Cover the baking dish with aluminum foil.
6. Place the baking dish with the egg mixture on the steamer basket.
7. Close the lid and set the vent to the Sealing position.
8. Press the Steam button and adjust the cooking time to 10 minutes.
9. Do natural pressure release.

Nutrition Facts Per Serving
Calories 161, Total Fat 13g, Saturated Fat 6g, Total Carbs 3g, Net Carbs 2.5g, Protein 9g, Sugar: 2g, Fiber: 0.5g, Sodium: 159mg, Potassium: 110mg, Phosphorus: 200mg

Biscuit Egg Bake

Prep time: 5 minutes, cook time: 15 minutes; Serves 5

Ingredients:

3 buttermilk biscuits

6 eggs

½ cup milk

2 tablespoons chives

½ cup salsa

1 tablespoon green chilies, chopped

¼ teaspoon garlic powder

¼ teaspoon dried oregano

Salt and pepper to taste

1 cup cheddar cheese, grated

Instructions

1. Place a trivet or steamer basket inside the Instant Pot and pour water over.
2. Line a baking dish that will fit inside the Instant Pot with buttermilk biscuits. Set aside.
3. In a mixing bowl, combine the eggs, milk, chives, salsa, green chilies, garlic powder, and dried oregano. Season with salt and pepper to taste.
4. Place the egg mixture into a baking dish that will fit inside the Instant Pot.
5. Sprinkle with grated cheese on top.
6. Cover the baking dish with aluminum foil.
7. Place the baking dish with the egg mixture on the steamer basket.
8. Close the lid and set the vent to the Sealing position.
9. Press the Steam button and adjust the cooking time to 15 minutes.
10. Do natural pressure release.

Nutrition Facts Per Serving

Calories 283, Total Fat 16g, Saturated Fat 5g, Total Carbs 20g, Net Carbs 18g, Protein 14g, Sugar: 6g, Fiber: 2g, Sodium: 669mg, Potassium: 377mg, Phosphorus: 357mg

Instant Pot Poached Egg

Prep time: 5 minutes, cook time: 5 minutes; Serves 5

Ingredients:

5 eggs

1 cup water

Instructions

1. Place a trivet or steamer basket inside the Instant Pot and pour water over.
2. Spray 5 silicone cups with cooking spray.
3. Crack each egg into each greased cup.
4. Place the silicone cups with eggs on the steamer.
5. Close the lid and set the vent to the Sealing position.
6. Press the Steam button and adjust the cooking time to 5 minutes.
7. Do quick pressure release.

Nutrition Facts Per Serving

Calories 130, Total Fat 10g, Saturated Fat 3g, Total Carbs 1g, Net Carbs 1g, Protein 9g, Sugar: 0.7g, Fiber: 0g, Sodium: 102mg, Potassium: 155mg, Phosphorus: 154mg

Deviled Eggs

Prep time: 10 minutes, cook time: 12 minutes; Serves 16

Ingredients:

8 large eggs

1 cup cold water

2 tablespoons full-fat mayonnaise

1 tablespoon olive oil

1 teaspoon Dijon mustard

1 teaspoon white vinegar

¼ teaspoon sriracha

Salt and pepper to taste

Instructions

1. Place a trivet or steamer basket inside the Instant Pot and pour water the water inside.
2. Place the eggs on the steamer basket.
3. Close the lid and set the vent to the Sealing position.
4. Press the Steam button. Set the pressure to Low and adjust the cooking time to 12 minutes.
5. Do quick pressure release.

6. Once the eggs are out, submerge in cold water for 5 minutes.
7. Crack open the eggshells.
8. Slice the eggs lengthwise and remove the yolks.
9. Place the yolks in a bowl and add in the rest of the ingredients.
10. Place the yolk mixture into piping bags and pipe carefully back into the depression within the egg whites.

Nutrition Facts Per Serving
Calories 42, Total Fat 4g, Saturated Fat 1g, Total Carbs 0.3g, Net Carbs 0.3g, Protein 2g, Sugar: 0.05g, Fiber: 0g, Sodium: 23mg, Potassium: 11mg, Phosphorus: 34mg

Orzo Soup with Eggs

Prep time: 5 minutes, cook time: 18 minutes; Serves 5

Ingredients:
6 cups vegetable broth
¾ cup uncooked orzo or small pasta
3 eggs
Juice from 2 lemons, freshly squeezed
salt and pepper to taste

Instructions
1. Place the broth and orzo into the Instant Pot.
2. Close the lid and set the vent to the Sealing position.
3. Press the Manual button.
4. Adjust the cooking time to 15 minutes.
5. Do quick pressure release.
6. Once the lid is removed, press the Sauté button and stir in the eggs and lemon juice.
7. Stir lightly and allow to simmer for 3 minutes.

Nutrition Facts Per Serving
Calories 108, Total Fat 6g, Saturated Fat 2g, Total Carbs 8g, Net Carbs 6g, Protein 6g, Sugar: 0.9g, Fiber: 1g, Sodium: 62mg, Potassium: 120mg, Phosphorus: 110mg

Hard Boiled Egg Loaf

Prep time: 5 minutes, cook time: 6 minutes; Serves 6

Ingredients:
6 eggs
salt and pepper to taste

Instructions
1. Grease the loaf pan that will fit inside the Instant pot.
2. Crack the eggs carefully into the greased pot.
3. Place a trivet or steamer basket inside the Instant Pot and pour water the water inside.
4. Place the loaf pan with the eggs on top of the steamer.
5. Close the lid and set the vent to the Sealing position.
6. Press the Steam button.
7. Adjust the cooking time to 6 minutes.
8. Do quick pressure release.

Nutrition Facts Per Serving
Calories 130, Total Fat 10g, Saturated Fat 3g, Total Carbs 1g, Net Carbs 1g, Protein 9g, Sugar: 0.7g, Fiber: 0g, Sodium: 102mg, Potassium: 155mg, Phosphorus: 154mg

Easy Shakshuka

Prep time: 5 minutes, cook time: 15 minutes; Serves 4

Ingredients:
1 onion, sliced
1 ½ cups sweet bell pepper, pureed
2 cans diced tomatoes
2 tablespoons red pepper flakes
4 eggs
½ cup flat-leaf parsley
Salt and pepper to taste

Instructions
1. Place the onions, sweet bell pepper puree, diced tomatoes, and red pepper flakes in the Instant Pot.
2. Season with salt and pepper to taste. Give a stir to combine everything.
3. Carefully crack the eggs inside the Instant Pot.
4. Sprinkle with half of the parsley.

5. Close the lid and set the vent to the Sealing position.
6. Press the Manual button and adjust the cooking time to 15 minutes.
7. Do natural pressure release.
8. Sprinkle with the remaining parsley.

Nutrition Facts Per Serving
Calories 177, Total Fat 12g, Saturated Fat 3g, Total Carbs 7g, Net Carbs 5g, Protein 12g, Sugar: 4g, Fiber: 2g, Sodium: 245mg, Potassium: 470mg, Phosphorus: 196mg

Pepperoni and Potato Frittata

Prep time: 10 minutes, cook time: 20 minutes; Serves 12

Ingredients:
3 medium-sized potatoes, unpeeled and sliced
1 onion, sliced
10 eggs
¼ cup milk
1 ½ tablespoons fresh thyme leaves
½ cup cheddar cheese
Salt and pepper to taste

Instructions
1. Place a trivet or steamer basket inside the Instant Pot and pour water.
2. Grease a baking dish that will fit in the Instant Pot.
3. Arrange the potatoes at the bottom of the baking dish. Add in the onions.
4. In a mixing bowl, combine the eggs and milk. Season with salt and pepper to taste. Add in the thyme.
5. Pour the egg mixture into the baking dish with the potatoes and salami.
6. Cover the baking dish with aluminum foil.
7. Place the baking dish with the egg mixture on the steamer basket.
8. Close the lid and set the vent to the Sealing position.
9. Press the Steam button and adjust the cooking time to 20 minutes.
10. Do natural pressure release.

Nutrition Facts Per Serving
Calories 205, Total Fat 10g, Saturated Fat 3g, Total Carbs 17g, Net Carbs 15g, Protein 11g, Sugar: 2g, Fiber: 2g, Sodium: 128mg, Potassium: 532mg, Phosphorus: 212mg

Eggs with Zucchini

Prep time: 5 minutes, cook time: 16 minutes; Serves 8

Ingredients:
8 eggs
½ cups milk
3 tablespoons butter, melted
2 cloves of garlic, minced
1 onion, chopped
2 zucchinis, sliced
1 tablespoon fresh oregano
1 ½ cups cheddar cheese, grated
Salt and pepper to taste

Instructions
1. In a mixing bowl, mix together the eggs and milk. Set aside.
2. Press the Sauté button on the Instant Pot. Heat the butter.
3. Sauté the garlic and onions until fragrant.
4. Add in the zucchini slices and oregano. Season with salt and pepper to taste.
5. Pour in the egg mixture.
6. Sprinkle with cheese on top.
7. Close the lid and set the vent to the Sealing position.
8. Press the Pressure Cook or Manual button and adjust the cooking time to 15 minutes.
9. Do natural pressure release.

Nutrition Facts Per Serving
Calories 285, Total Fat 23g, Saturated Fat 10g, Total Carbs 4g, Net Carbs 3.7g, Protein 16g, Sugar: 2g, Fiber: 0.3g, Sodium: 303mg, Potassium: 231mg, Phosphorus: 293mg

Dukkha Baked Eggs with Silverbeets

Prep time: 10 minutes, cook time: 10 minutes; Serves 4

Ingredients:

1 tablespoon olive oil
1 onion, chopped
2 cloves of garlic, chopped
1 can diced tomatoes
1 cup red bell pepper, chopped
1 bunch silverbeet, leaves chopped
4 eggs
1 cup feta cheese, crumbled
¼ cup mint leaves chopped
2 tablespoon lemon juice
salt and pepper to taste

Instructions

1. Press the Sauté button on the Instant Pot.
2. Heat the oil and sauté the onion and garlic until fragrant.
3. Stir in the tomatoes, red bell peppers, and silverbeet leaves.
4. Continue stirring until the silverbeet leaves have wilted.
5. Make 4 depressions in the mixture and, to each, crack open an egg.
6. Sprinkle with feta cheese and mint leaves on top.
7. Close the lid and set the vent to the Sealing position.
8. Press the Manual button.
9. Adjust the cooking time to 10 minutes.
10. Do natural pressure release.
11. Drizzle with lemon juice on top before serving.

Nutrition Facts Per Serving

Calories 288, Total Fat 21g, Saturated Fat 9g, Total Carbs 9g, Net Carbs 7g, Protein 15g, Sugar: 6g, Fiber: 2g, Sodium: 503mg, Potassium: 372mg, Phosphorus: 305mg

Chives and Egg Casserole

Prep time: 5 minutes, cook time: 15 minutes; Serves 8

Ingredients:

½ cups chives, chopped
8 eggs
½ cups milk
Salt and pepper to taste

Instructions

1. Place a trivet or steamer basket inside the Instant Pot and pour water over.
2. Grease a baking dish that will fit in the Instant Pot.
3. In a mixing bowl, combine all ingredients.
4. Pour the egg mixture into the baking dish.
5. Cover the baking dish with aluminum foil.
6. Place the baking dish with the egg mixture on the steamer basket.
7. Close the lid and set the vent to the Sealing position.
8. Press the Steam button and adjust the cooking time to 15 minutes.
9. Do natural pressure release.

Nutrition Facts Per Serving

Calories 139, Total Fat 10g, Saturated Fat 3g, Total Carbs 2g, Net Carbs 1.9g, Protein 10g, Sugar: 1g, Fiber: 0.1g, Sodium: 109mg, Potassium: 181mg, Phosphorus: 168mg

Parmesan and Spinach Eggs

Prep time: 5 minutes, cook time: 15 minutes; Serves 4

Ingredients:

1 cup spinach
½ cup parmesan
4 eggs
Salt and pepper to taste

Instructions

1. Place a trivet or steamer basket inside the Instant Pot and pour water over.
2. Grease a baking dish that will fit in the Instant Pot.
3. In a mixing bowl, combine all ingredients except for the French stick bread.
4. Pour the egg mixture into the baking dish.
5. Cover the baking dish with aluminum foil.
6. Place the baking dish with the egg mixture on the steamer basket.

7. Close the lid and set the vent to the Sealing position.
8. Press the Steam button and adjust the cooking time to 15 minutes.
9. Do natural pressure release.
10. Serve with the bread.

Nutrition Facts Per Serving
Calories 168, Total Fat 10g, Saturated Fat 3g, Total Carbs 5g, Net Carbs 4.9g, Protein 13g, Sugar: 0.8g, Fiber: 0.1g, Sodium: 223mg, Potassium: 257mg, Phosphorus: 228mg

Chinese Tea Eggs

Prep time: 5 minutes, cook time: 37 minutes; Serves 12
Ingredients:
12 large eggs
4 tablespoons soy sauce
2 bay leaves
1 teaspoon Sichuan peppercorns
1-star anise
1 cinnamon stick
2 teaspoons sugar
2 black tea bags
2 cups water
salt to taste
Instructions
1. Place eggs in the Instant Pot and pour water.
2. Close the lid and set the vent to the Sealing position.
3. Press the Steam button and adjust the cooking time to 7 minutes.
4. Do quick pressure release.
5. Open the lid and transfer the eggs into iced water. Set aside.
6. Clean the Instant Pot and place the remaining ingredients.
7. Close the lid and set the vent to the Sealing position.
8. Press the Broth/Soup button and cook for 30 minutes.
9. Do natural pressure release.
10. Remove the solids and place in a lidded container.
11. Slightly crack the eggs and place in the marinade. Allow to marinate in the fridge for 12 hours.
12. Peel the eggs before eating.

Nutrition Facts Per Serving
Calories 72, Total Fat5 g, Saturated Fat 1g, Total Carbs 0.4g, Net Carbs 0.4g, Protein 6g, Sugar: 0.4g, Fiber: 0g, Sodium: 70mg, Potassium: 67mg, Phosphorus: 54mg

Eggs and Peppers

Prep time: 5 minutes, cook time: 4 hours; Serves 4
Ingredients:
2 tablespoons olive oil
2 cloves of garlic
2 onions, chopped
1 red or green bell pepper, deseeded and sliced
2 red chilies, chopped
1 can crushed tomatoes
2 teaspoons caster sugar
Salt and pepper to taste
4 eggs, lightly beaten
1 bunch parsley, chopped
6 tablespoons creamy yogurt, for garnish
Instructions
1. Press the Sauté button on the Instant Pot and heat the oil.
2. Sauté the garlic and onions until fragrant.
3. Stir in the bell pepper, chilies, and tomatoes. Season with sugar, salt and pepper.
4. Pour in the eggs and parsley.
5. Close the lid but do not seal the vent.
6. Press the Slow Cook button and adjust the cooking time to 4 hours.
7. Garnish with yogurt on top.

Nutrition Facts Per Serving
Calories 235, Total Fat 16g, Saturated Fat 4g, Total Carbs 13g, Net Carbs 10g, Protein 10g, Sugar: 8g, Fiber: 3g, Sodium: 392mg, Potassium: 413mg, Phosphorus: 163mg

Coddled Eggs

Prep time: 5 minutes, cook time: 6 minutes; Serves 4

Ingredients:

3 tablespoons butter
1 onion, chopped
¼ cup white wine
1 cup vegetable stock
1 cup heavy cream
1 cup arugula leaves
4 eggs, lightly beaten
salt and pepper to taste

Instructions

1. Press the Sauté button on the Instant Pot.
2. Heat the butter and sauté the onion until fragrant.
3. Add in the white wine, stock, and heavy cream.
4. Close the lid and set the vent to the Sealing position.
5. Press the Manual button and adjust the cooking time to 6 minutes.
6. Do quick natural release.
7. Once the lid is open, press the Sauté button and select the high setting.
8. Add in the arugula leaves and eggs. Stir constantly until the mixture thickens.

Nutrition Facts Per Serving

Calories 308, Total Fat 28g, Saturated Fat 14g, Total Carbs 6g, Net Carbs 5.5g, Protein 9g, Sugar: 4g, Fiber: 0.5g, Sodium: 399mg, Potassium: 175mg, Phosphorus: 135mg

Egg Masala

Prep time: 5 minutes, cook time: 10 minutes; Serves 6

Ingredients:

6 eggs
2 tablespoons oil
1 onion, chopped
½ teaspoon turmeric powder
½ teaspoon chili powder
1 thumb-size ginger
1 green chili, sliced
½ teaspoon garam masala
1 can coconut milk
½ cup coriander leaves
salt and pepper to taste

Instructions

1. Place a trivet or steamer basket inside the Instant Pot and pour water over.
2. Arrange the eggs on the steamer basket.
3. Close the lid and set the vent to the Sealing position. Press the Steam button. Adjust the cooking time to 6 minutes. Do natural pressure release.
4. Peel the eggs and set aside.
5. Clean the inner pot and press the Sauté button.
6. Add in the oil and sauté the onion, turmeric powder, chili powder, ginger, chili, and garam masala until fragrant. Add in coconut milk and eggs.
7. Close the lid and set the vent to the Sealing position.
8. Press the Manual button and adjust the cooking time to 3 minutes.
9. Do quick pressure release.
10. Garnish with coriander leaves. Season.
11. Serve with rice.

Nutrition Facts Per Serving

Calories 185, Total Fat 14g, Saturated Fat 3g, Total Carbs 4g, Net Carbs g, Protein 10g, Sugar: 2g, Fiber: 0.9g, Sodium: 146mg, Potassium: 285mg, Phosphorus: 168mg

Savory Tomatoes and Eggs

Prep time: 5 minutes, cook time: 15 minutes; Serves 5

Ingredients:

4 eggs, beaten
1 cup vegetable stock
2 teaspoons olive oil
1 onion, chopped
2 cloves of garlic, minced
½ teaspoon smoked paprika
A dash of chili flakes
1 can crushed tomatoes
3 teaspoons red wine vinegar
Salt and pepper and pepper to taste
1 cup parmesan cheese

Instructions

1. In a mixing bowl, mix together the eggs and vegetable stock. Set aside.
2. Press the Sauté button on the Instant Pot and heat the oil.
3. Sauté the onion and garlic until fragrant.
4. Add in the paprika and chili flakes. Continue stirring for 3 minutes.
5. Add in the tomatoes and red wine. Season with salt and pepper to taste.
6. Pour in the egg mixture.
7. Close the lid and set the vent to the Sealing position.
8. Press the Manual button and adjust the cooking time to 15 minutes.
9. Do quick natural release.
10. Sprinkle with parmesan cheese on top.

Nutrition Facts Per Serving

Calories 221, Total Fat 15g, Saturated Fat 5g, Total Carbs 8g, Net Carbs 7g, Protein 14g, Sugar: 3g, Fiber: 1g, Sodium: 488mg, Potassium: 276mg, Phosphorus: 264mg

Instant Pot Egg Biryani

Prep time: 5 minutes, cook time: 20 minutes; Serves 5

Ingredients:

6 large eggs
2 tablespoons ghee
2 onions, sliced
1 tablespoon garam masala
2 teaspoon garlic, minced
1 teaspoon ginger, grated
1 tomato, diced
2 cups basmati rice, soaked overnight
½ cup cilantro leaves, chopped
¼ cup mint leaves
2 cups water
salt and pepper to taste

Instructions

1. Place the eggs in the Instant Pot and pour a cup of water. Close the lid and set the vent to the Sealing position. Press the Manual button and adjust the cooking time to 6 minutes. Do natural pressure release and allow the eggs to cool before removing the shell.
2. To the clean Instant Pot, press the Sauté button and heat the ghee.
3. Sauté the onion for 5 to 10 minutes until lightly brown. Remove from the pot and set aside.
4. Stir in the garlic and ginger for 30 seconds. Add the tomatoes and rice. Add the peeled boiled eggs.
5. Pour the water and season with salt and pepper to taste. Add in the cilantro leaves and mint leaves.
6. Close the lid and set the vent to the sealing position.
7. Press the Rice button and cook using the preset cooking time.

Nutrition Facts Per Serving

Calories 272, Total Fat 21g, Saturated Fat 5g, Total Carbs 26g, Net Carbs 16g, Protein 10g, Sugar: 1g, Fiber: 10g, Sodium: 15mg, Potassium: 805mg, Phosphorus: 882mg

Kale and Apple Frittata

Prep time: 5 minutes, cook time: 4 hours; Serves 9

Ingredients:

9 eggs
1 cup milk
1 tablespoon olive oil
1 onion, sliced
1 red apple, cored and chopped
1 cup kale sliced
salt and pepper to taste

Instructions

1. In a mixing bowl, combine the eggs and milk. Set aside.
2. Press the Sauté button on the Instant Pot.
3. Heat the oil and sauté the onions. Stir in the apples and kales.
4. Pour over the egg mixture.
5. Close the lid but do not seal the vent.
6. Press the Slow Cook button and adjust the cooking time to 4 hours.

Nutrition Facts Per Serving

Calories 171, Total Fat 12g, Saturated Fat 3g, Total Carbs 5g, Net Carbs 4.4g, Protein 10g, Sugar: 4g, Fiber: 0.6g, Sodium: 115mg, Potassium: 223mg, Phosphorus: 181mg

Mexican Eggs with Hash

Prep time: 5 minutes, cook time: 4 hours; Serves 4

Ingredients:

1 tablespoon oil
1 onion, chopped
½ pounds potatoes, grated
¼ cup chipotle chili sauce
1 can tomatoes, chopped
1/3 cup coriander, chopped
4 eggs, beaten
Salt and pepper to taste

Instructions

1. Press the Sauté button on the Instant Pot.
2. Sauté the onion for three minutes until fragrant.
3. Arrange the grated potatoes at the bottom of the Instant Pot.
4. Pour in the chipotle sauce, tomatoes and coriander.
5. Pour over beaten eggs.
6. Close the lid but do not seal the vent.
7. Press the Slow Cook button and adjust the cooking time to 4 hours.

Nutrition Facts Per Serving

Calories 238, Total Fat 13g, Saturated Fat 3g, Total Carbs 18g, Net Carbs 16g, Protein 11g, Sugar: 5g, Fiber: 2g, Sodium: 337mg, Potassium: 577mg, Phosphorus: 211mg

Eggs En Cocotte

Prep time: 10 minutes, cook time: 15 minutes; Serves 3

Ingredients:

3 tablespoons butter
3 tablespoons heavy cream
3 eggs, beaten
1 tablespoon chopped chive
salt and pepper to taste

Instructions

1. Pour water in the Instant Pot and place trivet inside.
2. Brush the ramekins with butter. Set aside.
3. In a bowl, mix the heavy cream and eggs. Stir in the remaining butter. Season with salt and pepper to taste.
4. Pour the egg mixture in the ramekin only until ¾ full.
5. Place the ramekins on the trivet.
6. Close the lid and set the vent to the Sealing position.
7. Press the Steam button and adjust the cooking time to 15 minutes.
8. Do natural pressure release.
9. Garnish with chives once cooked.

Nutrition Facts Per Serving

Calories 283, Total Fat 27g, Saturated Fat 13g, Total Carbs 2g, Net Carbs 2g, Protein 10g, Sugar: 1g, Fiber: 0g, Sodium: 199mg, Potassium: 173mg, Phosphorus: 167mg

Overnight Frittata Casserole

Prep time: 5 minutes, cook time: 6 hours; Serves 6

Ingredients:

6 large free-range eggs
1/3 cup heavy cream
¼ cup red bell pepper, diced
1/3 cup onion, minced
½ cup spinach, chopped
1 clove garlic, minced
½ cup grated white cheddar cheese
salt and pepper to taste

Instructions

1. In a bowl, mix the eggs and cream. Season with salt and pepper to taste.
2. Place the red bell pepper, onion, spinach, and garlic.
3. Pour over the egg mixture and top with grated cheese.
4. Close the lid but do not seal the vent.
5. Press the Slow Cook button and adjust the cooking time for 6 hours.

Nutrition Facts Per Serving

Calories 82, Total Fat 7g, Saturated Fat 3g, Total Carbs 2g, Net Carbs 1.8g, Protein 3g, Sugar: 0.6g, Fiber: 0.2g, Sodium: 13mg, Potassium: 55mg, Phosphorus: 75mg

Cheddar Egg Casserole

Prep time: 5 minutes, cook time: 6 hours; Serves 6

Ingredients:

6 eggs
½ cup half and half
1 cup frozen hash browns
2 handfuls spinach
1 cup grated cheddar cheese
salt and pepper to taste

Instructions

1. In a bowl, beat the eggs and half-and-half. Season with salt and pepper to taste.
2. Place the hash browns at the bottom of the pot. Add the spinach on top.
3. Pour in the egg mixture and top with cheddar cheese.
4. Close the lid but do not set the vent to the Sealing position.
5. Press the Slow Cook button and adjust the cooking time to 6 hours.

Nutrition Facts Per Serving

Calories 267, Total Fat 18g, Saturated Fat 8g, Total Carbs 9g, Net Carbs 9g, Protein 16g, Sugar: 7g, Fiber: 0g, Sodium: 281mg, Potassium: 257mg, Phosphorus: 313mg

Coconut Milk Yogurt

Prep time: 10 minutes, cook time: 12 hours; Serves 4

Ingredients:

2 14-ounce cans coconut milk
2 teaspoons agar agar
1 teaspoon yogurt starter

Instructions

1. Pour the coconut milk and agar in the Instant Pot. Close the lid.
2. Press the Yogurt button until it reads "Boil".
3. Press the Cancel button and allow the mixture to cool to 65^0C.
4. Add the yogurt starter and give a good stir.
5. Press the Yogurt button and allow to incubate. Adjust the time to 12 hours.
6. After 8 hours, transfer the yogurt in clean containers.
7. Keep in the fridge until ready to use.

Nutrition Facts Per Serving

Calories 209, Total Fat 23g, Saturated Fat 20g, Total Carbs 3g, Net Carbs 2.5g, Protein 2g, Sugar: 0.5g, Fiber: 0.5g, Sodium: 14mg, Potassium: 234mg, Phosphorus: 64mg

Buttered Mashed Potatoes

Prep time: 10 minutes, cook time: 10 minutes; Serves 4

Ingredients:

2 pounds potatoes, peeled and cubed
1 cup vegetable broth
1 cup milk
6 tablespoons butter
salt and pepper to taste

Instructions

1. Place tomatoes in the Instant Pot and pour in broth.
2. Close the lid and set the vent to the Sealing position.
3. Press the Pressure Cook or Manual button and adjust the cooking time to 15 minutes.
4. Do natural release once the timer sets off.
5. Open the lid and press the Sauté button.
6. Drain the potatoes and transfer into a bowl.
7. Stir in the rest of the ingredients and mash to the desired smoothness.

Nutrition Facts Per Serving

Calories 365, Total Fat 19g, Saturated Fat 12g, Total Carbs 43g, Net Carbs 38g, Protein 7g, Sugar: 5g, Fiber: 5g, Sodium: 177mg, Potassium: 1040mg, Phosphorus: 186mg

Instant Pot Mexican Queso

Prep time: 5 minutes, cook time: 8 minutes; Serves 16

Ingredients:

1 tablespoon olive oil
1 onion, chopped
2 tablespoon taco seasoning
1 10-ounce can fire-roasted tomatoes
1 32-ounce box Mexican cheese blend
½ cup half-and-half

Instructions

1. Press the Sauté button on the Instant Pot and heat the oil. Sauté the onion for 1 minute until fragrant.
2. Add in the taco seasoning and tomatoes. Stir for another 3 minutes.
3. Pour in the rest of the ingredients.
4. Close the lid and set the vent to the Sealing position.
5. Press the Pressure Cook or Manual button and cook on high for 5 minutes.
6. Do natural pressure release.

Nutrition Facts Per Serving

Calories178, Total Fat 7g, Saturated Fat 5g, Total Carbs 9g, Net Carbs 8.6g, Protein 19g, Sugar: 6g, Fiber: 0.4g, Sodium: 1020mg, Potassium: 657mg, Phosphorus: 322mg

Chapter 7 Rice and Grains Recipes

Barley-Cauliflower Risotto

Prep time: 10 minutes, cook time: 25 minutes; Serves 4

Ingredients:

1 head cauliflower, cut into florets
3 tablespoons olive oil
1 onion, chopped
2 cloves of garlic, minced
1 cup pearl barley, rinsed
3 cups vegetable broth
Salt and pepper to taste
1 tablespoon butter
½ cup parmesan cheese, grated

Instructions:

1. Press the Sauté button on the Instant Pot.
2. Pour the olive oil and sauté the onions and garlic until fragrant, around 3 minutes.
3. Add the pearl barley and vegetable broth. Give a good stir.
4. Season with salt and pepper to taste.
5. Close the lid, leave vent open, press the Multigrain button and adjust the cooking time to 20 minutes.
6. Press cancel and open lid.
7. Stir in the butter and sprinkle with parmesan cheese.
8. Serve and enjoy.

Nutrition Facts Per Serving

Calories 407, Total Fat 19g, Saturated Fat 6g, Total Carbs 49g, Net Carbs 39g, Protein 14g, Sugar: 3.6g, Fiber 10g, Sodium 857mg, Potassium 603mg, Phosphorus 289mg

Creamy Oatmeal with Peaches

Prep time: 5 minutes, cook time: 20 minutes; Serves 8

Ingredients:

4 cups old-fashioned oats
3 ½ cups water
3 ½ cups almond milk
1 teaspoon salt
1 teaspoon ground cinnamon
1/3 cup sugar
4 peaches

Instructions:

1. Place all ingredients in the Instant Pot.
2. Stir to combine.
3. Close the lid, place on vent position and press the Multigrain button.
4. Adjust the cooking time to 20 minutes.
5. Once done cooking, press cancel, open, serve and enjoy.

Nutrition Facts Per Serving

Calories 214, Total Fat 5g, Saturated Fat 5g, Total Carbs 53g, Net Carbs 44g, Protein 9g, Sugar: 20g, Fiber 9g, Sodium 369mg, Potassium 489mg, Phosphorus 380mg

Pumpkin & Spice Oatmeal

Prep time: 10 minutes, cook time: 20 minutes; Serves 6

Ingredients:

1 can pumpkin puree
1 ¼ cups steel-cut oats
3 tablespoons brown sugar
1 ½ teaspoons pumpkin pie spice
1 teaspoon ground cinnamon
¾ teaspoon salt
3 cups water
1 ½ cups almond milk

Instructions:

1. Place all ingredients in the Instant Pot.
2. Stir to combine.
3. Close the lid, place on vent position and press the Multigrain button.
4. Adjust the cooking time to 20 minutes.
5. Once done cooking, press cancel, open, serve and enjoy.

Nutrition Facts Per Serving

Calories 96, Total Fat 2g, Saturated Fat 1g, Total Carbs 23g, Net Carbs 19g, Protein 4g, Sugar: 10g, Fiber 4g, Sodium 337mg, Potassium 161mg, Phosphorus 156mg

Oatmeal with Spice and Apples

Prep time: 2 minutes, cook time: 6 minutes; Serves 2

Ingredients:

½ cup steel cut oats

1 medium apple, peeled and chopped

1 ½ cups water

1 teaspoon ground cinnamon

¼ teaspoon allspice

1/8 teaspoon nutmeg

3 tablespoons maple syrup

Instructions:

1. Place all ingredients in the Instant Pot.
2. Stir to combine.
3. Close the lid and press the Manual button.
4. Adjust the cooking time to 6 minutes.
5. Do natural pressure release.

Nutrition Facts Per Serving

Calories 188, Total Fat 2g, Saturated Fat 1g, Total Carbs 50g, Net Carbs 43g, Protein 5g, Sugar: 28g, Fiber 7g, Sodium 9mg, Potassium 303mg, Phosphorus 185mg

Oats with Walnut and Banana

Prep time: 5 minutes, cook time: 6 minutes; Serves 3

Ingredients:

1 cup steel-cut oats

2 cups water

1 cup almond milk

¼ cup walnut, chopped

2 tablespoons flaxseed

2 tablespoons chia seeds

1 large banana, sliced

2 tablespoons pure maple syrup

1 teaspoon cinnamon powder

1 teaspoon pure vanilla extract

A pinch of salt

Instructions:

1. Place all ingredients in the Instant Pot.
2. Stir to combine.
3. Close the lid and press the Manual button.
4. Adjust the cooking time to 6 minutes.
5. Do natural pressure release.

Nutrition Facts Per Serving

Calories 288, Total Fat 12g, Saturated Fat 12g, Total Carbs 48g, Net Carbs 39g, Protein 11g, Sugar: 19g, Fiber 9g, Sodium 44mg, Potassium 566mg, Phosphorus 376 mg

Coco-Nutty Oatmeal

Prep time: 5 minutes, cook time: 3 minutes; Serves 2

Ingredients:

1 cup steel-cut oats

2 cups water

1 cup coconut milk

½ cup coconut sugar

2 tbsp chopped cashews

Instructions:

1. Place all ingredients in the Instant Pot, except for cashews.
2. Stir to combine.
3. Close the lid and press the Manual button.
4. Adjust the cooking time to 3 minutes.
5. Do natural pressure release.
6. Serve with a sprinkle of chopped cashews.

Nutrition Facts Per Serving

Calories 288, Total Fat 13g, Saturated Fat 3g, Total Carbs 48g, Net Carbs 39g, Protein 11g, Sugar: 19g, Fiber 9g, Sodium 44mg, Potassium 566mg, Phosphorus 376mg

Creamy Millet Porridge

Prep time: 10 minutes, cook time: 20 minutes; Serves 2

Ingredients:

1 cup uncooked millet

1 cup almond milk

3 cups water

2 tablespoons maple syrup

1 tablespoon vanilla extract

1 tbsp chopped almonds, for garnish

4 strawberries, sliced for garnish

Instructions:

1. Place all ingredients in the Instant Pot.
2. Stir to combine.
3. Close the lid, place on vent position and press the Multigrain button.
4. Adjust the cooking time to 20 minutes.
5. Once done cooking, press cancel and open.

6. Serve and enjoy with chopped almonds and sliced strawberries.

Nutrition Facts Per Serving

Calories 534, Total Fat 9g, Saturated Fat 3g, Total Carbs 95g, Net Carbs 86g, Protein 15g, Sugar: 20g, Fiber 9g, Sodium 68mg, Potassium 449mg, Phosphorus 397mg

Porridge with Coconut and Dates

Prep time: 5 minutes, cook time: 10 minutes; Serves 3

Ingredients:

3 tablespoons of prepared millet
1 ½ cups coconut milk
2 Medjool dates, chopped
1 teaspoon cinnamon powder
1 teaspoon vanilla powder
A dash of salt

Instructions:

1. Place all ingredients in the Instant Pot.
2. Close the lid and press the Manual button.
3. Adjust the cooking time to 10 minutes.
4. Do a natural pressure release.
5. Serve and enjoy.

Nutrition Facts Per Serving

Calories 374, Total Fat 30g, Saturated Fat 1g, Total Carbs 28g, Net Carbs 23g, Protein 5g, Sugar: 15g, Fiber 5g, Sodium 71mg, Potassium 457mg, Phosphorus 166mg

Veggie 'n Mushroom Quinoa

Prep time: 10 minutes, cook time: 20 minutes; Serves 6

Ingredients:

3 tablespoons olive oil
1 onion, diced
1 carrot, peeled and chopped
2 cups button mushrooms, sliced
Zest of ½ lemon
2 tablespoons lemon juice
1 tablespoon salt
4 cloves of garlic, minced
1 cup quinoa, rinsed
1 cup vegetable stock

Instructions:

1. Place all ingredients in the Instant Pot.
2. Stir to combine.
3. Close the lid, place on vent position and press the Multigrain button.
4. Adjust the cooking time to 20 minutes.
5. Once done cooking, press cancel and open.
6. Serve and enjoy.

Nutrition Facts Per Serving

Calories 493, Total Fat 45g, Saturated Fat 31g, Total Carbs 23g, Net Carbs 20g, Protein 5g, Sugar: 1g, Fiber 3g, Sodium 1170mg, Potassium 228mg, Phosphorus 143mg

Quinoa Pilaf

Prep time: 10 minutes, cook time: 25 minutes; Serves 6

Ingredients:

3 tablespoons butter
2 tablespoons onion, chopped
1 tablespoon garlic, minced
2 tablespoons chopped celery
2 cups quinoa, rinsed
2 cups vegetable broth
¾ teaspoon garlic powder
¼ teaspoon paprika
Salt and pepper to taste
1 tablespoon parsley, chopped

Instructions:

1. Press the Sauté button on the Instant Pot.
2. Melt butter for a minute and sauté the onion, garlic, and celery until fragrant.
3. Add the quinoa, chicken broth, garlic, powder, and paprika.
4. Season with salt and pepper to taste.
5. Close the lid, place on vent position and press the Multigrain button.
6. Adjust the cooking time to 20 minutes

7. Once done cooking, press cancel and open.
8. Serve and enjoy with parsley on top.
Nutrition Facts Per Serving
Calories 894, Total Fat 82g, Saturated Fat 63g, Total Carbs 38g, Net Carbs 34g, Protein 8g, Sugar: 1g, Fiber 4g, Sodium 52mg, Potassium 374mg, Phosphorus 270mg

Fried Rice made of Quinoa

Prep time: 5 minutes, cook time: 20 minutes; Serves 6

Ingredients:
3 ½ cups quinoa, rinsed
3 cups water
1 tablespoon sesame oil
3 cloves of garlic, minced
1 onion, diced
1 cup frozen mixed vegetables
2 large eggs, beaten
2 tablespoons soy sauce
1 teaspoon red pepper flakes
Salt and pepper to taste

Instructions:
1. Place the quinoa and water in the Instant Pot.
2. Close the lid and press the Manual button. Adjust the cooking time to 12 minutes.
3. Do natural pressure release. Take the cooked quinoa out and set aside in another bowl.
4. Press the Sauté button on the pot.
5. Heat the sesame oil and sauté the garlic and onion until fragrant.
6. Add the vegetables and stir for 3 minutes. Push the vegetables to one side and add the eggs.
7. Scramble the eggs.
8. Stir in the cooked quinoa and season with soy sauce, red pepper flakes, salt, and pepper.
9. Stir to combine everything.
10. Serve warm.

Nutrition Facts Per Serving
Calories 745, Total Fat 47g, Saturated Fat 31g, Total Carbs 68g, Net Carbs 60g, Protein 16g, Sugar: 2g, Fiber 8g, Sodium 92mg, Potassium 638mg, Phosphorus 493mg

Cilantro Flavored Quinoa

Prep time: 10 minutes, cook time: 20 minutes; Serves 4

Ingredients:
2 tablespoons cilantro, chopped
½ clove of garlic, minced
1 tablespoon lime juice
2 tablespoons mayonnaise
1 tablespoons jalapeno, chopped
A pinch of salt
2 tablespoons olive oil
3 cloves of garlic, minced
1 onion, chopped
1 red pepper, diced
1 stalk of celery, diced
1 teaspoon cumin
1 teaspoon coriander seeds
1 teaspoon paprika
1 teaspoon oregano
1 cup raw quinoa, rinsed
Salt and pepper to taste
½ cup corn kernels
½ cup garden peas
½ cup tomato puree
½ cup water

Instructions:
1. Prepare the cilantro sauce first by combining in a small bowl the first 5 ingredients. Add salt, mix well, and set aside.
2. Press the Sauté button on the Instant Pot.
3. Heat the oil and sauté the onion and garlic until fragrant.
4. Add the pepper and celery. Season with cumin, coriander, paprika, and oregano.
5. Stir in the quinoa and season with salt and pepper to taste.
6. Dump the corn, peas, tomato puree, and water.
7. Close the lid and seal off the vent.
8. Press the Manual button and adjust the cooking time to 12 minutes.
9. Do natural pressure release.
10. Serve with cilantro sauce.

Nutrition Facts Per Serving
Calories 298, Total Fat 13g, Saturated Fat 2g, Total Carbs 40g, Net Carbs 34g, Protein 9g, Sugar: 5g, Fiber 6g, Sodium 116mg, Potassium 586mg, Phosphorus 250mg

Speedy Veggie 'n Quinoa

Prep time: 10 minutes, cook time: 2 minutes; Serves 4

Ingredients:

3 stalks of celery, chopped
1 bell pepper, chopped
1 ½ cups quinoa, rinsed
¼ teaspoon salt
4 cups spinach
1 ½ cups vegetable broth
½ cup feta cheese

Instructions:

1. Place all ingredients except the feta cheese in the Instant Pot.
2. Close the lid and seal off the vent.
3. Press the Manual button and adjust the cooking time to 2 minutes.
4. Do natural pressure release.
5. Once the lid is open, garnish with feta cheese on top.
6. Serve and enjoy.

Nutrition Facts Per Serving

Calories 302, Total Fat 8g, Saturated Fat 3g, Total Carbs 45g, Net Carbs 39g, Protein 13g, Sugar: 2g, Fiber 6g, Sodium 561mg, Potassium 609mg, Phosphorus 377mg

Your Basic Quinoa in Instant Pot

Prep time: 5 minutes, cook time: 20 minutes; Serves 6

Ingredients:

1 cup quinoa
2 1/2 cups water

Instructions:

1. Place all ingredients in the Instant Pot.
2. Stir to combine.
3. Close the lid, place on vent position and press the Multigrain button.
4. Adjust the cooking time to 20 minutes.
5. Once done cooking, press cancel and open.
6. Serve and enjoy.

Nutrition Facts Per Serving

Calories 104, Total Fat 2g, Saturated Fat 1g, Total Carbs 18g, Net Carbs 16g, Protein 4g, Sugar: 0g, Fiber 2g, Sodium 3mg, Potassium 160mg, Phosphorus 129mg

Porridge out of Buckwheat

Prep time: 10 minutes, cook time: 15 minutes; Serves 4

Ingredients:

1 cup buckwheat groats
3 cups almond milk
1 banana, sliced
¼ cup raisins
1 teaspoon ground cinnamon
½ teaspoon vanilla
¼ cup chopped nuts for garnish

Instructions:

1. Place all ingredients except the nuts in the Instant Pot.
2. Stir to combine.
3. Close the lid, place on vent position and press the Porridge button.
4. Adjust the cooking time to 15 minutes.
5. Once done cooking, press cancel and open.
6. Serve and enjoy with chopped nuts.

Nutrition Facts Per Serving

Calories 174, Total Fat 7g, Saturated Fat 9g, Total Carbs 18g, Net Carbs 16g, Protein 10g, Sugar: 10g, Fiber 2g, Sodium 86mg, Potassium 316mg, Phosphorus 205mg

Shiitake 'n Brown Rice Congee

Prep time: 10 minutes, cook time: 20 minutes; Serves 4

Ingredients:

½ cup brown rice
4 cups mushroom broth
2 cup shiitake mushrooms, sliced
2 tablespoons minced ginger
2 cloves of garlic, minced
3 cups warm water

Salt to taste

Instructions:

1. Place all ingredients in the Instant Pot.
2. Stir to combine.
3. Close the lid, place on vent position and press the Porridge button.
4. Adjust the cooking time to 20 minutes.
5. Once done cooking, press cancel and open.

6. If needed, add water to desired consistency. Congee should be thick.
7. Before serving, adjust salt seasoning to taste.

Nutrition Facts Per Serving

Calories 117, Total Fat 1g, Saturated Fat 0g, Total Carbs 24g, Net Carbs 22g, Protein 5g, Sugar: 3g, Fiber 2g, Sodium 10mg, Potassium 398mg, Phosphorus 151mg

Congee for Cold Days

Prep time: 10 minutes, cook time: 30 minutes; Serves 6

Ingredients:

1 ½ cups short-grain rice

6 cups vegetable broth

2 cups water

2 thumb-size ginger, julienned

3 cloves garlic

2 tablespoons soy sauce

1 tsp salt

1 tsp freshly ground pepper

1 lemon, cut into wedges

Instructions:

1. Place all ingredients in the Instant Pot, except for lemon wedges.
2. Stir to combine.
3. Close the lid, place on vent position and press the Porridge button.

4. Adjust the cooking time to 20 minutes.
5. Once done cooking, press cancel and let pot rest for 10 minutes before opening.
6. If needed, add water to desired consistency. Congee should be thick.
7. Before serving, adjust salt and pepper seasoning to taste.
8. Serve with lemon wedges.

Nutrition Facts Per Serving

Calories 287, Total Fat 3g, Saturated Fat 1g, Total Carbs 57g, Net Carbs 53g, Protein 8g, Sugar: 5g, Fiber 4g, Sodium 1037mg, Potassium 490mg, Phosphorus 136mg

Butternut Squash Risotto

Prep time: 10 minutes, cook time: 15 minutes; Serves 6

Ingredients:

2 tablespoons butter

3 cloves of garlic, minced

1 onion, chopped

3 tablespoons fresh sage, chopped

2 cups butternut squash, peeled and cubed

1 ½ cups Arborio rice

1/4 cup white wine

2 cups water

2 cups vegetable stock

Salt and pepper to taste

1 cup goat cheese, grated

Instructions:

1. Press the Sauté button on the Instant Pot and melt butter.
2. Sauté the garlic, onions, and sage until fragrant.

3. Add the butternut squash and sauté for 5 minutes.
4. Add the Arborio rice and white wine.
5. Allow simmering for 3 minutes until the wine has reduced.
6. Pour in water and stock.
7. Season with salt and pepper to taste.
8. Close the lid and press the Manual button.
9. Adjust the cooking time to 4 minutes.
10. Do quick pressure release.
11. Once the lid is open, sprinkle goat cheese on top and let rest for 2 minutes before serving.

Nutrition Facts Per Serving

Calories 259, Total Fat 18g, Saturated Fat 8g, Total Carbs 24g, Net Carbs 16g, Protein 12g, Sugar: 3g, Fiber 8g, Sodium 291mg, Potassium 811mg, Phosphorus 666mg

Barley, Carrot and Mushroom Soup

Prep time: 10 minutes, cook time: 30 minutes; Serves 6

Ingredients:
1 tablespoon olive oil
4 cloves of garlic, minced
2 onions, chopped
1 stalk of celery, chopped
4 large carrots, chopped
1-lb cremini mushrooms, washed
1 bay leaf
1 cup pearl barley, rinsed
4 cups vegetable stock
Salt and pepper to taste

Instructions:
1. Press the Sauté button on the Instant Pot.
2. Heat the oil and sauté the garlic, onions, and celery for 3 minutes.
3. Add the carrots and mushrooms. Cook for 3 minutes more.
4. Stir in the bay leaf and pearl barley, sauté for 3 minutes.
5. Pour in stock. Season with salt, and pepper.
6. Close the lid.
7. Press the Soup button and cook for 20 minutes.
8. Do a quick pressure release.
9. Serve and enjoy.

Nutrition Facts Per Serving
Calories 1652, Total Fat 149g, Saturated Fat 119g, Total Carbs 92g, Net Carbs 76g, Protein 12g, Sugar: 6g, Fiber 16g, Sodium 50mg, Potassium 1476mg, Phosphorus 327mg

Butternut Squash Risotto

Prep time: 10 minutes, cook time: 15 minutes; Serves 6

Ingredients:
2 tablespoons butter
3 cloves of garlic, minced
1 onion, chopped
3 tablespoons fresh sage, chopped
2 cups butternut squash, peeled and cubed
1 ½ cups Arborio rice
1/4 cup white wine
2 cups water
2 cups vegetable stock
Salt and pepper to taste
1 cup goat cheese, grated

Instructions:
12. Press the Sauté button on the Instant Pot and melt butter.
13. Sauté the garlic, onions, and sage until fragrant.
14. Add the butternut squash and sauté for 5 minutes.
15. Add the Arborio rice and white wine.
16. Allow simmering for 3 minutes until the wine has reduced.
17. Pour in water and stock.
18. Season with salt and pepper to taste.
19. Close the lid and press the Manual button.
20. Adjust the cooking time to 4 minutes.
21. Do quick pressure release.
22. Once the lid is open, sprinkle goat cheese on top and let rest for 2 minutes before serving.

Nutrition Facts Per Serving
Calories 259, Total Fat 18g, Saturated Fat 8g, Total Carbs 24g, Net Carbs 16g, Protein 12g, Sugar: 3g, Fiber 8g, Sodium 291mg, Potassium 811mg, Phosphorus 666mg

Barley and Spinach Soup

Prep time: 10 minutes, cook time: 25 minutes; Serves 6

Ingredients:
3 cups vegetable stock
2 cups water
2 cups carrots, diced
1 cup red potatoes, peeled and diced
1 cup onion, diced
¾ cup celery
½ cup pearl barley, rinsed and drained
1 tablespoon oregano
1 bay leaf
2 cups spinach leaves, washed and drained
Salt and pepper to taste

Instructions:

1. Place all ingredients in the Instant Pot.
2. Give a good stir.
3. Close the lid and seal the vent.
4. Press the Soup button and adjust the cooking time to 20 minutes.
5. Do quick pressure release.
6. Stir in spinach leaves and let it sit for 3 minutes.
7. Serve and enjoy.

Nutrition Facts Per Serving
Calories 146, Total Fat 2g, Saturated Fat 1g, Total Carbs 27g, Net Carbs 22g, Protein 6g, Sugar: 5g, Fiber 5g, Sodium 223mg, Potassium 520mg, Phosphorus 111mg

Barley and Root Veggie Soup

Prep time: 10 minutes, cook time: 20 minutes; Serves 4

Ingredients:
1 onion, chopped
1 carrot, chopped
1 leek, sliced
1 zucchini, sliced
½ butternut squash, diced
¾ cup pearl barley, soaked and rinsed
2 tablespoons tomato paste
7 cups vegetable broth
1 teaspoon cumin
1 teaspoon paprika
½ teaspoon parsley
Salt and pepper to taste

Instructions:

1. Place all ingredients in the Instant Pot.
2. Give a good stir.
3. Close the lid and seal the vent.
4. Press the Soup button and adjust the cooking time to 20 minutes.
5. Do quick pressure release.
6. Serve and enjoy.

Nutrition Facts Per Serving
Calories 200, Total Fat 2g, Saturated Fat 1g, Total Carbs 40g, Net Carbs 32g, Protein 8g, Sugar: 6g, Fiber 8g, Sodium 1642mg, Potassium 430mg, Phosphorus 135mg

Goat Cheese & Spinach Risotto

Prep time: 10 minutes, cook time: 15 minutes; Serves 8

Ingredients:
1 tablespoon olive oil
¾ cup onion, chopped
2 cloves of garlic, minced
1 ½ cups Arborio rice
½ cup white wine
3 ½ cup hot vegetable broth
Salt and pepper to taste
2 tablespoons lemon juice, freshly squeezed
1 cup spinach leaves, chopped
½ cup parmesan cheese, grated

Instructions:
1. Press the Sauté button on the Instant Pot.
2. Pour the olive oil and sauté the onions and garlic until fragrant.
3. Add the Arborio rice and white wine.
4. Allow simmering for a minute before pouring in the hot vegetable broth.
5. Season with salt and pepper to taste
6. Close the lid and seal off the vent.
7. Press the Manual button and adjust the cooking time to 3 minutes.
8. Do quick pressure release.
9. Once the lid is open, press the Sauté button.
10. Add the lemon juice and spinach. Give a good stir and allow the spinach to wilt.
11. Sprinkle with parmesan cheese on top.

Nutrition Facts Per Serving
Calories 129, Total Fat 8g, Saturated Fat 2g, Total Carbs 14g, Net Carbs 9g, Protein 6g, Sugar: 1g, Fiber 5g, Sodium 509mg, Potassium 472mg, Phosphorus 435mg

Asparagus Risotto

Prep time: 10 minutes, cook time: 25 minutes; Serves 5

Ingredients:

1 tablespoon olive oil
1 shallot, chopped
1 clove of garlic, minced
1 ½ cup Arborio rice
1/3 cup white wine
3 cups vegetable broth
1 teaspoon lemon zest
2 teaspoon thyme leaves
Salt and pepper to taste
1 bunch asparagus spears, trimmed
1 tablespoons butter
2 tablespoons parmesan cheese, grated

Instructions:

1. Press the Sauté button on the Instant Pot.
2. Pour the olive oil and sauté the shallot and garlic until fragrant

3. Add the Arborio rice and stir for 30 seconds before adding the white wine.
4. Pour in the vegetable broth. Season with salt and pepper to taste.
5. Stir in the lemon zest and thyme leaves.
6. Close the lid, leave vent open, and press rice button.
7. Once done cooking, open lid and stir in the asparagus spears and butter.
8. Cover and let it rest for 5 minutes.
9. Fluff rice and sprinkle with parmesan cheese.
10. Serve and enjoy.

Nutrition Facts Per Serving

Calories 195, Total Fat 14g, Saturated Fat 5g, Total Carbs 20g, Net Carbs 12g, Protein 9g, Sugar: 2g, Fiber 8g, Sodium 524mg, Potassium 713mg, Phosphorus 660mg

Porcini Mushroom Risotto

Prep time: 10 minutes, cook time: 15 minutes; Serves 6

Ingredients:

1 tablespoon olive oil
½ cup onions, chopped
1-ounce porcini mushrooms, sliced
1 ½ cups Arborio rice
½ cup dry white wine
3 ½ cups vegetable broth
Salt and pepper to taste
1 cup frozen peas
½ cup parmesan cheese

Instructions:

1. Press the Sauté button on the Instant Pot.
2. Pour the oil and sauté the onions until fragrant. Stir in the mushrooms and cook for 2 minutes.
3. Add the rice, white wine and half of the vegetable broth. Season with salt and pepper to taste.

4. Allow simmering for 3 minutes.
5. The rice should turn from solid white to translucent.
6. Pour the rest of the broth.
7. Close the lid and press the Manual button and adjust the cooking time to 4 minutes.
8. Do natural pressure release.
9. Press the Sauté button and stir in the peas and parmesan cheese. Allow to cook for 5 minutes.

Nutrition Facts Per Serving

Calories 212, Total Fat 13g, Saturated Fat 4g, Total Carbs 25g, Net Carbs 17g, Protein 10g, Sugar: 3g, Fiber 8g, Sodium 621mg, Potassium 621mg, Phosphorus 618mg

Shiitake 'n Cremini Mushroom Risotto

Prep time: 10 minutes, cook time: 15 minutes; Serves 6

Ingredients:

3 tablespoons olive oil
4 tablespoons unsalted butter
1 onion, chopped
4 cloves of garlic, minced
3 shiitake mushrooms, sliced

1 cremini mushrooms, sliced
2 cups Arborio rice
4 ½ cups vegetable stock
1 cup parmesan cheese, grated
3 tablespoons light soy sauce

¾ cup dry white wine
Salt and pepper to taste
Instructions:
1. Press the Sauté button on the Instant Pot.
2. Heat the oil and butter.
3. Sauté the onion and garlic until fragrant.
4. Add the mushrooms.
5. Stir in the Arborio rice and half of the vegetable stock.
6. Stir until the stock has boiled.
7. Add the rest of the ingredients and give a boil.
8. Close the lid and seal off the vent.
9. Press the Manual button and adjust the cooking time to 3 minutes.
10. Do natural pressure release.
11. Once the lid is open, press the Sauté button and continue stirring until the amount of liquid has reduced and the rice has thickened.

Nutrition Facts Per Serving
Calories 407, Total Fat 30g, Saturated Fat 11g, Total Carbs 28g, Net Carbs 19g, Protein 19g, Sugar: 3g, Fiber 9g, Sodium 920mg, Potassium 956mg, Phosphorus 944mg

Broccoli-Carrot Rice

Prep time: 10 minutes, cook time: 15 minutes; Serves 6
Ingredients:
2 tablespoons butter
2 cloves of garlic, minced
1 onion, chopped
Salt and pepper to taste
1 1/3 cups long grain rice
1 1/3 cups vegetable broth
½ cup almond milk
1 cup broccoli florets
2 medium carrots, peeled and cubed
½ cup cheddar cheese, grated
Instructions:
1. Press the Sauté button on the Instant Pot.
2. Melt the butter and add garlic and onion. Season with salt and pepper to taste.
3. Continue stirring for 3 minutes.
4. Add the rice and chicken broth. Stir in the milk.
5. Stir in the broccoli florets, carrots. and cheddar cheese.
6. Close the lid and keep vent open.
7. Press cancel, press rice button, and press cancel once done cooking.
8. Serve and enjoy.

Nutrition Facts Per Serving
Calories 226, Total Fat 6g, Saturated Fat 3g, Total Carbs 39g, Net Carbs 36g, Protein 6g, Sugar: 4g, Fiber 3g, Sodium 237mg, Potassium 289mg, Phosphorus 180mg

Creamy Mushroom Wild Rice Soup

Prep time: 10 minutes, cook time: 45 minutes; Serves 6
Ingredients:
5 carrots, chopped
5 stalks of celery, chopped
1 onion, chopped
3 cloves of garlic, minced
1 cup uncooked wild rice, rinsed
8 ounces mushrooms, diced
4 cups chicken broth
1 teaspoon salt
1 teaspoon dried thyme
6 tablespoons butter
½ cup flour
1 ½ cups milk
Instructions:
1. Put all ingredients in the Instant Pot except the butter, flour, and milk.
2. Close the lid and press the soup button. Adjust the cooking time to 20 minutes.
3. Meanwhile, prepare the sauce by melting the butter in a saucepan over medium flame. Whisk in the flour and add the milk gradually. Continue stirring until the sauce thickens.
4. Once the Instant Pot timer beeps, do natural pressure release.
5. Mix in the creamy sauce. Stir to combine.
6. Serve and enjoy.

Nutrition Facts Per Serving
Calories 566, Total Fat 26g, Saturated Fat 12g, Total Carbs 41g, Net Carbs 37g, Protein 44g, Sugar: 8g, Fiber 4g, Sodium 1215mg, Potassium 771mg, Phosphorus 452mg

Mexican Rice

Prep time: 10 minutes, cook time: 10 minutes; Serves 12

Ingredients:

2 tablespoons olive oil
¼ cup onion, chopped
4 cloves of garlic, chopped
2 cups long grain white rice, rinsed
A dash of salt
¾ cup crushed tomatoes
2 ½ cups chicken stock
½ teaspoon cumin
½ teaspoon smoked paprika
¼ cup sun-dried tomatoes

Instructions:

1. Press the Sauté button on the Instant Pot.
2. Pour the oil and sauté the onion and garlic until fragrant.
3. Add the rest of the ingredients and stir to combine everything.
4. Close the lid, leave vent open and press the rice button.
5. Once done cooking, serve and enjoy.

Nutrition Facts Per Serving

Calories 158, Total Fat 3g, Saturated Fat 1g, Total Carbs 29g, Net Carbs 28g, Protein 4g, Sugar: 2g, Fiber 1g, Sodium 90mg, Potassium 160mg, Phosphorus 58mg

Japanese Style Fried Rice

Prep time: 10 minutes, cook time: 20 minutes; Serves 6

Ingredients:

2 cups Jasmine rice, rinsed and drained
2 cups water
1 tablespoon butter
3 eggs, beaten
1 onion, chopped
1 cup frozen peas
1 cup corn kernels
2 tablespoons soy sauce
2 tablespoons sesame oil

Instructions:

1. Place the rice and water in the Instant Pot.
2. Close the lid and press rice button.
3. Once done cooking, Fluff the rice and transfer to a serving bowl.
4. Press the Sauté button.
5. Use the same inner pot and melt the butter.
6. Scramble the eggs for a minute or two then set aside in a bowl.
7. Add the onions, peas, and corn. Sauté for 3 minutes or until heated through.
8. Stir in the cooked rice and drizzle with soy sauce.
9. Add the scrambled eggs and continue stirring until the vegetables are cooked.
10. Drizzle with sesame oil last.
11. Serve and enjoy.

Nutrition Facts Per Serving

Calories 298, Total Fat 21g, Saturated Fat 5g, Total Carbs 29g, Net Carbs 19g, Protein 12g, Sugar: 3g, Fiber 10g, Sodium 202mg, Potassium 788mg, Phosphorus 774mg

Spanish Style Rice

Prep time: 10 minutes, cook time: 15 minutes; Serves 8

Ingredients:

½ onion, chopped
½ red bell pepper, chopped
1 ½ cups white rice, rinsed
2 cups vegetable broth
½ teaspoon chili powder
¼ teaspoon ground cumin
1 cup salsa

Instructions:

1. Place everything in the pot and give a good stir.
2. Close the lid and press the Rice button.
3. Fluff the rice before serving.

Nutrition Facts Per Serving

Calories 152, Total Fat 1g, Saturated Fat 1g, Total Carbs 32g, Net Carbs 30g, Protein 5g, Sugar: 2g, Fiber 2g, Sodium 431mg, Potassium 196mg, Phosphorus 58mg

Cajun Fried Rice

Prep time: 10 minutes, cook time: 10 minutes; Serves 5

Ingredients:

1 tablespoon oil
1 onion, diced
3 cloves of garlic, minced
1 tablespoon tomato paste
1 cup canned black beans, drained and rinsed well
1 tablespoon Cajun seasoning
2 cups vegetable broth
1 ½ cups white rice, rinsed
1 bell pepper, chopped

Instructions:

1. Press the Sauté on the Instant Pot and pour the oil.
2. Sauté the onion and garlic until fragrant.
3. Stir in black beans and tomato paste. Season with Cajun seasoning.
4. Continue cooking for 3 minutes.
5. Add the tomato paste and chicken broth. Dissolve the tomato paste before adding the rice and bell pepper.
6. Close the lid and press the rice button.
7. Once done cooking, serve and enjoy.

Nutrition Facts Per Serving

Calories 314, Total Fat 4g, Saturated Fat 1g, Total Carbs 59g, Net Carbs 53g, Protein 10g, Sugar: 2g, Fiber 6g, Sodium 442mg, Potassium 368mg, Phosphorus 133mg

Shawarma Flavored Rice

Prep time: 10 minutes, cook time: 15 minutes; Serves 5

Ingredients:

1 tablespoon oil
1 cup onion, chopped
5 cloves of garlic, minced
½-lb vegetarian ground beef substitute
1 ½ cups water
1 ½ cups basmati rice, rinsed and drained
4 cups cabbage, shredded
3 tablespoons shawarma spice
1 teaspoon salt
¼ cup cilantro, chopped

Instructions:

1. Place all ingredients in the Instant Pot except for the cilantro.
2. Give a good stir and close the lid.
3. Press the rice button.
4. Once done cooking, open pot and stir in cilantro.
5. Serve and enjoy.

Nutrition Facts Per Serving

Calories 288, Total Fat 17g, Saturated Fat 5g, Total Carbs 28g, Net Carbs 17g, Protein 18g, Sugar: 5g, Fiber 11g, Sodium 674mg, Potassium 999mg, Phosphorus 734mg

Cilantro-Lime Rice

Prep time: 10 minutes, cook time: 20 minutes; Serves 10

Ingredients:

1 can vegetable broth
¾ cup water
2 tablespoons canola oil
2 cups long grain white rice, rinsed
Zest of 1 lime
½ teaspoon salt
3 tablespoons juice of lime juice
½ cup cilantro, chopped

Instructions:

1. Place everything in the pot except for lime juice and cilantro and give a good stir.
2. Press the Rice button and let pot cook.
3. Once done, add the lime juice and cilantro.
4. Fluff and mix well before serving.

Nutrition Facts Per Serving

Calories 166, Total Fat 3g, Saturated Fat 1g, Total Carbs 31g, Net Carbs 30g, Protein 3g, Sugar: 1g, Fiber 1g, Sodium 197mg, Potassium 78mg, Phosphorus 52mg

Vegetable Rice Indian Style

Prep time: 10 minutes, cook time: 10 minutes; Serves 6

Ingredients:

1 tablespoon olive oil
¼ cup shallots, chopped
1 clove of garlic, minced
1 ½ cups basmati rice, rinsed
½ cup carrots, chopped
2 teaspoons curry powder
2 cups chicken broth
Salt and pepper to taste
1 cup frozen peas

Instructions:

1. Heat the oil in the Instant Pot by pressing the Sauté button.
2. Sauté the shallots and garlic until fragrant.
3. Add the rest of the ingredients.
4. Give a stir and scrape the bottom of the pot.
5. Close the lid and leave vent open.
6. Press the Rice button and let it cook.
7. Once done, open lid, serve and enjoy.

Nutrition Facts Per Serving

Calories 261, Total Fat 14g, Saturated Fat 3g, Total Carbs 20g, Net Carbs 11g, Protein 22g, Sugar: 1g, Fiber 9g, Sodium 339mg, Potassium 663mg, Phosphorus 623mg

Irish Style Oatmeal

Prep time: 10 minutes, cook time: 10 minutes; Serves 3

Ingredients:

4 cups almond milk
1 ¾ cup steel-cut oats
½ cup dried cherries
½ cup maple syrup
½ teaspoon salt
¼ teaspoon ground allspice
4 cups water
½ cup blueberries
1/3 cup pecans, chopped

Instructions:

1. Place all ingredients except for the pecans in the Instant Pot.
2. Give a good stir.
3. Close the lid and seal off the vent.
4. Press the Porridge button and adjust the cooking time to 15 minutes.
5. Do natural pressure release.
6. Prior to serving, give the oatmeal and good stir.
7. Garnish with pecans on top.

Nutrition Facts Per Serving

Calories 598, Total Fat 23g, Saturated Fat 8g, Total Carbs 102g, Net Carbs 91g, Protein 22g, Sugar: 62g, Fiber 11g, Sodium 547mg, Potassium 955mg, Phosphorus 716mg

Blueberries and Oats

Prep time: 10 minutes, cook time: 6 minutes; Serves 1

Ingredients:

1/3 cup old-fashioned oats
1/3 cup almond milk, unsweetened
1/3 cup Greek yogurt
1/3 cup blueberries
1 tablespoon chia seeds
2 tablespoons brown sugar
A dash of salt
A dash of cinnamon

Instructions:

1. Place all ingredients in the Instant Pot and give a good stir.
2. Close the lid and seal the vent.
3. Press the Manual button and adjust the cooking time to 6 minutes.
4. Do natural pressure release.
5. Give a good stir before serving.

Nutrition Facts Per Serving

Calories 311, Total Fat 8g, Saturated Fat 4g, Total Carbs 63g, Net Carbs 57g, Protein 11g, Sugar: 42g, Fiber 6g, Sodium 231mg, Potassium 441mg, Phosphorus 380mg

Oatmeal Coffee Cake

Prep time: 10 minutes, cook time: 5 minutes; Serves 8

Ingredients:

4 ½ cups water

1 ½ cups steel cut oats

1 ½ cups pumpkin puree

2 teaspoons cinnamon

1 teaspoon allspice

1 teaspoon vanilla

¾ cup brown sugar

Instructions:

1. Place all ingredients except the brown sugar in the Instant Pot.
2. Give a good stir.
3. Close the lid and seal off the vent.
4. Press the Manual button and cook for 3 minutes.
5. Do natural pressure release.
6. Once cooked, do natural pressure release.
7. Top with brown sugar.

Nutrition Facts Per Serving

Calories 252, Total Fat 12g, Saturated Fat 2g, Total Carbs 36g, Net Carbs 31g, Protein 10g, Sugar: 21g, Fiber 5g, Sodium 66mg, Potassium 308mg, Phosphorus 391mg

Cornmeal Porridge Jamaican Style

Prep time: 10 minutes, cook time: 20 minutes; Serves 4

Ingredients:

4 cups water, divided

1 cup yellow cornmeal

1 cup milk

2 sticks of cinnamon

3 pimento berries

1 teaspoon vanilla extract

½ teaspoon nutmeg, ground

½ cup sweetened condensed milk

Instructions:

1. In a bowl, combine half of the water and cornmeal. Set aside.
2. Press the Porridge button on the Instant Pot.
3. Add the remaining water and milk into the Instant Pot. Stir in the cinnamon, pimento berries, vanilla extract, and nutmeg.
4. Pour in the cornmeal mixture then stir.
5. Close the lid and adjust the cooking time to 15 minutes.
6. Do natural pressure release.
7. Drizzle with condensed milk on top.

Nutrition Facts Per Serving

Calories 252, Total Fat 12g, Saturated Fat 2g, Total Carbs 36g, Net Carbs 21g, Protein 10g, Sugar: 21g, Fiber 5g, Sodium 66mg, Potassium 308mg, Phosphorus 391mg

Espresso Oatmeal

Prep time: 5 minutes, cook time: 10 minutes; Serves 4

Ingredients:

2 ½ cups water

1 cup milk

1 cup oats

2 tablespoons sugar

1 teaspoon espresso powder

¼ teaspoon salt

2 teaspoons vanilla extract

A dollop of whipped cream

2 tablespoons grated chocolate

Instructions:

1. Place all ingredients except for the whipped cream and chocolate shavings in the Instant Pot.
2. Stir to combine everything.
3. Lock the lid and close the vent.
4. Press Manual and set the cooking time to 10 minutes.
5. Once done, do quick pressure release
6. Serve with whip cream and sprinkle with chocolate shavings on top.

Nutrition Facts Per Serving

Calories 173, Total Fat 4g, Saturated Fat 2g, Total Carbs 36g, Net Carbs 32g, Protein 7g, Sugar: 18g, Fiber 4g, Sodium 190mg, Potassium 266mg, Phosphorus 251mg

Spicy Black Beans & Brown Rice Salad

Prep time: 10 minutes, cook time: 10 minutes; Serves 8

Ingredients:

1 cup brown rice
¼ teaspoon salt
1 ½ cups water
12 grape tomatoes, halved
1 can black beans, drained and rinsed
¼ cup minced cilantro
1 avocado, diced
3 tablespoon lime juice
2 teaspoon Tabasco sauce
1 teaspoon honey
2 garlic cloves
1/8 teaspoon salt
3 tablespoon olive oil

Instructions:

1. Place the rice, salt, and water in the Instant Pot.
2. Close the lid and press the Rice button.
3. Once done cooking, place rice in a bowl. Let the rice cool for at least 30 minutes.
4. Once the rice has cooled off, add tomatoes, black beans, cilantro, and avocado. Mix well and set aside.
5. Prepare the dressing by mixing together the remaining ingredients.
6. Pour the dressing over the rice salad.

Nutrition Facts Per Serving

Calories 96, Total Fat 9g, Saturated Fat 1g, Total Carbs 5g, Net Carbs 3g, Protein 1g, Sugar: 2g, Fiber 2g, Sodium 122mg, Potassium 151mg, Phosphorus 17mg

Vanilla-Apple Quinoa

Prep time: 10 minutes, cook time: 10 minutes; Serves 2

Ingredients:

1 cup quinoa, rinsed
1 ½ cups water
¼ teaspoon salt
1 apple, seeded and chopped
2 tablespoons cinnamon
½ teaspoon vanilla

Instructions:

1. Add all ingredients to the Instant Pot.
2. Close the lid and seal the vent.
3. Choose the Manual button and adjust the cooking time to 8 minutes.
4. Do natural pressure release.

Nutrition Facts Per Serving

Calories 382, Total Fat 6g, Saturated Fat 1g, Total Carbs 64g, Net Carbs 52g, Protein 13g, Sugar: 10g, Fiber 12g, Sodium 300mg, Potassium 611mg, Phosphorus 404mg

Olives and Basil Rice Salad

Prep time: 15 minutes, cook time: 20 minutes; Serves 5

Ingredients:

2 cups Arborio rice
4 cups water
A pinch of salt
A dash of olive oil
2 fresh tomatoes, chopped
3 hard-boiled eggs, chopped
1 cup black olives, chopped
1 bunch basil, chopped
4 ounces of cooked ham, diced
1 mozzarella ball, sliced
3 tablespoon pickled capers
A dash of olive oil

Instructions:

1. Place the rice, water, salt and olive oil inside the Instant Pot.
2. Close the lid and press the Rice button.
3. Once done cooking, transfer the rice to a salad bowl and allow to cool for at least 30 minutes.
4. Once cooled, add the remaining ingredients.
5. Toss to combine.
6. Serve and enjoy.

Nutrition Facts Per Serving

Calories 291, Total Fat 20g, Saturated Fat 4g, Total Carbs 29g, Net Carbs 17g, Protein 17g, Sugar: 2g, Fiber 12g, Sodium 679mg, Potassium 1028mg, Phosphorus 957mg

Kale and Grains Salad

Prep time: 10 minutes, cook time: 20 minutes; Serves 12

Ingredients:

1 package of harvest grains of your choice
1 teaspoon salt
2 ½ cups water
1/3 cup red onion, diced
3 cups kale leaves, torn
4 tablespoon lemon juice
1/3 cup extra-virgin olive oil
Zest of 1 lemon
Salt and pepper to taste
¼ cup feta cheese, crumbled

Instructions:

1. Place the harvest grains, salt, and water in the Instant Pot.
2. Close the lid and press the Rice button.
3. Once done cooking, transfer grains to a bowl and allow the grains to cool down a bit.
4. Add the rest of the ingredients into bowl of grains. Mix well to combine everything.
5. Serve warm.

Nutrition Facts Per Serving

Calories 38, Total Fat 3g, Saturated Fat 1g, Total Carbs 2g, Net Carbs 1g, Protein 1g, Sugar: 1g, Fiber 1g, Sodium 277mg, Potassium 50mg, Phosphorus 19mg

Greek Couscous Salad

Prep time: 10 minutes, cook time: 15 minutes; Serves 4

Ingredients:

½ cup whole wheat couscous
1 ½ cups water
2 tbsp finely chopped fresh dill
3 tbsp lemon juice
½ cup crumbled feta
1 medium cucumber, peeled and chopped
2 medium tomatoes, chopped
2 tsp extra virgin olive oil

Instructions:

1. Add water and couscous in Instant Pot.
2. Press rice button and cook.
3. Once done cooking, transfer to a large bowl and let it cool.
4. Add remaining ingredients and toss well to mix.
5. Serve and enjoy.

Nutrition Facts Per Serving

Calories 110, Total Fat 6g, Saturated Fat 3g, Total Carbs 12g, Net Carbs 9g, Protein 5g, Sugar: 4g, Fiber 3g, Sodium 198mg, Potassium 285mg, Phosphorus 114mg

Spicy Quinoa Salad Thai Style

Prep time: 10 minutes, cook time: 30 minutes; Serves 8

Ingredients:

1 cup quinoa
1 ½ cups water
½ teaspoon salt
1 carrot, shredded
6 green onions, chopped
1 cucumber, chopped
1 cup edamame
2 cups red cabbage, shredded
¼ cup lime juice
1 tablespoon soy sauce
1 tablespoon vegetable oil
2 tablespoons sugar
1 tablespoon sesame oil
1 tablespoon ginger, grated
½ cup peanuts, toasted and chopped
A pinch of red pepper flakes
2 tablespoons basil, chopped
¼ cup cilantro, chopped

Instructions:

1. Place the quinoa, water, and salt in the Instant Pot.
2. Close the lid and press the Multigrain button.
3. Adjust the cooking time to 30 minutes. Once done cooking, do quick pressure release.
4. Transfer the quinoa to a bowl and let it cool for at least 30 minutes.

5. Once cooled, mix quinoa with carrots, onions, cucumber, edamame, and cabbage. Mix well to combine. Set aside.
6. In another mixing bowl, mix together the lime juice, soy sauce, vegetable oil, sugar, sesame oil, ginger, peanuts, red pepper flakes, basil, and cilantro.
7. Pour the sauce over the quinoa salad.

Nutrition Facts Per Serving
Calories 271, Total Fat 13g, Saturated Fat 2g, Total Carbs 32g, Net Carbs 26g, Protein 12g, Sugar: 9g, Fiber 6g, Sodium 296mg, Potassium 563mg, Phosphorus 231mg

Polenta with Sun-Dried Tomatoes

Prep time: 10 minutes, cook time: 10 minutes; Serves 8

Ingredients:
2 tablespoons olive oil
2 cloves of garlic, minced
½ cup onion, chopped
4 cups vegetable stock
1/3 cup sun-dried tomatoes, finely chopped
1 bay leaf
1 teaspoon salt
2 tablespoons parsley, chopped
2 teaspoons oregano, chopped
3 tablespoons basil, chopped
1 teaspoon rosemary, chopped
1 cup polenta

Instructions:
1. Press the Sauté button on the Instant Pot and add the oil.
2. Sauté the garlic and onions for 3 minutes until fragrant.
3. Add the stock, sun-dried tomatoes, bay leaf, salt, parsley, oregano, basil, and rosemary. Stir to combine.
4. Evenly add polenta on top but do not stir.
5. Close the lid and adjust the cooking time to 5 minutes.
6. Do natural pressure release.

Nutrition Facts Per Serving
Calories 88, Total Fat 5g, Saturated Fat 1g, Total Carbs 9g, Net Carbs 8g, Protein 4g, Sugar: 2g, Fiber 1g, Sodium 546mg, Potassium 280mg, Phosphorus 85mg

Cherry and Farro Salad

Prep time: 10 minutes, cook time: 10 minutes; Serves 5

Ingredients:
1 cup raw grain farro
3 cups water
1 tablespoon apple cider vinegar
1 teaspoon lemon juice
¼ teaspoon salt
1 tablespoon olive oil
¼ cup chives, minced
¼ cup dried cherries, chopped
8 mint leaves, minced
2 cups fresh cherries, pitted and halved

Instructions:
1. Place the faro in the Instant Pot and add 3 cups of water.
2. Close the lid and press the Rice button.
3. Adjust the cooking time to 40 minutes.
4. Do natural pressure release.
5. Allow the farro grains cool for a few minutes.
6. Place in a salad bowl and combine the remaining ingredients.
7. Toss to mix well.

Nutrition Facts Per Serving
Calories 208, Total Fat 6g, Saturated Fat g, Total Carbs 35g, Net Carbs 31g, Protein 6g, Sugar: 9g, Fiber 4g, Sodium 129mg, Potassium 312mg, Phosphorus 227mg

Miso Risotto

Prep time: 10 minutes, cook time: 10 minutes; Serves 6

Ingredients:

6 tablespoon olive oil
1 medium onion, chopped finely
3 cloves garlic, chopped
2 cups Arborio or risotto rice
2 teaspoon soy sauce
¾ cup dry sake
¼ cup miso paste
½ teaspoon juice of 1 lemon
4 cups vegetable stock
Salt to taste
Chives for garnish

Instructions:

1. Press the Sauté button on the Instant Pot.
2. Heat the oil and sauté the onion and garlic until fragrant.
3. Stir in the Arborio rice and add the rest of the ingredients except for the chives.
4. Close the lid and press the Rice button.
5. Once done cooking, fluff rice.
6. Garnish with chopped chives and serve.

Nutrition Facts Per Serving

Calories 332, Total Fat 24g, Saturated Fat 4g, Total Carbs 32g, Net Carbs 22g, Protein 11g, Sugar: 9g, Fiber 10g, Sodium 709mg, Potassium 918mg, Phosphorus 779mg

Parsley-Cucumber Tabbouleh

Prep time: 10 minutes, cook time: 10 minutes; Serves 4

Ingredients:

½ cup bulgur
1 cup water
4 scallions, thinly sliced
1 small cucumber, peeled, seeded and diced
2 tomatoes, diced
¼ cup chopped fresh mint
2 cups finely chopped flat-leaf parsley
Pepper to taste
¼ tsp salt
½ tsp minced garlic
2 tbsp extra virgin olive oil
¼ cup lemon juice

Instructions:

1. In Instant pot, add water and bulger.
2. Press rice button and cook.
3. Once done cooking, transfer to a large bowl and allow to cool until warm.
4. Add remaining ingredients into bowl. Toss well to coat and mix. Allow to cool in fridge and to meld all flavors for an hour.
5. Serve and enjoy.

Nutrition Facts Per Serving

Calories 110, Total Fat 6g, Saturated Fat 2g, Total Carbs 12g, Net Carbs 10g, Protein 5g, Sugar: 4g, Fiber 2g, Sodium 198mg, Potassium 285mg, Phosphorus 114mg

Chapter 8 Dessert Recipes

Apple Pudding

Prep time: 5 minutes, cook time: 10 minutes; Serves 6

Ingredients:
½ cup coconut sugar
2 cups milk
¼ teaspoon all spice
¼ teaspoon nutmeg, ground
2 teaspoon cinnamon
2 tablespoon lemon juice
6 medium apples, deseeded and chopped
½ cup raw honey
2 teaspoon vanilla
1 teaspoon sea salt

Instructions
1. Place all ingredients in the Instant Pot.
2. Give a good stir.
3. Close the lid and set the vent to the Sealing position.
4. Press the Pressure Cook or Manual button.
5. Adjust the cooking time to 10 minutes.
6. Do natural pressure release.

Nutrition Facts Per Serving
Calories 271, Total Fat 3g, Saturated Fat 2g, Total Carbs 62g, Net Carbs 57g, Protein 3g, Sugar: 55g, Fiber: 5g, Sodium: 38mg, Potassium: 329mg, Phosphorus: 91mg

Baked Apples in Instant Pot

Prep time: 5 minutes, cook time: 10 minutes; Serves 6

Ingredients:
6 apples, cored
½ cup brown sugar
1 cup red wine
¼ cup raisins
1 teaspoon cinnamon powder

Instructions
1. Place the apples on the bottom of the pressure cooker.
2. Add the rest of the ingredients on top.
3. Do not stir the mixture
4. Close the lid and set the vent to the Sealing position.
5. Press the Manual button.
6. Adjust the cooking time to 10 minutes.
7. Do natural pressure release.

Nutrition Facts Per Serving
Calories 168, Total Fat 0.3g, Saturated Fat 0g, Total Carbs 44g, Net Carbs 39g, Protein 0.7g, Sugar: 37g, Fiber: 5g, Sodium: 10mg, Potassium: 255mg, Phosphorus: 27mg

Instant Pot Date-Sweetened Carrot Cake

Prep time: 10 minutes, cook time: 5 hours; Serves 8

Ingredients:
2 cups whole wheat pastry flour
¾ teaspoon baking powder
¾ teaspoon baking soda
½ teaspoon ground cinnamon
¼ teaspoon ground cardamom
¼ teaspoon ground all spice
¼ teaspoon ground ginger
2 eggs
½ cup butter, melted
1 cup milk
1 cup shredded carrots
½ cup chopped dates

Instructions
1. Line the bottom of the inner pot with parchment paper.
2. In a bowl, mix together the flour, baking powder, baking soda, cinnamon, cardamom, all spice, and ginger. Set aside.
3. In another bowl, mix the eggs, butter, and milk.
4. Pour the wet ingredients to the dry ingredients and mix well.

5. Fold in carrots and dates until all ingredients are well-incorporated.
6. Stir in the carrots and dates. Mix again.
7. Pour the batter onto the parchment-lined Instant Pot.
8. Close the lid but do not seal the vent.
9. Press the Slow Cook button and adjust the cooking time to 5 hours.

Nutrition Facts Per Serving
Calories 288, Total Fat 16g, Saturated Fat 9g, Total Carbs 32g, Net Carbs 27g, Protein 8g, Sugar: 8g, Fiber: 5g, Sodium: 260mg, Potassium: 346mg, Phosphorus: 218mg

Vegan Rice Pudding

Prep time: 5 minutes, cook time: 20 minutes; Serves 3
Ingredients:
3 cups almond milk
2/3 cup jasmine rice, rinsed
1/3 cup granulated sugar
1 ½ teaspoons vanilla
½ teaspoon salt
Instructions
1. Place all ingredients in the Instant Pot. Give a good stir.
2. Close the lid but do not seal the vent.
3. Press the Rice button and cook for 20 minutes.
4. Do natural pressure release.

Nutrition Facts Per Serving
Calories 281, Total Fat 13g, Saturated Fat 6g, Total Carbs 36g, Net Carbs 30g, Protein 11g, Sugar: 24g, Fiber: 6g, Sodium: 107mg, Potassium: 717mg, Phosphorus: 647mg

Instant Pot Peach Cobbler

Prep time: 10 minutes, cook time: 6 hours; Serves 2
Ingredients:
2 medium peaches, pitted and sliced
2 teaspoons + 2 tablespoons sugar
1/8 teaspoon ground cinnamon
1/8 teaspoon ground nutmeg
¾ cup all-purpose flour
1/8 teaspoon salt
½ teaspoon baking powder
2 tablespoons milk
2 tablespoons softened butter
½ teaspoon turbinado sugar
Instructions
1. In a bowl, toss the peaches with 2 teaspoons sugar, cinnamon, and nutmeg.
2. Distribute into ramekins. Set aside.
3. In another bowl, mix the flour, salt, remaining sugar, baking powder, milk, and butter. Mix to create crumbly dough.
4. Sprinkle on top of the peaches.
5. Sprinkle with turbinado sugar last.
6. Place into the Instant Pot.
7. Pour ½ cup water around the ramekins.
8. Close the lid but do not seal the vent.
9. Press the Slow Cook button and adjust the cooking time to 6 hours.

Nutrition Facts Per Serving
Calories 298, Total Fat 13g, Saturated Fat 8g, Total Carbs 41g, Net Carbs 40g, Protein 5g, Sugar: 4g, Fiber: 1g, Sodium: 100mg, Potassium: 201mg, Phosphorus: 153mg

Apple Pecan Crumble

Prep time: 10 minutes, cook time: 6 hours; Serves 8
Ingredients:
5 apples, peeled and sliced
1 lemon juice
1 teaspoon vanilla
2 tablespoons arrowroot powder
1/3 cup coconut sugar
2 teaspoons cinnamon
1 teaspoon ground ginger
½ teaspoon all spice
¼ teaspoon nutmeg
¼ teaspoon cloves
½ cup pecans
¾ cup all-purpose flour

½ teaspoon baking powder
2 tablespoons milk
2 tablespoons softened butter
½ teaspoon turbinado sugar

Instructions

1. In a bowl, toss the apples, lemon juice, vanilla, arrowroot powder, coconut sugar, cinnamon, ginger, all spice, nutmeg, cloves, and pecans.
2. Distribute into ramekins. Set aside.
3. In another bowl, mix the flour, salt, remaining sugar, baking powder, milk, and butter. Mix to create crumbly dough.
4. Sprinkle on top of the apples.
5. Sprinkle with turbinado sugar last.
6. Place into the Instant Pot.
7. Pour ½ cup water around the ramekins.
8. Close the lid but do not seal the vent.
9. Press the Slow Cook button and adjust the cooking time to 6 hours.

Nutrition Facts Per Serving
Calories 420, Total Fat 25g, Saturated Fat 13g, Total Carbs 53g, Net Carbs g, Protein 4g, Sugar: 37g, Fiber: 6g, Sodium: 365mg, Potassium: 190mg, Phosphorus: 23mg

Carrot Cake Oatmeal

Prep time: 5minutes, cook time: 10 minutes; Serves 5

Ingredients:
1 cup steel-cut oats
1 cup milk
2 medium carrots, grated
¼ cup golden raisins
2 tablespoons maple syrup
1 ½ teaspoon cinnamon
½ teaspoon nutmeg
1 ½ teaspoon vanilla extract
2 cups water
A dash of salt

Instructions
1. Place all ingredients in the Instant Pot.
2. Give a good stir to combine everything.
3. Close the lid and set the vent to the Sealing position.
4. Press the Pressure Cook or Manual button and adjust the cooking time to 10 minutes.
5. Do natural pressure release.

Nutrition Facts Per Serving
Calories 155, Total Fat 4g, Saturated Fat 2g, Total Carbs 30g, Net Carbs 26g, Protein 7g, Sugar: 14g, Fiber: 4g, Sodium: 63mg, Potassium: 350mg, Phosphorus: 208mg

Coconut Rice Kheer

Prep time: 5 minutes, cook time: 20 minutes; Serves 6

Ingredients:
½ cup white rice
3 cups coconut milk
½ cup shredded coconut meat
½ cup sugar
1 teaspoon cardamom powder
1/8 teaspoon saffron
1/8 teaspoon nutmeg powder
2 tablespoons raisins
1 ½ cups water

Instructions
1. Place all ingredients in the Instant Pot.
2. Give a good stir to combine everything.
3. Close the lid and set the vent to the Sealing position.
4. Press the Rice button and adjust the cooking time to 20 minutes.
5. Do natural pressure release.

Nutrition Facts Per Serving
Calories 281, Total Fat 20g, Saturated Fat 18g, Total Carbs 28g, Net Carbs 26g, Protein 2g, Sugar: 20g, Fiber: 2g, Sodium: 73mg, Potassium: 728mg, Phosphorus: 129mg

Pumpkin Date Brown Rice Pudding

Prep time: 5 minutes, cook time: 20 minutes; Serves 6

Ingredients:

1 cup brown rice

3 cups coconut water

½ cup pitted dates, chopped

2 stick cinnamon

1 cup pumpkin puree

1 teaspoon pumpkin spice mix

½ cup maple syrup

1 teaspoon vanilla

½ cup water

1/8 teaspoon salt

Instructions

1. Place all ingredients irn the Instant Pot.
2. Give a good stir to combine everything.
3. Close the lid and set the vent to the Sealing position.
4. Press the Rice button and adjust the cooking time to 20 minutes.
5. Do natural pressure release.

Nutrition Facts Per Serving

Calories 356, Total Fat 11g, Saturated Fat 2g, Total Carbs 58g, Net Carbs 53g, Protein 10g, Sugar: 28g, Fiber: 5g, Sodium: 182mg, Potassium: 663mg, Phosphorus: 366mg

Instant Pot Baked Apples

Prep time: 5 minutes, cook time: 4 hours; Serves 4

Ingredients:

4 small Gala apples

4 tablespoons chopped walnuts

1 teaspoon brown sugar

1 teaspoon cinnamon

8 frozen cranberries

1 teaspoon coconut oil

Instructions

1. Place all ingredients in the Instant Pot.
2. Close the lid but do not seal the vent.
3. Press the Slow Cook button and adjust the cooking time to 4 hours.
4. Cook on low and make sure to give a good stir halfway through the cooking time.

Nutrition Facts Per Serving

Calories 132, Total Fat 7g, Saturated Fat 1g, Total Carbs 16g, Net Carbs g, Protein 1g, Sugar: 11g, Fiber: 3g, Sodium: 1mg, Potassium: 152mg, Phosphorus: 185mg

Overnight Pineapple Jam

Prep time: 5 minutes, cook time: 5 hours; Serves 4

Ingredients:

2 pounds pineapples, peeled and chopped finely

½ cup coconut sugar

1 teaspoon lime rind, grated

1/8 teaspoon salt

Instructions

1. Place all ingredients in the Instant Pot and give a good stir.
2. Close the lid but do not seal the vent.
3. Press the Slow Cook button and adjust the cooking time to 5 hours.

Nutrition Facts Per Serving

Calories 185, Total Fat 0.2g, Saturated Fat 0g, Total Carbs 48g, Net Carbs 46g, Protein 1g, Sugar: 45g, Fiber: 2g, Sodium: 3mg, Potassium: 278mg, Phosphorus: 14mg

Sweetened Rhubarb

Prep time: 5 minutes, cook time: 10 minutes; Serves 6

Ingredients:

½ cups strawberries, fresh and cleaned

2 medium lemon, juiced

1 teaspoon vanilla

1 medium orange, juiced

1 ½ pounds rhubarb, sliced into segments

1 cup water

2 cups raw honey

Instructions

1. Place all ingredients in the Instant Pot.
2. Give a good stir.
3. Close the lid and set the vent to the Sealing position.
4. Press the Manual button.
5. Adjust the cooking time to 10 minutes.
6. Do natural pressure release.

7. Once the lid is open, press the Sauté button and simmer to reduce the sauce.

Nutrition Facts Per Serving
Calories 484, Total Fat 0.1g, Saturated Fat 0g, Total Carbs 130g, Net Carbs 127g, Protein 0.9g, Sugar: 126g, Fiber: 3g, Sodium: 7mg, Potassium: 204mg, Phosphorus: 18mg

Pumpkin Spice Chocolate Chip Cookies

Prep time: 15 minutes, cook time: 30 minutes; Serves 6

Ingredients:
½ cup chocolate chips, semi-sweet
1 tablespoon pumpkin pie spice
1 teaspoon baking soda
2 teaspoon vanilla
¼ cup coconut oil
¼ cup raw honey
3 tablespoon almond butter
½ cup pumpkin puree
1 ½ cup all-purpose flour

Instructions
1. Place a steamer basket in the Instant Pot.
2. In a mixing bowl, combine all ingredients.

3. Pour in a baking dish that will fit in the Instant Pot.
4. Place aluminum foil on top.
5. Place on top of the steamer basket.
6. Close the lid and press the Steam button.
7. Adjust the cooking time to 30 minutes.
8. Do natural pressure release.

Nutrition Facts Per Serving
Calories 400, Total Fat 24g, Saturated Fat 15g, Total Carbs 41g, Net Carbs 38g, Protein 7g, Sugar: 14g, Fiber: 3g, Sodium: 74mg, Potassium: 188mg, Phosphorus: 179mg

Fruit Salad Jam

Prep time: 5 minutes, cook time: 10 minutes; Serves 6

Ingredients:
½ teaspoon cinnamon
1 medium apple, diced
1 medium oranges, peeled
1 cup blueberries
1 cup sugar
Zest from ½ lemon
1 ½ cups water

Instructions
1. Place all ingredients in the Instant Pot.
2. Give a good stir.
3. Close the lid and set the vent to the Sealing position.

4. Press the Manual button.
5. Adjust the cooking time to 10 minutes.
6. Do natural pressure release.
7. Once the lid is open, press the Sauté button and simmer to reduce the sauce.

Nutrition Facts Per Serving
Calories 140, Total Fat 0.3g, Saturated Fat 0g, Total Carbs 35g, Net Carbs 33g, Protein 0.7g, Sugar: 32g, Fiber: 2g, Sodium: 4mg, Potassium: 129mg, Phosphorus: 15mg

Apple Cinnamon Cake

Prep time: 10 minutes, cook time: 30 minutes; Serves 6

Ingredients:
1 teaspoon fresh nutmeg, grated
1 tablespoon vanilla
1 medium peeled apple, cored and diced
1 large egg
½ cup raw honey
¼ cup coconut oil, melted

1 teaspoon cinnamon
¼ cup arrowroot powder
½ teaspoon baking soda
½ teaspoon salt
2 cups almond flour

Instructions

1. Place a steamer basket in the Instant Pot.
2. In a mixing bowl, combine all ingredients.
3. Pour in a baking dish that will fit in the Instant Pot.
4. Place aluminum foil on top.
5. Place on top of the steamer basket.
6. Close the lid and set the vent to the Sealing position.
7. Press the Steam button.
8. Adjust the cooking time to 30 minutes.
9. Do natural pressure release.

Nutrition Facts Per Serving

Calories 204, Total Fat 10g, Saturated Fat 8g, Total Carbs 29g, Net Carbs 27g, Protein 0.9g, Sugar: 27g, Fiber: 1g, Sodium: 303mg, Potassium: 82mg, Phosphorus: 24mg

Dark Chocolate Cake

Prep time: 10 minutes, cook time: 25 minutes; Serves 6

Ingredients:

4 drops liquid stevia
2 tablespoon raw cacao nibs
¼ cups unsweetened applesauce
2 tablespoon almond milk, unsweetened
½ cup coconut milk, full fat
1 large egg
½ teaspoon vanilla
½ cup cacao powder
½ cup raw honey
2 tablespoon tapioca flour
1 cup almond flour

Instructions

1. Place a steamer basket in the Instant Pot.
2. In a mixing bowl, combine all ingredients.
3. Pour in a baking dish that will fit in the Instant Pot.
4. Place aluminum foil on top.
5. Place on top of the steamer basket.
6. Close the lid and set the vent to the Sealing position.
7. Press the Steam button.
8. Adjust the cooking time to 30 minutes.
9. Do natural pressure release.

Nutrition Facts Per Serving

Calories 178, Total Fat 7g, Saturated Fat 5g, Total Carbs 33g, Net Carbs 30g, Protein 3g, Sugar: 25g, Fiber: 3g, Sodium: 9mg, Potassium: 267mg, Phosphorus: 90mg

Caramel Pear Pudding

Prep time: 5 minutes, cook time: 15 minutes; Serves 6

Ingredients:

½ cup sugar
½ teaspoon ground cinnamon
1 ½ teaspoons baking powder
1/8 teaspoon ground cloves
¼ teaspoon salt
3/4 cup milk
4 medium pears, peeled and cubed
½ cup pecans, chopped
¾ cup brown sugar
¼ cup softened butter

Instructions

1. Place all ingredients in the Instant Pot.
2. Give a good stir to incorporate all ingredients.
3. Close the lid and set the vent to the Sealing position.
4. Press the Manual button.
5. Adjust the cooking time to 15 minutes
6. Allow to chill in the fridge before serving.

Nutrition Facts Per Serving

Calories 316, Total Fat 15g, Saturated Fat 6g, Total Carbs 47g, Net Carbs 42g, Protein 2g, Sugar: 42g, Fiber: 5g, Sodium: 180mg, Potassium: 339mg, Phosphorus: 147mg

Coconut, Cranberry, And Quinoa

Prep time: 5 minutes, cook time: 20 minutes; Serves 4

Ingredients:

2 ½ cups coconut water
¼ cup slivered almonds
½ cup coconut meat

1 cup quinoa, rinsed
½ cup dried cranberries
1 tablespoon vanilla

¼ cup honey

Instructions

1. Place all ingredients except the whipping cream in the Instant Pot.
2. Give a good stir to incorporate all ingredients.
3. Close the lid and press the Manual button.
4. Adjust the cooking time to 20 minutes

5. Allow to chill in the fridge before serving.

Nutrition Facts Per Serving

Calories 312, Total Fat 6g, Saturated Fat 4g, Total Carbs 56g, Net Carbs 163g, Protein 5g, Sugar: 26g, Fiber: 6g, Sodium: 163mg, Potassium: 671mg, Phosphorus: 237mg

Sweet Rice Pudding

Prep time: 5 minutes, cook time: 15 minutes; Serves 4

Ingredients:

1 ¼ cups milk
½ cup uncooked rice
½ cups brown sugar
½ cup raisin
1 teaspoon ground cinnamon
1 teaspoon butter, melted
2 eggs, beaten
1 teaspoon vanilla extract
¾ teaspoon lemon extract
1 cup heavy whipping cream

Instructions

1. Place all ingredients except the whipping cream in the Instant Pot.

2. Give a good stir to incorporate all ingredients.
3. Close the lid and set the vent to the Sealing position.
4. Press the Manual button.
5. Adjust the cooking time to 15 minutes
6. Allow to chill in the fridge before serving.
7. Serve with whipping cream

Nutrition Facts Per Serving

Calories 379, Total Fat 22g, Saturated Fat 11g, Total Carbs 40g, Net Carbs 37g, Protein 10g, Sugar: 32g, Fiber: 3g, Sodium: 111mg, Potassium: 463mg, Phosphorus: 409mg

Instant Pot Crème Brulee

Prep time: 10 minutes, cook time: 30 minutes; Serves 3

Ingredients:

3 large egg yolks, beaten
½ cup packed brown sugar
¼ teaspoon ground cinnamon
1 1/3 cups heavy whipping cream, warm
½ teaspoon maple flavoring
1 ½ teaspoon sugar for topping

Instructions

1. Place a steamer in the Instant Pot and pour a cup of boiling water.
2. In a bowl, whisk the yolks, sugar, and cinnamon. Stir in the warm cream to the yolk mixture.
3. Stir in the maple flavoring.

4. Ladle the mixture into ramekins and sprinkle sugar for topping.
5. Place the ramekins on the steamer basket.
6. Close the lid and press the Steam button.
7. Adjust the cooking time to 30 minutes.
8. Do natural pressure release.
9. Remove the ramekins and allow to cool in the fridge for 10 minutes.

Nutrition Facts Per Serving

Calories 380, Total Fat 24g, Saturated Fat g, Total Carbs 38g, Net Carbs 38g, Protein 4g, Sugar: 37g, Fiber: 0g, Sodium: 39mg, Potassium: 109mg, Phosphorus: 101mg

Grapefruit Cheesecake

Prep time: 10 minutes, cook time: 30 minutes; Serves 6

Ingredients:

¾ cup graham cracker crumbs
1 tablespoon + 2/3 cup sugar, divided
1 teaspoon grated grapefruit peel
¼ teaspoon ground ginger

2 ½ tablespoons butter, melted
2 packages cream cheese, softened
½ cup sour cream
2 tablespoons pink grapefruit juice

2 large eggs, beaten

Instructions

1. Place a steamer basket in the Instant Pot and pour a cup of water.
2. Wrap a spring form pan with foil to prevent the cheesecake from leaking from the pan. Make sure that the pan will fit inside the Instant Pot.
3. In a bowl, mix the graham cracker crumbs, 1 tablespoon sugar, grapefruit peel, ginger, and butter. Mix until well combined. Press the crust mixture into the base of the spring form pan. Set aside to cool inside the fridge.
4. In another bowl, beat the remaining sugar and cream cheese. Add in the sour cream, grapefruit juice, and eggs. Whisk until well combined.
5. Pour the cheesecake mixture into the spring form pan.
6. Place on top of the steamer rack and close the lid. Set the vent to the Sealing position.
7. Press the Steam button and adjust the cooking time to 30 minutes.
8. Do natural pressure release.

Nutrition Facts Per Serving

Calories 162, Total Fat 9g, Saturated Fat 5g, Total Carbs 20g, Net Carbs 19.9g, Protein 2g, Sugar: 17g, Fiber: 0.1g, Sodium: 66mg, Potassium: 63mg, Phosphorus: 42mg

Berry Cobbler

Prep time: 5 minutes, cook time: 30 minutes; Serves 8

Ingredients:

1 ¼ cups whole wheat flour, divided
1 cup and 2 tablespoons sugar, divided
¼ teaspoon ground cinnamon
1 teaspoon baking powder
1 large eggs
2 tablespoons canola oil
¼ cups fat-free milk
1/8 teaspoon salt
2 cups fresh raspberries
2 cups fresh blueberries

Instructions

1. Place a steamer in the Instant Pot and pour a cup of water.
2. In a mixing bowl, combine 1 cup of flour, 2 tablespoons of sugar, cinnamon, and baking powder.
3. In another bowl, mix the egg, oil, and milk.
4. Add the wet ingredients to the dry ingredients and stir constantly until well combined.
5. Pour the batter on a dish that will fit inside the Instant Pot.
6. In another bowl, toss together salt and the berries.
7. Spread berries on top of the batter.
8. Place aluminum foil on top of the baking dish.
9. Place on the steamer rack.
10. Close the lid and set the vent to the Sealing position.
11. Press the Steam button and adjust the cooking time to 30 minutes.
12. Do natural pressure release.

Nutrition Facts Per Serving

Calories 268, Total Fat 5g, Saturated Fat 0.6g, Total Carbs 56g, Net Carbs 51g, Protein 4g, Sugar: 39g, Fiber: 5g, Sodium: 48mg, Potassium: 170mg, Phosphorus: 95mg

Easy Apple Cinnamon

Prep time: 5 minutes, cook time: 6 hours; Serves 5

Ingredients:

5 apples, cored and sliced
½ cup brown sugar
1 tablespoon cinnamon
A dash of nutmeg

Instructions

1. Place all ingredients in the Instant Pot.
2. Give a good stir.
3. Close the lid and do not seal the vent.
4. Press the Slow Cook button and adjust the cooking time to 6 hours.

Nutrition Facts Per Serving

Calories 182, Total Fat 0.33g, Saturated Fat 0g, Total Carbs 48g, Net Carbs 43g, Protein 0.5g, Sugar: 40g, Fiber: 5g, Sodium: 8mg, Potassium: 231mg, Phosphorus: 22mg

Gingerbread Pudding

Prep time: 15 minutes, cook time: 30 minutes; Serves 8

Ingredients:

1 cup water
½ cup molasses
¼ cup butter, softened
¼ cup granulated sugar
1 large egg white
1 teaspoon vanilla extract
1 ¼ cups whole wheat flour
¾ teaspoon baking soda
¼ teaspoon salt
½ teaspoon ground ginger
½ teaspoon ground cinnamon
1/8 teaspoon ground nutmeg
¼ teaspoon ground all spice
½ cup chopped pecans

Instructions

1. Place a steamer in the Instant Pot and pour a cup of water.
2. Combine water and molasses in a mixing bowl. Stir in the softened butter, granulated sugar, egg white, and vanilla. Mix until fluffy.
3. In another bowl, combine the flour, baking soda, and salt. Add the ginger, cinnamon, nutmeg, and all spice.
4. Mix the wet ingredients to the dry ingredients until well combined.
5. Fold in the pecans.
6. Pour into a baking dish that will fit inside the Instant Pot and sprinkle on top brown sugar.
7. Put aluminum foil on top of the baking dish.
8. Place on the steamer rack
9. Close the lid and set the vent to the Sealing position.
10. Press the Steam button.
11. Adjust the cooking time to 30 minutes.
12. Do natural pressure release.

Nutrition Facts Per Serving

Calories 235, Total Fat 11g, Saturated Fat 4g, Total Carbs 34g, Net Carbs 31g, Protein 4g, Sugar: 19g, Fiber: 3g, Sodium: 254mg, Potassium: 413mg, Phosphorus: 93mg

Coffee Cake

Prep time: 15 minutes, cook time: 30 minutes; Serves 6

Ingredients:

1 ¾ cups packed brown sugar, divided
1 cup whole wheat flour
5 tablespoons baking cocoa, divided
2 teaspoons baking powder
½ teaspoon salt
2 tablespoon butter, melted
½ cup milk
½ teaspoon vanilla extract
1/8 teaspoon almond extract
½ cup boiling water
4 teaspoon instant coffee granules

Instructions

1. Place a steamer in the Instant Pot and pour a cup of water.
2. In a bowl, mix all the ingredients until well combined.
3. Pour the batter on a dish that will fit inside the Instant Pot.
4. Put aluminum foil on top.
5. Place on the steamer and close the lid. Set the vent to the Sealing position.
6. Press the Manual button and adjust the cooking time for 30 minutes.
7. Do natural pressure release.

Nutrition Facts Per Serving

Calories 385, Total Fat 6g, Saturated Fat 3g, Total Carbs 84g, Net Carbs 80g, Protein 5g, Sugar: 64g, Fiber: 4g, Sodium: 262mg, Potassium: 335mg, Phosphorus: 142mg

Instant Pot Apple Streusel

Prep time: 5 minutes, cook time: 30 minutes; Serves 6

Ingredients:

6 cups sliced, peeled, and cored tart apples
½ cup all-purpose flour
¼ teaspoon ground all spice
1 ¼ teaspoon ground cinnamon
¼ teaspoon ground nutmeg
¾ cup milk
2 tablespoon butter, softened
¾ cup brown sugar

2 large eggs, beaten
1 teaspoon vanilla extract
1/3 cup packed brown sugar
3 tablespoons cold butter
½ cup sliced almonds

Instructions

1. Place a steamer rack in the Instant Pot and pour a cup of water.
2. Place the apples in a baking dish that will fit in the Instant Pot.
3. In a mixing bowl, combine flour, all spice, cinnamon, nutmeg, milk, butter, ¾ cup brown sugar, eggs, and vanilla extract. Mix until well combined.
4. Pour over the apples and toss to coat.
5. In another bowl, combine the brown sugar, butter, and almonds.
6. Sprinkle the mixture on top of the apples.
7. Cover the baking dish with aluminum foil.
8. Close the lid and set the vent to the Sealing position.
9. Press the Steam button.
10. Adjust the cooking time to 30 minutes.
11. Do natural pressure release.

Nutrition Facts Per Serving
Calories 427, Total Fat 13g, Saturated Fat 7g, Total Carbs 77g, Net Carbs 72g, Protein 4g, Sugar: 64g, Fiber: 5g, Sodium: 106mg, Potassium: 244mg, Phosphorus: 76mg

Instant Pot Cheesecake

Prep time: 10 minutes, cook time: 30 minutes; Serves 6

Ingredients:
3 8-ounce cream cheese, room temperature
1 cup white sugar
3 eggs
½ tablespoon vanilla extract

Instructions

1. Place a steamer in the Instant Pot and pour a cup of water.
2. In a bowl, mix all the ingredients until well combined.
3. Pour the batter on a spring form pan that will fit inside the Instant Pot.
4. Put aluminum foil on top.
5. Place on the steamer and close the lid.
6. Press the Manual button and adjust the cooking time for 30 minutes.
7. Do natural pressure release.

Nutrition Facts Per Serving
Calories 467, Total Fat 37g, Saturated Fat 22g, Total Carbs 21g, Net Carbs 21g, Protein 13g, Sugar: 21g, Fiber: 0g, Sodium: 546mg, Potassium: 207mg, Phosphorus: 180mg

Instant Pot Mocha Pudding

Prep time: 10 minutes, cook time: 30 minutes; Serves 3

Ingredients:
¾ cup butter, cut into chunks
2 ounces unsweetened chocolate, chopped
½ cup heavy cream
2 tablespoon instant coffee
1 teaspoon vanilla extract
1/3 cup all purpose
4 tablespoon cocoa powder, unsweetened
1/8 teaspoon salt
5 large eggs
2/3 cup white sugar

Instructions

1. Place a steamer in the Instant Pot and pour a cup of water.
2. In a bowl, mix all the ingredients until well combined.
3. Pour the batter on a dish that will fit inside the Instant Pot.
4. Put aluminum foil on top.
5. Place on the steamer and close the lid. Set the vent to the Sealing position.
6. Press the Manual button and adjust the cooking time for 30 minutes.
7. Do natural pressure release.

Nutrition Facts Per Serving
Calories 825, Total Fat 70g, Saturated Fat 38g, Total Carbs 45g, Net Carbs 41g, Protein 11g, Sugar: 33g, Fiber: 4g, Sodium: 509mg, Potassium: 469mg, Phosphorus: 280mg

Cinnamon Blondie Pecan Bars

Prep time: 6 minutes, cook time: 30 minutes; Serves 16

Ingredients:

1 cup white sugar
6 tablespoon unsalted butter, melted
3 large eggs
2 teaspoon vanilla extract
1 ½ cups all-purpose flour
¼ teaspoon salt
1 tablespoon cinnamon
1 teaspoon baking powder
2 tablespoon unsalted butter
¼ cup heavy whipping cream
1 cup pecans, chopped

Instructions

1. Place a steamer in the Instant Pot and pour a cup of water.
2. In a bowl, whisk the sugar and butter until well combined.
3. Add in the eggs and vanilla extract.
4. Stir in the flour, salt, cinnamon, baking powder, and butter.
5. Pour the batter on a dish that will fit inside the Instant Pot.
6. Put aluminum foil on top.
7. Place on the steamer and close the lid. Set the vent to the Sealing position.
8. Press the Manual button and adjust the cooking time for 30 minutes.
9. Do natural pressure release.
10. Allow to cool in the fridge.
11. Garnish with whip cream and pecans on top.

Nutrition Facts Per Serving

Calories 164, Total Fat 10g, Saturated Fat 4g, Total Carbs 17g, Net Carbs 13g, Protein 3g, Sugar: 7g, Fiber:1 g, Sodium: 42mg, Potassium: 51mg, Phosphorus: 46mg

Steamed Choco Cake

Prep time: 10 minutes, cook time: 30 minutes; Serves 10

Ingredients:

1 cup all-purpose flour
½ cup cocoa powder
½ cup white sugar
3 tablespoon whey protein powder, unflavored
1 ½ teaspoon baking powder
¼ teaspoon salt
3 large eggs
2/3 cup unsweetened almond milk
6 tablespoon butter, melted
¾ teaspoon vanilla extract
1/3 cup sugar-free chocolate chips

Instructions

1. Place a steamer in the Instant Pot and pour a cup of water.
2. In a bowl, mix all the ingredients except for the chocolate chips.
3. Pour the batter on a dish that will fit inside the Instant Pot.
4. Sprinkle with the chocolate chips on top and give a swirl.
5. Put aluminum foil on top.
6. Place on the steamer and close the lid. Set the vent to the Sealing position.
7. Press the Manual button and adjust the cooking time for 30 minutes.
8. Do natural pressure release.

Nutrition Facts Per Serving

Calories 166, Total Fat 11g, Saturated Fat 6g, Total Carbs 15g, Net Carbs 13g, Protein 4g, Sugar: 2g, Fiber: 2g, Sodium: 125mg, Potassium: 238mg, Phosphorus: 139mg

Pumpkin Pie Pudding

Prep time: 5 minutes, cook time: 10 minutes; Serves 6

Ingredients:

2 cups pumpkin, mashed
2 cups full-fat milk
¾ cup brown sugar
½ cup whole wheat flour
2 large eggs, beaten
2 tablespoon grass-fed butter
2 ½ teaspoon pumpkin pie extract
2 teaspoon vanilla extract

Instructions

1. Place all ingredients in the Instant Pot.

2. Give a good stir.
3. Close the lid and set the vent to the Sealing position.
4. Press the Manual button and adjust the cooking time for 10 minutes.
5. Do natural pressure release.

Nutrition Facts Per Serving
Calories 214, Total Fat 3g, Saturated Fat 2g, Total Carbs 41g, Net Carbs 40g, Protein 5g, Sugar: 32g, Fiber: 1g, Sodium: 50mg, Potassium: 331mg, Phosphorus: 152mg

Steamed Vanilla Cake

Prep time: 10 minutes, cook time: 30 minutes; Serves 12

Ingredients:
1 ½ cups all-purpose flour
¾ cup stevia sweetener
2/3 cup protein powder, vanilla powder
¼ teaspoon salt
2 teaspoon baking powder
½ cup unsalted butter, melted
¾ cup heavy cream
4 large eggs
1 teaspoon vanilla extract

Instructions
1. Place a steamer in the Instant Pot and pour a cup of water.
2. In a bowl, mix all the ingredients until well combined.
3. Pour the batter on a dish that will fit inside the Instant Pot.
4. Put aluminum foil on top.
5. Place on the steamer and close the lid. Set the vent to the Sealing position.
6. Press the Manual button and adjust the cooking time for 30 minutes.
7. Do natural pressure release.

Nutrition Facts Per Serving
Calories 189, Total Fat 11g, Saturated Fat 6g, Total Carbs 14g, Net Carbs 13g, Protein 7g, Sugar: 1g, Fiber: 1g, Sodium: 90mg, Potassium: 147mg, Phosphorus: 110mg

Choco Lava Cake

Prep time: 10 minutes, cook time: 15 minutes; Serves 12

Ingredients:
1 ½ cup white sugar, divided
½ cup all-purpose flour
5 tablespoon unsweetened cocoa powder
½ teaspoon salt
1 teaspoon baking powder
3 whole eggs
3 egg yolks
½ cup butter, melted
1 teaspoon vanilla extract
2 cups hot water
4 ounces sugar-free chocolate chips

Instructions
1. Place a steamer in the Instant Pot and pour a cup of water.
2. In a bowl, mix all the ingredients until well combined.
3. Pour the batter on a dish that will fit inside the Instant Pot.
4. Place on the steamer and close the lid. Set the vent to the Sealing position.
5. Press the Manual button and adjust the cooking time for 15 minutes.
6. Do natural pressure release.

Nutrition Facts Per Serving
Calories 238, Total Fat 19g, Saturated Fat 7g, Total Carbs 15g, Net Carbs g13, Protein 5g, Sugar: 3g, Fiber: 2g, Sodium: 227mg, Potassium: 151mg, Phosphorus: 109mg

Steamed Lemon Cake

Prep time: 10 minutes, cook time: 30 minutes; Serves 12

Ingredients:
½ cup all-purpose flour
1 ½ cups almond flour
3 tablespoon white sugar
2 teaspoon baking powder
½ teaspoon xanthan gum
½ cup whipping cream

½ cup butter, melted
1 tablespoon juice, freshly squeezed
Zest from one large lemon
2 eggs

Instructions
1. Place a steamer in the Instant Pot and pour a cup of water.
2. In a bowl, mix all the ingredients until well combined.
3. Pour the batter on a dish that will fit inside the Instant Pot.
4. Put aluminum foil on top.
5. Place on the steamer and close the lid. Set the vent to the Sealing position.
6. Press the Manual button and adjust the cooking time for 30 minutes.
7. Do natural pressure release.

Nutrition Facts Per Serving
Calories 125, Total Fat 10g, Saturated Fat 3g, Total Carbs 7g, Net Carbs 6.8g, Protein 2g, Sugar: 3g, Fiber: 0.2g, Sodium: 78mg, Potassium: 44mg, Phosphorus: 37mg

Raspberry Curd

Prep time: 10 minutes, cook time: 10 minutes; Serves 6

Ingredients:
12 ounces raspberries
2 tablespoon lemon juice
1 cup sugar
2 egg yolks
2 tablespoon butter

Instructions
1. Place the raspberries, lemon juice and sugar in the Instant Pot.
2. Close the lid and set the vent to the Sealing position.
3. Press the Manual button.
4. Adjust the cooking time to 5 minutes.
5. Once the pressure cooker stops cooking, do natural pressure release and open the lid.
6. Strain the raspberries to puree and remove large lumps and seeds. Discard the seeds.
7. In another bowl, beat the egg yolks and add the raspberry puree. Return to the Instant Pot.
8. Without the lid on, press the Sauté button and stir constantly.
9. Add the butter and wait for the mixture to thicken.

Nutrition Facts Per Serving
Calories 170, Total Fat 5g, Saturated Fat 3g, Total Carbs 30g, Net Carbs 28g, Protein 1g, Sugar: 28g, Fiber: 2g, Sodium: 35mg, Potassium: 66mg, Phosphorus: 29mg

Steamed Double Chocolate Cake

Prep time: 10 minutes, cook time: 30 minutes; Serves 12

Ingredients:
¾ cup stevia sweetener
1 ½ cups all-purpose flour
¼ cup protein powder, chocolate or vanilla flavor
2/3 cup cocoa powder, unsweetened
¼ teaspoon baking powder
¼ teaspoon salt
½ cup unsalted butter, melted
4 large eggs
¾ cup heavy cream
1 teaspoon vanilla extract

Instructions
1. Place a steamer in the Instant Pot and pour a cup of water.
2. In a bowl, mix the sweetener, flour, protein powder, cocoa powder, baking powder, and salt.
3. Add the butter, eggs, cream, and vanilla extract.
4. Pour the batter on a dish that will fit inside the Instant Pot.
5. Place on the steamer and close the lid. Set the vent to the Sealing position.
6. Press the Manual button and adjust the cooking time for 30 minutes.
7. Do natural pressure release.

Nutrition Facts Per Serving
Calories 174, Total Fat 11g, Saturated Fat 6g, Total Carbs 16g, Net Carbs 14g, Protein 6g, Sugar: 0.6g, Fiber:2 g, Sodium: 71mg, Potassium: 208mg, Phosphorus: 113mg

Cherry Compote

Prep time: 5 minutes, cook time: 15 minutes; Serves 8

Ingredients:

1 package frozen cherry
2 tablespoon lemon juice
¾ cup sugar
2 tablespoon cornstarch
2 tablespoon water
¼ teaspoon almond extract

Instructions

1. Place the cherries, lemon juice and sugar in the Instant Pot. Stir to combine everything.
2. Close the lid and set the vent to the Sealing position.
3. Press the Manual button. Adjust the cooking time to 10 minutes.
4. Do natural pressure release.
5. Meanwhile, mix the cornstarch, water and almond extract.
6. Once the lid is open, press the Sauté button and pour the slurry over the cherries.
7. Stir and allow to simmer until the sauce thickens

Nutrition Facts Per Serving

Calories 77, Total Fat 0.08g, Saturated Fat 0g, Total Carbs 19g, Net Carbs 18.2g, Protein 0.4g, Sugar: 16g, Fiber: 0.8g, Sodium: 1mg, Potassium: 75mg, Phosphorus: 6mg

Pumpkin Chocolate Cake

Prep time: 15 minutes, cook time: 50 minutes; Serves 8

Ingredients:

1 ½ cups all-purpose flour
½ teaspoon pumpkin pie spice
1 teaspoon ground cinnamon
¼ teaspoon salt
½ teaspoon baking soda
½ teaspoon baking powder
½ cup butter, softened
1 cup granulated sugar
2 eggs
1 cup pumpkin puree
¾ cup mini chocolate chips

Instructions

1. Place a trivet or steamer rack in the Instant Pot and a cup of water.
2. In a mixing bowl, mix the flour, pumpkin pie spice, cinnamon, salt, baking soda and baking powder.
3. In another bowl, beat in the rest of the ingredients until fluffy.
4. Mix the dry ingredients and wet ingredients.
5. Pour the batter on greased Bundt pan that will fit inside the Instant Pot. Cover with aluminum foil.
6. Place on top of the steamer and close the lid. Set the vent to the Sealing position.
7. Press the Steam button and adjust the cooking time to 50 minutes.
8. Do natural pressure release.

Nutrition Facts Per Serving

Calories 354, Total Fat 21g, Saturated Fat 9g, Total Carbs 33g, Net Carbs 31g, Protein 9g, Sugar: 13g, Fiber: 2g, Sodium: 234mg, Potassium: 218mg, Phosphorus: 262mg

Carrot Pudding

Prep time: 10 minutes, cook time: 50 minutes; Serves 8

Ingredients:

1 cup brown sugar
¼ cup molasses
2 eggs
½ cup flour
½ teaspoon cinnamon
½ teaspoon allspice
½ teaspoon nutmeg
½ teaspoon baking soda
¼ teaspoon salt
2/3 cup shortening, frozen and grated
½ cup carrots, grated
½ cup raisins
1 cup breadcrumbs
½ cup pecans, chopped
4 tablespoon butter
¼ cup cream
2 tablespoon rum
¼ teaspoon cinnamon, ground

Instructions

1. Place a steamer rack in the Instant Pot and add a cup of water.

2. In a mixing bowl, whisk ½ cup of brown sugar, molasses, and eggs.
3. Pour in the flour and the spices, baking soda, salt, shortening, carrots, breadcrumbs, and pecans.
4. Pour the batter in a baking dish that will fit the pressure cooker. Cover with aluminum foil and place on the steamer.
5. Close the lid and press the Steam button.
6. Adjust the cooking time to 50 minutes.
7. Prepare the rum sauce by mixing in a saucepan the remaining brown sugar, butter, cream, rum and cinnamon. Heat over low flame until reduced.
8. Once the pressure cooker beeps, do natural pressure release.
9. Pour over the rum sauce on top.
10. Allow to cool before serving.

Nutrition Facts Per Serving
Calories 424, Total Fat 32g, Saturated Fat 10g, Total Carbs 31g, Net Carbs 30g, Protein 4g, Sugar: 21g, Fiber: 1g, Sodium: 257mg, Potassium: 269mg, Phosphorus: 83mg

Coco Pina Colada Pudding

Prep time: 10 minutes, cook time: 11 minutes; Serves 8

Ingredients:
1 cup Arborio rice
1 ½ cups water
1 tablespoon coconut oil
¼ teaspoon salt
1 can coconut milk
2 eggs
½ cup milk
½ teaspoon vanilla extract
1 can pineapple tidbits, drained

Instructions
1. Mix the rice, water and oil in the Instant Pot. Season with salt.
2. Close the lid and press the Rice button. Adjust the cooking time to 6 minutes.
3. Do natural pressure release to open the lid.
4. Meanwhile, beat the eggs, milk and vanilla. Pour over the sieve to remove any lumps.
5. Once the lid is open, press the Sauté and pour over the coconut milk and sugar. Stir to mix everything.
6. Add the egg mixture until it thickens.
7. Stir in the pineapples last.

Nutrition Facts Per Serving
Calories 157, Total Fat 8g, Saturated Fat 3g, Total Carbs 21g, Net Carbs 17g, Protein 5g, Sugar: 14g, Fiber: 4g, Sodium: 134mg, Potassium: 470mg, Phosphorus: 311mg

Hazelnut Flan

Prep time: 15 minutes, cook time: 50 minutes; Serves 5

Ingredients:
1 1/4 cups granulated sugar
¼ cup water
3 eggs
2 egg yolks
A pinch of salt
2 cups milk
½ cup whipping cream
1 teaspoon vanilla extract
2 tablespoon hazelnut syrup

Instructions
1. Prepare the caramel base by heating the ¾ cup sugar and ¼ cup water. Bring to a boil and place on ramekins before it hardens. Set aside.
2. Place a trivet or steamer basket in the pressure cooker and a cup of water.
3. In a mixing bowl, beat the eggs, yolks and the remaining cup of sugar. Add a pinch of salt.
4. Heat milk in a saucepan over medium heat until it bubbles. Add milk to eggs to temper the eggs.
5. Stir in the cream, vanilla and Hazelnut syrup.
6. Pour mixture on ramekins and cover with tin foil.
7. Place on the steamer basket and close the lid. Set the vent to the Sealing position.
8. Press the Steam button and adjust the cooking time to 50 minutes.
9. Do natural pressure release.

Nutrition Facts Per Serving
Calories 299, Total Fat 12g, Saturated Fat 5g, Total Carbs 38g, Net Carbs 38g, Protein 10g, Sugar: 37g, Fiber: 0g, Sodium: 113mg, Potassium: 240mg, Phosphorus: 206mg

Instant Pot Dulce De Leche

Prep time: 5 minutes, cook time: 50 minutes; Serves 4

Ingredients:

1 can sweetened condensed milk

Instructions

1. Place a steamer basket in the Instant Pot and add 8 cups of water.
2. Pour the condensed milk into a 16 ounce of canning jar.
3. Place the jar with the condensed milk on the steamer rack.
4. Place the jar with condensed milk on the steamer rack.
5. Close the lid and press the Steam button.
6. Adjust the cooking time to 50 minutes.
7. Do natural pressure release.

Nutrition Facts Per Serving

Calories 150, Total Fat 0.4g, Saturated Fat 0.2g, Total Carbs 22g, Net Carbs 22g, Protein 15g, Sugar: 22g, Fiber:0 g, Sodium: 221mg, Potassium: 637mg, Phosphorus: 374mg

Key Lime Pie

Prep time: 15 minutes, cook time: 15 minutes; Serves 8

Ingredients:

¾ cup graham cracker crumbs

3 tablespoon butter, melted

1 tablespoon sugar

1 can condensed milk

4 large egg yolks

½ cup key lime juice

1/3 cup sour cream

2 tablespoon key lime zest

Instructions

1. Place a trivet or steamer rack in the Instant Pot and pour a cup of water.
2. Coat a spring form pan that will fit in the pressure cooker with cooking spray.
3. In a bowl, mix together the graham crackers, butter and sugar. Press evenly on the bottom of the pan to form the crust. Place inside the fridge to set.
4. In another bowl, beat the egg yolks until light yellow.
5. Stir in the condensed milk. Beat in the lime juice and beat until smooth. Stir the sour cream and lime zest.
6. Pour the batter in the spring form pan and cover the top with aluminum foil.
7. Place on the steamer rack and close the lid.
8. Press the Steam button and adjust the cooking time to 15 minutes.
9. Do natural pressure release.
10. Allow to cool in the fridge before serving.

Nutrition Facts Per Serving

Calories 92, Total Fat 8g, Saturated Fat 4g, Total Carbs 4g, Net Carbs 3.9g, Protein 2 g, Sugar: 2g, Fiber: 0.1g, Sodium: 53mg, Potassium: 51mg, Phosphorus: 46mg

Coconut Tapioca

Prep time: 5minutes, cook time: 10 minutes; Serves 8

Ingredients:

1 cup pearl tapioca, rinsed

5 cups coconut milk

16-inch lemon grass, smashed

2 teaspoon ginger, grated

1 cup sugar

4 egg yolks

½ teaspoon salt

1 cup cashew nuts, toasted

Instructions

1. Place tapioca pearls and coconut milk in the Instant Pot.
2. Stir in lemon grass and ginger.
3. Close the lid and press the Rice button.
4. Adjust the cooking time to 6 minutes.
5. Do natural pressure release.
6. Meanwhile, mix the sugar, egg yolks and salt in a mixing bowl.
7. Once the lid is open, press the Sauté button and pour the egg mixture.
8. Allow to simmer until the mixture thickens.
9. Top with toasted cashew nuts.

Nutrition Facts Per Serving

Calories 331, Total Fat 15g, Saturated Fat 5g, Total Carbs 42g, Net Carbs 41.3g, Protein 9g, Sugar: 21g, Fiber: 0.7g, Sodium: 120mg, Potassium: 317mg, Phosphorus: 248mg

Cranberry Pudding

Prep time: 5 minutes, cook time: 25 minutes; Serves 6

Ingredients:

4 eggs, beaten
½ cup granulated sugar
 cups milk
1 teaspoon vanilla
3 cups bread cubes
1/3 cup dried cranberries
1/3 cup pecans, chopped

Instructions

1. Place a trivet or steamer rack in the pressure cooker. Pour a cup of water.
2. Grease a ramekin dish that will fit inside the pressure cooker.
3. In a mixing bowl, combine the eggs, sugar and milk using a whisk.
4. Stir in the vanilla.
5. Arrange the bread cubes and cranberries in the ramekin dish.
6. Pour the custard mixture. Place tin foil on top of the dish.
7. Place the dish on the steamer rack.
8. Close the lid in place and press the Steam button. Adjust the cooking time to 25 minutes.
9. Do natural pressure release. Top with pecans and refrigerate for at least 8 hours to harden.

Nutrition Facts Per Serving

Calories 237, Total Fat 12g, Saturated Fat 3g, Total Carbs 22g, Net Carbs 21g, Protein 9g, Sugar: 14g, Fiber: 1g, Sodium: 172mg, Potassium: 205mg, Phosphorus:169 mg

Rice-Pumpkin Pudding

Prep time: 10 minutes, cook time: 35 minutes; Serves 6

Ingredients:

1 cup short grain rice
3 cups milk
½ cup water
½ cups pitted dates, chopped
1 stick cinnamon stick
1/8 teaspoon salt
1 cup pumpkin puree
1 teaspoon pumpkin spice mix
½ cup maple syrup
1 teaspoon vanilla extract

Instructions

1. Soak rice with water and let it rest for at least 10 minutes.
2. Without the lid on, press the Sauté button on the Instant Pot and add milk and water. Add in the rice. Bring to a boil and add rice, dates, and cinnamon. Season with salt.
3. Lock the lid and set the vent to the Sealing position. Press the Rice button.
4. Adjust the cooking time to 20 minutes.
5. Do natural pressure release to open the lid.
6. Once the lid is open, press the Sauté button and add the pumpkin puree, spice mix, maple syrup and vanilla extract.
7. Allow to simmer for 5 minutes
8. Remove the cinnamon stick before serving.

Nutrition Facts Per Serving

Calories 412, Total Fat 14g, Saturated Fat 4g, Total Carbs 62g, Net Carbs 61g, Protein 12g, Sugar: 30g, Fiber: 3g, Sodium: 107mg, Potassium: 480mg, Phosphorus: 374mg

Sugared Plantains

Prep time: 5 minutes, cook time: 10 minutes; Serves 3

Ingredients:

½ large ripe plantain, peeled and sliced thickly
½ cup brown sugar
1 cup water

Instructions

1. Place all ingredients in the Instant Pot.
2. Give a good stir.
3. Close the lid and set the vent to the Sealing position.
4. Press the Pressure Cook or Manual button and adjust the cooking time to 10 minutes.
5. Do natural pressure release.

Nutrition Facts Per Serving

Calories 145, Total Fat 0.01g, Saturated Fat 0g, Total Carbs 37g, Net Carbs 36.9g, Protein 0.08g, Sugar: 36g, Fiber: 0.1g, Sodium: 23mg, Potassium: 70mg, Phosphorus: 3mg

Peach Compote

Prep time: 5 minutes, cook time: 30 minutes; Serves 5

Ingredients:

3 cups peaches, pitted and chopped

½ cup sugar

Instructions

1. Place all ingredients in the Instant Pot. Give a good stir.
2. Close the lid and set the vent to the Sealing position.
3. Press the Pressure Cook or Manual button. Adjust the cooking time to 30 minutes.
4. Do natural pressure release.

Nutrition Facts Per Serving

Calories 155, Total Fat 0.2g, Saturated Fat 0g, Total Carbs 41g, Net Carbs 39g, Protein 0.7g, Sugar: 39g, Fiber: 2g, Sodium: 10mg, Potassium: 145mg, Phosphorus: 17mg

Asian Coconut Sweet Rice

Prep time: 5 minutes, cook time: 10 minutes; Serves 8

Ingredients:

1 ½ cups sticky rice

¾ cup sugar

3 cups coconut milk

1 stalk pandan leaf

½ teaspoon salt

Instructions

1. Put everything in the Instant Pot.
2. Give a good stir.
3. Close the lid and press the Rice button.
4. Adjust the cooking time to 10 minutes.
5. Do natural pressure release.
6. Discard the pandan leaf.

Nutrition Facts Per Serving

Calories 166, Total Fat 8g, Saturated Fat 3g, Total Carbs 25g, Net Carbs 20g, Protein 6g, Sugar: 14g, Fiber: 5g, Sodium: 44mg, Potassium: 496mg, Phosphorus: 457mg

Oreo Cheesecake

Prep time: 10 minutes, cook time:10 minutes; Serves 8

Ingredients:

12 Oreo cookies, crushed

2 tablespoon butter, melted

16 ounces cream cheese

½ cup granulated sugar

2 large eggs

1 tablespoon all-purpose flour

¼ cup heavy cream

2 teaspoon vanilla extract

8 whole Oreo cookies, chopped

Instructions

1. Place a steamer rack in the Instant Pot and pour a cup of water.
2. Get a spring form pan that will fit inside the Instant Pot. Wrap a spring-form pan in foil and spray the inside of the pan with oil. Set aside.
3. In a mixing bowl, mix the crushed Oreo cookies and melted butter. Press the crumbs on the bottom of the pan. Refrigerate the pan.
4. In a bowl, beat the cream cheese until smooth. Add in the sugar and eggs slowly until well combined. Add in flour, cream and vanilla. Fold in the chopped Oreo cookies.
5. Pour the batter in the prepared crust.
6. Place an aluminum foil on top of the spring form pan.
7. Place the pan inside the pressure cooker and close the lid. Set the vent to the Sealing position.
8. Press the Steam button and adjust the cooking time to 10 minutes.
9. Do natural pressure release.
10. Allow to cool before serving.

Nutrition Facts Per Serving

Calories 401, Total Fat 29g, Saturated Fat g16, Total Carbs 31g, Net Carbs 30.2g, Protein 7g, Sugar: 20g, Fiber: 0.8g, Sodium: 380mg, Potassium: 136mg, Phosphorus: 105mg

CPSIA information can be obtained
at www.ICGtesting.com
Printed in the USA
LVHW020508121220
674004LV00009B/155

9 781952 832291